KT-152-050

The Architecture of Europe

The Nineteenth and Twentieth Centuries

Also by Doreen Yarwood

Published

Forthcoming

THE LIBRARY
GUILDFORD COLLEGE
of Further and Higher Education

The Architecture of Europe

The Nineteenth and Twentieth Centuries

Doreen Yarwood

B. T. Batsford Ltd, London

71010
720 YAR
7 day loan

Doreen Yarwood 1991
First published 1991

All rights reserved. No part of this publication
may be reproduced in any form or by any means
without permission from the Publisher.

Typeset by
Servis Filmsetting Ltd, Longsight, Manchester
and printed in Great Britain
by Butler & Tanner Ltd
Frome, Somerset
for the publishers
B. T. Batsford Ltd
4 Fitzhardinge Street
London W1H 0AH

A CIP catalogue record for this book is
available from the British Library

ISBN 0 7134 6605 7 (cased)

Contents

Preface

There are many books available on the architecture of Europe, most of which cover a specific area or period of time. It is rare for one to deal with Europe as a whole; generally only western Europe is discussed and, within this context, a carefully chosen selection of western European countries. This was, until comparatively recently, understandable, especially in the light of the older, academic approach to the subject, for it was long considered that only such countries as France and Italy, with possibly Germany and the Low Countries, had been instrumental in influencing and forming British architectural history.

Since 1945, with increasing leisure time, the expansion of higher education and, above all, a greater facility of travel, the whole of Europe has slowly opened up to tourists and students and, in consequence, academic study has broadened its base. Because of this rising interest, the publishers invited me to write an illustrated book which would narrate the history of European architecture from early times within the geographical boundaries of the Continent.

This was an immense canvas, even for a 600-page book, so there could be no pretence of comprehensiveness or detail. The aim was to present as clear a picture as possible of the general evolution of style and construction, of taste and design, in the different areas, so illustrating the trends – political, social, climatic and religious – which influenced development. Half the space was devoted to illustration, for architecture is a visual subject. My husband, John Yarwood, and I travelled some 67,000 miles by car in Europe over a ten-year period, visiting all the buildings illustrated and discussed in the various countries. My husband took over 25,000 photographs, from which the illustrations, both line drawings and photographic plates, were made. Only by this method was it possible to present an accurate account of the current condition, even existence, of all these monuments, for many had suffered grievously in the Second World War as well as from the passage of time.

The resulting book, *The Architecture of Europe*, was first published by Batsford in 1974. It has remained in print until the present time, being widely disseminated in Europe as well as in the English-speaking world. The time has come, though, for it to be updated and the publishers intend to produce the complete work in four separate volumes. Each volume will contain an increased selection of photographic plates and will have its own index and glossary, making it possible to purchase them singly or together. The final volume, devoted to architecture of the nineteenth and twentieth centuries, has been completely re-written. It is greatly enlarged and the historical account extends to 1990.

I should like to express my appreciation to the many colleagues and friends who have helped and advised me over the years, and to Miss Kate Johnston for typing this demanding manuscript. Most of all, I wish to acknowledge my deep debt to my late husband, Professor John Yarwood, not only for accompanying me on all the travels and for taking the photographs but also for developing and printing them which was much more of a chore.

Most of the photographic plates were taken by Professor Yarwood and, later, by myself. For the remaining, newer plates, the author and publishers wish to thank the Austrian National Tourist Office (29), Barnaby's Picture Library, London (1 and 36), Bildarchiv Foto, Marburg (28), Richard Bryant (30), Janet Gill (33), Greater London Record Office (34) and the Novosti Press Agency (47).

Doreen Yarwood
East Grinstead, 1991

I

The Nineteenth Century: Eclecticism

Introduction

The merging of one architectural style into another rarely coincides with the birth of a new century, the accession of a new monarch or establishment of a different political system. The first few years after 1800 though, marked, to a limited extent, the emergence of a changed attitude towards architectural design. The nineteenth century was, artistically and architecturally, a time of eclecticism and regurgitation of an extended compass of past styles derived from the ancient Egyptian and classical worlds, Byzantium and the Middle Ages.

Since the advent of the Renaissance in fifteenth-century Italy, architectural form and structure had been inspired by the earlier classical work, but the designers of the Renaissance, Baroque, Rococo and Neo-classical buildings had brought to their interpretations something new and personal, re-creating the styles of antiquity but changing them to suit the post-Renaissance world. The variations on the classical theme created by such men as Brunelleschi and Bernini, Mansart and Wren were inspired by Rome; they represented an interpretation not a reproduction. The architects of the nineteenth century western world also adapted the original source material to their own needs which, with growing industrialization, urbanization and increasing population, created new challenges for them. Again, their large-scale schemes were not mere copies, but, with the exception of the few outstanding men, the innovatory genius of application was missing, and the buildings, though many were of high quality, lacked the aesthetic vision of earlier work.

A considerable proportion of nineteenth-century architecture is in the classical style; in the first three decades of the century this was almost entirely so. Until the mid eighteenth century the source of this classical form had been the antique world of Rome. Since then, however, extensive archaeological studies in Greece, Turkey and the Middle East had introduced the earlier, purer yet simpler form of Greek classical architecture to western Europe. In reaction to the extrovert and decorative boldness of Baroque design, architects had veered towards this more restrained interpretation of both Greek and Roman sources in what is generally referred to as Neo-classicism.

From the late 1790s this form was gradually superseded by Romantic Classicisim. This varied from country to country and according to individual architects, but in general the work was more picturesque and dramatic than previously. From 1800 to the 1830s the model was more frequently the Greek classical form, creating bold, clear buildings, utilizing the Greek Doric Order – the columns fluted and without base – and, less often the Ionic Order. Such buildings were to be seen all over Europe.

By 1830 the factors that, since the later eighteenth century, had been gradually altering the structure of western society were accelerating, necessitating in the building and architecture of urban areas a much faster rate of construction. With the impetus of the Industrial Revolution, now not just in England and France but also in Germany, the Low Countries, Scandinavia and Italy, urbanization had speeded up. Factories were built to mass-produce goods, and by 1900 ornament and mouldings, furniture and fittings were being applied ready-made to the insides and exteriors of buildings. A hardness of finish and sameness of design invaded more and more the domain previously governed by aesthetic considerations and produced by the craftsmen.

In the 1840s workers trekked from the land where mechanization of agriculture had deprived them of a living towards the towns where they could earn a wage. Here, living standards in housing, necessarily built around the factory area because of lack of civic transport, were, in the main, extremely low, and overcrowding was rife. Small towns became cities almost overnight it seemed, and decades were to pass before a semblance of adequacy in amenities such as house interiors, water supply, sewage disposal, town administration and essential food and clothing supplies became tolerable.

Despite these low living standards, medical advances were gradually eliminating long-standing killer diseases – smallpox, for example – and population figures rose dramatically; this was due not to increased births but largely to longer survival, especially of young children. London's population multiplied four times during the nineteenth century, and this reflected the general European pattern.

Meanwhile speculative builders were profiting from the desperate need for housing. They bought land in industrial cities and built houses, packing them close together in ugly rows without providing adequate sanitation and other necessary amenities. Life in these houses was miserable; and the standard of health and hygiene was abysmally low. The countryside of Europe was slowly eaten into by areas of small, ugly dwellings, factories, slag heaps and other detritus from man's progress from an agricultural lifestyle to an industrial one.

But not all home building was like this. There were philanthropists, visionaries and architects of social purpose, ahead of their time and thought. In Germany there was Krupp in Essen, in England Sir Titus Salt in Yorkshire. Such men built ideal townships for their workers, with housing, shops and amenities near to the factories. These were the pioneers of the twentieth century 'new town' and 'garden city'.

To meet the needs of the population explosion, as well as the changing character of life in cities, new building materials were experimented with and, in conjunction with these, new methods of construction. The most notable advance in both of these fields was the adoption of iron and glass, used separately at first but increasingly, as time passed, together. This ferrovitreous-type of construction had been made possible by technical advances in both materials which had been taking place since the later eighteenth century and which had accelerated in the nineteenth.

Iron had been regarded as a durable, utilitarian material since the Middle Ages. It was first hammered into wrought iron and later, with the evolution of the improved design of blast furnace, it became possible to pour it molten into moulds to produce cast iron. The switchover to coal as a smelting fuel in the early seventeenth century

because of diminishing timber supplies initially caused technical problems, but, after Abraham Darby's experiments from 1709 in England, which showed that the coal must first be coked to remove sulphurous impurities, iron was increasingly used for the construction of bridges and factories to house heavy machinery. Two further vital advances were due to John Wilkinson, the great ironmaster who in 1776 installed a Boulton and Watt steam engine in his Shropshire works, so improving the power potential, and Henry Cort who, in 1784, introduced the action of puddling into the manufacturing process. In this the molten iron was stirred to free it from further impurities and so render it less brittle.

The way was then clear for an extensive use of iron in building for railings, balconies, staircase balustrades then, later, structurally for supporting columns, complete staircases, galleries and roofing. As the most developed industrial nation, England was world leader in the development of all these fields of construction.

The second half of the nineteenth century saw the increasing use of iron for heavy structural work. Beams for floors, lintels and roof trusses that would withstand heavy loads were manufactured for use in railway stations, civic and industrial buildings. In 1848, *James Bogardus* (1800–74) in New York created the first four-storeyed structure made of iron piers and lintels, going on to undertake more ambitious urban buildings using iron. Others followed his example for factories, textile mills, department stores and apartment blocks. In particular iron was used extensively for roofing as it was deemed to be more fireproof than earlier wood constructions. The new dome for the *United States Capitol* in *Washington* was a notable example, as was *Barry's* roofing for the new *Palace of Westminster* (**Plate 1**).

Advances in technique and practice were simultaneously making the production of suitable larger panes of glass available at a lower cost than previously. During the nineteenth century a number of factories were established to manufacture cast plate glass, a process earlier developed by the French in which molten glass was run directly on to a table where it was rolled out. This was a faster process and produced lustrous glass but, due to its contact with the table surface, was costly to manufacture as it still had to be ground and polished. A cheaper glass process was developed

Plate 1   The Palace of Westminster. London, 1836–65,
Sir Charles Barry. Photograph Geoff Ward

on the Continent from the old cylinder method. Called sheet glass, this was ideal for glazing as large panes could be produced.

Ferrovitreous construction was widely experimented with during the nineteenth century. At first used particularly for glasshouses and factories, it was later realized that the combined materials were ideal for structures such as railway stations, glass roofing and shopping arcades and galleries. In the later decades of the century such structures were built in cities all over Europe.

Increasing urbanization led to city centre replanning on a large scale. Much of the work was in classical form, from the Romantic Classicism of cities such as *Munich* and *Trieste* laid out in the 1830s and 1840s to the monumentality of the new capital of *Helsinki* and the later grand-scale redevelopment of *Paris* and *Vienna*. After mid-century

this Second Empire style, so termed from the creation of the *Grandes Boulevards* and *rond-points* of Napoleon III's Paris, moved closer to neo-Baroque in Franz Josef's *Ringstrasse* in *Vienna*. These extensive schemes served as a pattern for the whole of Europe later in the century.

Concurrently the revived medieval forms of construction had gained increasing favour for building of all types in the years 1850–80. First initiated as a literary then theological movement, the Gothic Revival was most marked in England but was then gradually taken up in northern Europe. By the 1840s the movement had become more serious and archaeologically correct. Utilized then chiefly for ecclesiastical and university building, after 1855 the style was increasingly adopted for all types of structure including civic design, railway architecture and housing.

It is only now, in the late twentieth century, that a balanced evaluation of nineteenth century architecture is being made. In the first half of the twentieth century historians and critics were too close to the previous age to assess its contribution dispassionately. Most condemned the work as derivative, mass-produced, overdecorated and in poor taste. A few, in contrast, praised fulsomely. It is undoubtedly true that all over Europe the nineteenth century perpetrated much ugly, tasteless building, permitted large, uncontrolled expansion of cities and created for posterity great areas of slums. On the other side of the coin, a fair quantity of fine, if eclectic, architecture was produced, much of which, despite widespread later demolition in cities and the holocaust of two world wars, survives. This is partly due to the vast quantity of buildings erected – more than in any comparative previous period in history. It is to be hoped that the over-enthusiasts of today do not succeed in their aim of preserving the total surviving heritage: but concentrate only on the best of it.

Contemporaneously with the later medieval and classical eclecticism evolved a minority splinter movement, contributed to by architects all over Europe (but particularly in England) who were endeavouring to design in a new way, one that was less derivative and shackled to the past. With the development of the use of new materials and consequent construction techniques, notably iron, glass and concrete, such a movement might have been expected to arise earlier, but, despite a multiplicity of ideas and experiments, these nineteenth-century attempts to design differently were hesitant and unsure. Outside the United States there was little evidence of the understanding of the design possibilities inherent in such materials. Although the buildings erected in this way provided a jumping-off ground for twentieth century concepts, at the time many of them appeared to be blind alleys.

The earliest group of designers searching for a new architectural form tended to look backwards rather than forwards. They were reacting against overdecoration, monumentality and polychromy, and wanted to return to the simpler vernacular forms of architecture that had prevailed in their own countries in an earlier age. The back-to-craftsmanship approach inspired by an abhorrence of the machine age that was initiated by *William Morris* in England and developed into the *Arts and Crafts Movement* strongly influenced many architects of the years 1870–1900.

By 1890 the search for new terms of architectural reference was producing more original and diverse ideas which led to a variety of different but related themes being manifested between the years 1890-1910. Such themes included the *Art Nouveau*, movement, of the *Sezession* architects and the greatly contrasting talented achievement of those two highly personalized architects: *Gaudì* in Spain and *Mackintosh* in Scotland.

Britain

As in other European countries, architecture in Britain in the first three decades of the century was mainly of Romantic Classical design. The two chief exponents, Soane and Nash, provided a great contrast in their work and in their personalities. *Sir John Soane* (1753–1837) was a highly original architect, a perfectionist and dedicated to his profession. He travelled widely before taking up practice, spending some years in Italy, north and south.

Soane's career had really begun with his appointment as Surveyor to the *Bank of England* in 1788, a post which he held until 1833 and in which he made his greatest contribution. His work here (almost completely lost in the rebuilding of the 1930s) was monumental, stripped of all superfluous ornament and relying upon simple, pure lines and fine proportions. Soane was a classicist but his inspiration was multi-centred; he took. for instance, structural themes and decorative features from Byzantine sources. This was to be seen particularly in his interiors where he fused these differing concepts into a highly personalized architectural style. In his later work especially, his architecture became increasingly austere and linear, his domes and arches becoming shallower, more segmental. His spatial handling and lighting were outstandingly original (**1**). The simplicity of his barely ornamented masses shared a common theme with Schinkel's work in Germany and Latrobe's in the United States (pp. 23–5).

Soane's town and country houses illustrate his appreciation of the Greek classical form combined, in some instances with other influences. Notable are *Tyringham Hall*, Buckinghamshire (c. 1796) and *Pitzhanger Manor* in Ealing (1800–3). His

1 Bank of England interior, c. *1800, Sir John Soane*

2 Hanover Terrace, Regent's Park, London, 1822–3, John Nash

3 Brunswick Terrace, Hove, c. *1825, Amon Wilds and Charles Busby*

mature style may be seen in his London home, *13 Lincoln's Inn Fields* (now the Sir John Soane Museum) and in the *Art Gallery and Mausoleum* at Dulwich (1811–14).

John Nash (1752–1835), an exact contemporary of Soane, was a contrast to him in every way. He was not austere and restrained but an ebullient extrovert. Whereas Soane's architecture was personally original and particularly adapted to effective interiors, Nash was in his element handling the large-scale exterior scheme. A man of his time, Nash experimented with all past styles from the picturesque and castellar to revived Gothic and Italian Renaissance.

Nash spent much of the last 30 years of his life working on extensive schemes for his patron the Prince Regent. The most colourfully flamboyant – and very successful – of these was the Royal Pavilion at Brighton, (1816–20) created in a blend of oriental forms which might be described as 'Indian Gothic with a flavour of Chinese', especially in the interiors.

Nash's great opportunity came in 1811 when, in London, Marylebone Park reverted to the Crown and, with the support of the Prince Regent, this area of farmland was made available for building development. Nash submitted an ambitious scheme which was accepted. He envisaged a 'garden city' for the wealthy near to the centre of the metropolis. The concept included a park with summer palace, villas, a lake, a canal encircled by terraces of town houses and intermittent focal centres. From this area – the Regent's Park – a royal route – Regent Street – would provide a link to the Regent's town palace in the Mall (Carlton House).

Nash began work in 1812. When he died 23 years later much of this vast concept had been realized. The terraces and crescents were built between 1812 and 1832 and, between 1827 and 1832, Nash replaced Carlton House with Carlton House Terrace. Not least successful was his Regent Street with All Souls' Church near one end and the Quadrant near the other (2).

The next generation of architects followed, in general, the path of Romantic Classicism. *William Wilkins* (1778–1839) and *Sir Robert Smirke* (1781–1867) both designed their most important structures in Greek Revival form, with Wilkins responsible for the *National Gallery* in Trafalgar Square, London (1832–8) and Smirke the *British Museum* (1825–47). However, architects of this period also suited their architectural style to the needs of the individual commission, reverting to Italian Renaissance or Gothic when they felt that this was warranted, as in, for example, Wilkins' work at Cambridge University.

The eclecticism springing from this variety of source material was clearly demonstrated in the Commissioners' Churches. Little church building had been undertaken since the early eighteenth century, and 100 years later the population had both greatly increased and been redistributed. New centres of population had sprung up from the migration of workers from country to town. To meet this situation in 1818 the Church Building Society was formed, and, with Parliamentary support, a Church Building Act was passed which provided for £1 million to be spent to build new churches, with a further £500,000 allocated some years later. The Church Commissioners supervised the scheme.

The final total of churches built was 214, the majority of which were in the London suburbs and the industrial areas of the Midlands and the north. Few were aesthetically or architecturally notable, being primarily large to accommodate big congregations. Of the total, 174 were Gothic and the remainder classical.

A small proportion of Commissioners' Churches were interesting and well designed. Most notable, for example, are Sir John Soane's *Holy Trinity Marylebone*, and *S. John, Bethnal Green* both built 1824–5 in London; *John Nash's All Souls'* off Regent Street (1822–4); *Sir Robert Smirke's S. Mary, Wyndham Place, London* (1823–4) and *S. Philip, Salford* (1825), *Thomas Hardwick's* parish church of *S. Marylebone* and *Sir Charles Barry's S. Peter, Brighton* (1824–8 Gothic) and *S. Andrew, Hove* (1827–8, Italian Renaissance). The finest Greek Revival church is that of *S. Pancras* in *London* by the *Inwoods*, father and son (1819–22). The body of the church is based upon the Erechtheion in Athens (Vol. 1) and the steeple upon the Tower of the Winds in the same city (Vol. 1). A fine early Gothic example and one of the first attempts to design a stone church according to medieval type of construction is *S. Luke, Chelsea* (1820–4) by *James Savage* (5).

Urban domestic buildings in terrace form had been initiated in the second half of the eighteenth century in Bath and by Adam in London and Edinburgh (Vol. 3). After 1800 the rising population and increasing urbanization made necessary a much faster pace of such construction. At this time (apart from Nash's Regent's Park scheme, (pp. 5–6), the need was fulfilled by two notable speculative builders: *James Burton* (1761–1837) and *Thomas Cubitt* (1788–1855). Their contribution was in London, Burton building mainly in *Bloomsbury* followed from the 1820s onwards by Cubitt.

Cubitt is famous particularly as the founder of the modern-style building firm. Until his time work in different trades had been sub-contracted – bricklaying, masonry, carpentry, etc. – and, whereas the system had worked well enough previously, it was now too slow. Cubitt bought land and workshops and set up a firm that included all craftsmen necessary to the building trade, employed on a permanent wage basis. To keep his firm financially solvent, he had to provide continuous work for them. This he did by large-scale speculative building. Cubitt's estates were, unlike later developments which have devalued the term 'speculative building', of high architectural and structural standard. Many stand today as fine, elegant and sound as they were 150 years ago. All his life Cubitt used his influence to combat the abuses of architectural, building and living standards to which such expansion is heir. He was especially determined to keep up high standards in drainage, sewage disposal, street lighting and construction.

Cubitt began his development at *Highbury Park* and *Stoke Newington*, moving on to *St Pancras* and *Euston*. His most extensive and best-known enterprise was his creation of *Belgravia*. When Buckingham Palace was built he realized that the area was suited to wealthy development. He leased a plot of swampy ground from Lord Grosvenor and converted it into aristocratic squares, employing architects to design the houses. *Belgrave Square* is a typical example, designed by *George Basevi*.

Such development was also taking place outside London. In *Edinburgh* the *New Town* was finally being laid out. Planned in the 1780s by Robert Adam but delayed by the Napoleonic Wars among other reasons, it was finally built by the next generation of architects on a classical grid pattern of streets in Greek Revival style. It covered a rectangular area parallel to but north of the Royal Mile: it was termed 'Athens of the North'. As in Bath, it was a homogeneous scheme, built in one style and one material. The city had, at last, awakened to the advantages of its topography and had utilized this to the full instead of complaining, as in the previous century, of not possessing a city built on flat ground where it was easy to expand.

Urban expansion was also taking place for recreational purposes in seaside resorts and spas. *Brighton* and *Hove*, popularized by the Prince Regent, developed from the village of Brighthelmstone between 1800 and 1850 into a magnificent terraced sea front, with squares behind, some 2–3 miles (4–5 km) long. Here is the culmination of Nash's Regent's Park terraces: there is no local feeling present. The work is mainly painted stucco-faced, as in London, and many architects contributed. Of particular quality and distinction is the work of *Charles Busby* and *Amon Wilds*, (*Brunswick Terrace*) and *Decimus Burton* (*Adelaide Crescent*) (**3**).

Decimus Burton (1800–81) had designed a quantity of work for Nash in Regent's Park. He also worked closely with his father, *James Burton* (1761–1837) in developing *Hastings, St Leonards* and *Tunbridge Wells*.

Cheltenham expanded as a spa in the early nineteenth century as Bath had done in the eighteenth. The architects most closely associated with this were *John B. Papworth* (1775–1847) and *John B. Forbes* (b. 1795) who, between them, largely laid out the *Montpellier, Lansdown* and *Pittville Estates* in the town. The style was Greek Revival, though the two notable *Pump Room* buildings were based on the Roman Bath concept.

In nineteenth-century Britain the revival of the medieval forms of architectural design was a strong and enduring movement; indeed, medievalism and its expression in Gothic architecture had never completely died out. From about 1750 a literary, romantic version (Gothick) arose, encouraged by the pattern books of Batty Langley and stimulated by Horace Walpole's villa, Strawberry Hill. By the 1780s, it was employed more often, and in a less romantic manner, by such architects as *James Wyatt, Sanderson Miller* and *Henry Keene*.

During the first decade of the nineteenth century the study of Gothic architecture was not taken very seriously, but more and more architects were using the style to design churches and university buildings. They adopted its decorative media and general features but took liberties with the proportions and the materials used. They approached medievalism in a similar manner to that adopted by the Elizabethans when they took up Renaissance design. Gothic builders in the years 1800–40 supported their vaults on slender iron columns and constructed the actual vaults in plaster. Typical are *William Wilkins'* work at *Cambridge University*, the *New Court* at *Corpus Christi College* (1823) and his screen and gateway to *King's College* (1822–4), *Sir Charles Barry's S. Peter's Church* in *Brighton* (p. 6) and *Edward Garbett's Theale Church* (1820–30).

From the 1840s the Gothic Revival became more serious. Archaeological study made the work more competent and the buildings more closely related to their medieval prototypes. The great building of this age is the *Palace of Westminster*, redesigned and built after a fire in 1834 by *Sir Charles Barry* (1795–1860) and *A. W. N. Pugin* (1815–52). Based on the later Perpendicular style, this is a masterly design and representative of its age. It is fundamentally a classical building in Gothic dress that incorporates modern materials such as cast iron for roofing – Barry was bearing in mind the fate of its predecessor (**Plate 1**).

The Revival was seriously established in Britain by idealists and thinkers rather than architects. The movement was espoused primarily by men

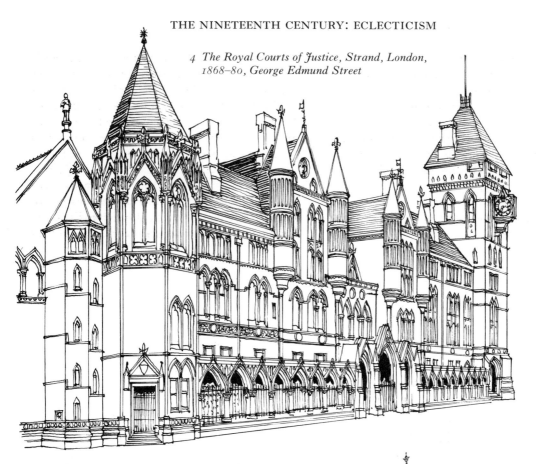

4 *The Royal Courts of Justice, Strand, London,
1868–80, George Edmund Street*

5 *S. Luke's Church, Chelsea, 1820–4,
James Savage*

6 *S. Augustine's Church, Kilburn,
1870–80, John Loughborough
Pearson*

who advanced it on moral and theological grounds. Such men believed that the Middle Ages was the greatest period of human endeavour and human spirit and that the arts and architecture of the time were the most beautiful. They aimed to recreate this age and, in so doing, recommended the use only of materials that had been available at the time. The dominating influences of the years 1845–65 were the ecclesiological movement stemming from Oxford and Cambridge Universities, the writings and architecture of Pugin and the works of *John Ruskin*.

It took time to learn to recreate authentic medieval workmanship and to relate it, however unsuitably, to buildings of completely different function from those needed in the Middle Ages: town halls, public schools, railway stations, hotels, department stores, etc. Barry and Pugin had to train a new school of craftsmen to build the Palace of Westminster and to transform Pugin's meticulous drawings into carved stone and painted glass.

The Gothic Revival in Britain was at its height between 1855 and 1885. In this High Victorian Gothic period architects such as *Sir George Gilbert*

7 *The Town Hall, Manchester, 1869–77, Alfred Waterhouse*

Scott (1811–78), *George Edmund Street* (1824–81), *William Butterfield* (1814–1900), *Alfred Waterhouse* (1830–1905) and many more covered the country with Gothic structures intended for all purposes. Pressure was put upon architects by the Ecclesiological Society to design only with medieval materials in thirteenth and fourteenth-century style, but by 1865 architects were using all medieval styles, from Romanesque to Tudor in English, French and Italian interpretations, and their buildings were constructed in a variety of materials but predominantly polychrome brickwork decorated with terracotta (**Plates 2**, **3**, **figs 4**, **6**, **7**).

As the leader of European industrialization from the mid eighteenth century onwards, Britain was a pioneer in the use of iron and glass for a wide variety of structures. From the early years of the nineteenth century on, these materials were found to be especially suited to factory and commercial building and to the construction of bridges, docks and railway stations. Employed together, iron and glass were regarded as being more fireproof than wood and glass, although by 1850 it was being realized that an iron skeleton structure could collapse dangerously if it reached a certain temperature in a fire.

Iron – wrought and cast – had been utilized extensively for railings, balconies and staircase balustrades during the eighteenth and early nineteenth centuries but after this its use was rapidly extended. Some textile mills contained a comprehensive iron skeleton – for example, *Sir Titus Salt's* magnificent new *mill* at *Saltaire* in Yorkshire (1854) – and iron was being adopted as a suitable material for complete staircases or for Gothic vaults as in John Nash's 'Chinese-style' *staircase* at the *Royal Pavilion* at Brighton (*c.* 1818) and *Thomas Hopper's* fan-vaulted *conservatory* at *Carlton House* in London (1811–12). In 1851 at *Balmoral Castle*, the Prince Consort ordered a prefabricated iron ballroom.

The great nineteenth-century engineers, such as

Plate 2 St Pancras Station Midland Hotel, London, 1868–76, Sir George Gilbert Scott

Plate 3 Keble College Chapel, Oxford, 1873–6,
    William Butterfield

Telford, Rennie, Stephenson and *Brunel*, had shown from early in the nineteenth century by their bridges and aqueducts what could be attained with iron and steel. Among such pioneering examples is the remarkable *Pont-Cysylltau aqueduct*, an iron superstructure supported on stone piers, which carries the canal across the River Dee and over 1000 ft (300 m) of countryside in the *Vale of Llangollen* (1805, Telford). Bridges of a span greater than this which had been attempted hitherto include those across the *Menai Straits* separating Wales from Anglesey, *Isambard Kingdom Brunel's Clifton Suspension Bridge* over the gorge at Bristol (1836–54) and his *Royal Albert Bridge* over the *River Tamar* (1859) which divides Devon from Cornwall.

The nineteenth century was also the railway age and here also Britain led the way in designing the great railway termini for which ferrovitreous construction was ideally suited. Iron was utilized for brackets, trusses, cantilevers and all other purposes, from the great train shed roofs and supports to decorative detail, whether as classical capitals and columns or Gothic cusped panelling. Early stations were unpretentious – *Crown Street, Liverpool* (1830) for example. Gradually becoming more elaborate and extensive, these were followed by *Euston, London* (1836–9), *Lime Street, Liverpool* (1839), *Brighton* (1841) and *Carlisle* (1848). Among the impressive survivors (in a not-too-unaltered condition) of later years may be numbered the London termini of *St Pancras, Paddington* and *King's Cross*.

Ferrovitreous construction was also found to be suited to a wide range of roofing structures. Most notable of these was the *Coal Exchange* in *London* by *J. B. Bunning*, built 1846–9 but now, sadly, demolished and the *Reading Room* which *Sydney Smirke* added in 1854–5 over the court of his brother's *British Museum*. Then, in 1851, came the

*8 The Grand Hotel, Scarborough, 1863–7,
Cuthbert Brodrick*

*9 Glasgow School of Art, 1897,
Charles Rennie Mackintosh*

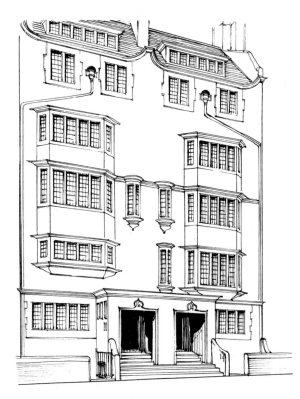

*10 14–16 Hans Road, London, 1891,
C. F. A. Voysey*

11 The Crystal Palace, Hyde Park, London, 1850–2, Sir Joseph Paxton

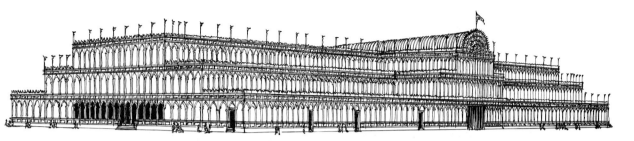

full realization of the potential of these materials for prefabrication when the *Crystal Palace* was erected in *Hyde Park* in less than five months. Built here to house the Great Exhibition of that year, this giant glasshouse was 1,848 ft (565 m) long and contained 3,300 iron columns, 2,150 girders, 24 miles (38 km) of guttering and 900,000 sq.ft. (84,000 sq. m) of glass. In 1852 it was dismantled and reassembled at Sydenham in south London where it remained until its spectacular conflagration in 1936: a destruction hastened by the 600,000 cu. ft. (17,000 cu. m) of timber contained in its roof (**11**).

In the last three decades of the nineteenth century in Britain a number of architects were in rebellion against the over-ornamentation, polychromy and endless eclecticism of the majority of building of the time. The work of these men was also eclectic but it was a return to a simpler, vernacular form of architecture, based very much on English work of the sixteenth and seventeenth centuries. There were a number of versions of this but predominant was the so-called 'Queen Anne' style of which *Richard Norman Shaw* (1831–1912) was the premier exponent. Shaw had a very large practice concerned with domestic and civic building. His work showed a personal, fresh approach which lent individuality to his buildings. He used half timber and brick mainly with stone dressings for windows, gables and doorways. Shaw's office contained many pupils, a number of whom, in turn, became talented architects; Shaw always encouraged originality in all his pupils.

Shaw's earlier work, especially in his country houses, was informal and based upon late medieval traditional designs. Typical are *Grim's Dyke, Harrow Weald* (1872), *'Wispers', Midhurst* (1875) and *Pierrepoint, Farnham* (1876). He revived the concepts of the two-storeyed hall and the ingle-

nook fireplace as at his large house in Northumberland, *Cragside* near *Rothbury* (1869–84). Later, in the 1890s, Shaw turned to more classical themes, as at *Bryanston House* in *Dorset*.

Shaw designed many town houses – detached and terraced – for example, *Swan House* on the *Chelsea Embankment* (1876), as well as blocks of flats. He also built office blocks (the *First Alliance Assurance Building, Pall Mall*, 1882–3) but his best-known London building was his *New Scotland Yard* at *Westminster* (1887–1900), planned in castellar form using granite with, above, horizontal banding in brick and Portland Stone (**12**). His last work, in Italian Renaissance style, is the entrance façade in stone of the *Piccadilly Hotel*, completed in 1908.

A whole school of architects followed Shaw's lead, all eschewing over-ornamentation and reverting to the simpler vernacular forms,

12 New Scotland Yard, London, 1887–90, Richard Norman Shaw

especially in brick with stone dressings. They demanded a high standard of craftsmanship, good design and, where possible, the use of local materials. A strong influence on such architects was the contemporary Arts and Crafts Movement. Similarly motivated but different in their approach were such men as Webb and Voysey.

Philip Webb (1831–1915), in contrast to Shaw, had a small practice and concentrated almost entirely on domestic work. He was a perfectionist, taking infinite pains and designing the house down to its last interior decorative detail. Like Shaw, he reverted to the English vernacular, but his work was plain, almost astringent, and stripped of all needless decoration. An early commission was his *Red House, Bexleyheath* which he was asked to build in 1859 by his friend William Morris for the latter's wedding. This is a plain red-brick house with steeply-sloping tiled roofs. The house plan is irregular and informal, reflecting the disposition of the rooms within. It is a blend of past English styles: Georgian sash windows, seventeenth-century tall chimneystacks and brick bonding.

Webb's last house and the only one to survive almost unaltered was *Standen* in *East Grinstead* (1891-4). This is a charming, unpretentious house, well-built and carefully designed with quality materials and attractive interior detail – a house ahead of its time.

The contribution of *C. F. A. Voysey* (1857–1941) at the end of the century was also in the domestic field and, again, his style was intensely personal.He too used traditional building materials and his work paid tribute to the English vernacular but was simple, almost austere, and looked forward to modern architectural concepts. His façades were unpretentious with low elevations, sloping, asymmetrical rooflines, the rough-cast faced walls broken by rectangular, mullioned windows, (**10**). Probably his best house is *Broadleys* on the shores of Lake Windermere in Cumbria (1898-9).

The most original and uncompromising of these *fin-de-siècle* architects was *Charles Rennie Mackintosh* (1868–1928). His work pointed the way towards modern architecture and exerted a marked influence upon its later exponents. Mackintosh was a Scot, and most of his work is in or near Glasgow. His masterpiece is the *Glasgow School of Art*, an austere, almost functionalist building, constructed in two phases (1897–9 and 1907–9) (**9**).

France

The French Revolution not only brought architectural construction to a halt but also caused extensive damage to individual buildings, especially cathedrals and châteaux. Complete areas of city centres were devastated in reprisal for royalist support; the Place Bellecour in Lyons, for example, became a casualty. From 1806 Napoleon Bonaparte endeavoured to get a building programme re-started, partly to leave some fine monuments in Paris and other cities as evidence of his reign and partly to ease the unemployment situation. He began many schemes, but most were completed after his death. Fortunately his successors broadly continued the work and, in turn, in the second half of the century, Napoleon III initiated and completed a further and more ambitious building programme.

Bonaparte's chief architects were *Charles Percier* (1764–1839) and *Pierre Fontaine* (1762–1853). Their work followed the Romantic Classical line, typically French in its low-key interpretation, with the fine detailing and carefully proportioned arcades repeated along the length of the newly laid-out street façades. This was in marked contrast to the more richly-ornate interiors. Napoleon's first urban plan carried out by these architects comprised the *Rue de Rivoli* fronting the Tuileries gardens and leading out of the earlier Place de la Concorde (Vol. 3). The other end of the road terminated in the *Rue des Pyramids* and *Place des Pyramids*. Also built was the cross street of the *Rue de Castiglione*, which debouches into the Place Vendôme.

Percier and Fontaine also built the elegant *Arc de Triomphe du Carrousel*, planned as a gateway to the Tuileries gardens. The arch (1806–8) is in marble, a version of that of Septimius Severus in the Forum Romanum in Rome (Vol. 1). The original crowning quadriga represented Napoleon and incorporated the four Greek horses from St Mark's Cathedral in Venice (Vol. 2). The horses were returned to their original position there by the British after the fall of Napoleon. For Bonaparte, Percier and Fontaine also worked on the palaces at Compiègne, Fontainbleau and Versailles.

The best known monument to the First Empire in Paris is the *Arc de Triomphe de L'Etoile*, commissioned in 1806 by Napoleon to be built in

Plate 4 Arc de Triomphe de L'Etoile, Paris, 1806–35. Sculpture Le Départ, *1833, by Rude*

Plate 5 The Opera House, Paris. Sculpture 1861–5 by Carpeaux

honour of the French armies: a true symbol of imperialism. Several architects were involved, but the arch was finally built largely to the design of *Jean Francis Chalgrin* (1739–1811). It is a vast arch, 164 ft (50 m) high and 148 ft (45 m) wide. Based upon the triumphal arch theme of ancient Rome, this overshadows even the Arch of Constantine there, which measures 80 by 69 ft (24 by 21 m). The Etoile arch is astylar, its decoration comprising a frieze extending round all sides and containing hundreds of 6-ft (1.8-m) figures depicting the departure and triumphal return of the French armies in the Napoleonic Wars. The four great sculptural groups are the work of different sculptors. The best of these works is *Le Départ de 1792* by Rude (but commonly called *La Marseillaise*) (1833); this is on the left side facing the Champs Elysées (**Plate 4**). Under the arch is the eternal flame, marking the resting place of France's 'Unknown Soldier'.

When Napoleon commissioned the arch (which was only finally completed in 1836), the *Place de L'Etoile* (p. 19) was in the form of a five-pointed star, in the centre of which the arch was set. The great avenue of the *Champs Elysées*, which extends from L'Etoile to the *Place de la Concorde* (see Gabriel, Vol. 3), had been developed over many years. The avenue and the square were taken over by the City of Paris in 1828, when fountains were constructed and gardens laid out. Before this, in 1807, Napoleon commissioned *Bernard Poyet* (1742–1824) to create a new façade to the older *Palais Bourbon* situated on the opposite bank of the Seine in order to make the building style and line conform with those in the square and to harmonize with the proposed Madeleine Church at the other end of the Rue Royale vista. Poyet achieved this result by the addition of a large Corinthian portico and steps. The palace later housed the Legislative Assembly (*Chambre des Députés*) and since became

Plate 6 The Madeleine Church, Paris, 1806–12,
Pierre Vignon

the residence of the President of the National Assembly.

The site of a church to be dedicated to the *Magdalen* had been planned in the eighteenth century, when Gabriel had designed the Place de la Concorde and the Rue Royale (Vol. 3). The church was to stand at the end of this vista. Napoleon decided early in the nineteenth century to build here a Roman Corinthian temple of glory, standing upon a podium. It was designed on these lines in 1808 by *Pierre Vignon* (1762–1828) and is now a Paris landmark on this impressive site. The exterior is severely monumental, finely proportioned and sculptured (**Plate 6**). Like the Arc de Triomphe de L'Etoile, the building of the Madeleine was interrupted and was only finally completed by Huvé in 1845. Napoleon had changed his mind after the beginning of construction, deciding that it should be a church after all. Inside, the

church is entered through a caissoned barrel-vaulted vestibule and, beyond, three caissoned saucer domes cover the nave. The east end is apsidal; below the conch of the apse is a panel of painted figures – Byzantine in style – and below this is an Ionic colonnade. The main order of the church is Corinthian, with altars between the columns. The whole interior is richly, boldly Roman, painted and gilded, presenting a marked contrast to the formal, monumental exterior (**13**).

Another great monument to Romantic Classicism in the central area of Paris is the *Bourse* (Exchange). The designer in 1808 was *A. T. Brogniart* (1739–1813), who created a large colonnaded structure on square plan in the Corinthian Order, which lost something of its impact when it was enlarged in 1903.

An extensive influence on the architecture of the first half of the century was exerted by the first

13 Interior, The Madeleine

professor of the new École Polytechnique founded by Napoleon Bonaparte in 1795. *Jean Nicholas Louis Durand* (1760–1834) had served as an engineer in Napoleon's army and his approach to the subject of architecture was, therefore, more pragmatic and practical than that of his predecessors in the Académie before the Revolution. His publications *Recueil et parallèle des edifices en tout genre, anciens et modernes* (1801) and *Précis des leçons d'architecture données à L'École Polytechnique* (1802–5) put forward his theories on the adaptation of classical, medieval and Renaissance forms to modern use. He demonstrated this standardization of the eclectic approach, suiting the choice of style to the commission, in standard bays shown in plan and elevation. It was a practical if not inspiring method and was taken up widely by European architects, notably in urban planning. The strongest influence of the Durand thesis was, strangely, not so much in France as in Germany and Denmark.

The majority of French architecture of the half-century from 1825 was classical in derivation, carefully Italian Renaissance in the early years but gradually, as elsewhere in Europe, becoming heavier and more monumental as time passed, though less over-ornamented than in England or Germany, for example. The rebuilding of the *Hôtel de Ville* in Paris illustrates this development. The fine, slightly Mannerist early-Renaissance sixteenth-century building was extended and restored in 1837–49 by *Godde* and *Lesueur* – the Mannerist touches being carefully deleted – then, after being fired by the insurgents in 1871, a further, but coarser, rebuilding and extension took place from 1874 by *Ballu* and *Deperthes*.

The population increase and urbanization necessitated the building of a number of new churches at this time and a similar pattern may be discerned in all of them. The best of the earlier churches is *S. Vincente de Paul* in *Paris*, begun in 1824 by *Charles Lepère* and completed 20 years later by his son-in-law, *Jacques Ignace Hittorff*. This Romantic Classical church has a fine site. From flights of steps rises a Grecian central Ionic portico flanked by twin square towers. In the interior, based upon the early-Christian basilican model, an imposing Ionic colonnade divides nave from aisles, this echoed above by a smaller-scale Corinthian one. The apse is decorated by frescoes of Christ Pantocrator. This church, like later examples, is dark inside, the small windows filled with richly-coloured glass.

Two Paris churches in the 1860s illustrate the later trend: *La Trinité* by Théodore Ballu (1861–7) and S. Augustin by Victor Balthard (1860–8). Both are large, well-constructed, solid and heavy buildings. *La Trinité* is a blend of Romanesque and classical forms, the triple portico with rose window above on the entrance front surmounted by a tall multi-stage classical tower. The interior of this cruciform church is dark, with coloured glass in the small window openings. *S. Augustin* is classical/Byzantine in concept, a massive central dome rising on a classical drum and surmounted by a lantern. Its four corner turrets above apses on three sides have a Germanic appearance. The interior is impressive, the wide nave and triumphal chancel arch leading into the short choir.

French architecture of the 1850s to the 1880s was dominated by the Second Empire mode established in Paris under Napoleon III. This was the French equivalent of the English High Victorian Gothic – in both cases the maturity of the style. Characteristic of Second Empire design is the mansard roof and the corner and centre pavilions projecting from the façades and capped by taller mansards. A late-sixteenth-century style (Vol. 3), the mansard roof had never quite died out in France. It was revived with enthusiasm in this period and its popularity spread to most countries of Europe.

The main layout of the centre of Paris (apart from the Medieval Île de la Cité and the Île S. Louis) is the product of the Second Empire. Napoleon III became Emperor in 1852 and for almost the next 20 years, under *Haussmann* and his colleagues, the Grandes Boulevards of Paris, with their *ronds-point* and flamboyant buildings set at significant places, were constructed. The schemes were extensive, the quality of work high, the façades along the boulevards homogeneous and imposing. An urban masterpiece was created, the finest in Europe in this century. Apart from one or two exceptions, the individual buildings are not outstanding. It is the town planning, the layout and the harmonious handling of the whole that is effective. The structures are mainly of stone or stucco, with shops on the ground floor and flats above, covered by mansard roofs. The roofline is even, the fenestration uniform. The whole is classical, often neo-Baroque.

One of the most impressive landscaping schemes was the enlargement of the *Place de L'Étoile* (p. 15) planned by Haussmann. *Georges Eugène Haussmann* (1809–91) worked for Napoleon III from 1853. He was not an architect but a government administrator and urban planner. He was made Prefect of the Seine Department by Napoleon and, later, a baron. His remodelling of Paris was extensive, driving boulevards through older, crowded districts and establishing railway stations, parklands and civic and commercial structures in their place. In 1854 Haussmann began the redesigning of the *Place de L'Étoile*, creating 12 avenues radiating from the central arch to replace the earlier five. The uniform buildings round the Place were designed by *Hittorff*, who carried out a considerable part of Haussmann's programmes for the capital.

Plate 7 The New Louvre, Paris, 1852–7, L. T. J. Visconti and H. M. Lefuel

Napoleon III's first priority after becoming Emperor was the completion of the old palace of the *Louvre* and connection of it to the Tuileries. The old Renaissance Louvre had been initiated by Francis I in 1546 and had been altered and added to ever since (Vol. 3). The rulers of France had long since taken up residence in the Tuileries Palace (burnt down in 1871) and the Louvre had accommodated various ministries and the great art gallery. The *New Louvre* planned by Napoleon was intended for similar purposes. The work was begun by *L. T. J. Visconti* (1791–1853) in 1852 and completed five years later by *H. M. Lefuel* (1810–80). The façades continued the design of earlier work but are coarser and more plastic, especially in the sculpture and convex mansard roofs (**Plate 7**).

The most flamboyant and successful scheme of the period is the *Avenue* and *Place de l'Opéra*. The Place was laid out from 1858 onwards with buildings by *Charles Rohault de Fleury* (1801–75) and *Henri Blondel* (1832–97). The Opera House itself, designed by *Jean Louis Charles Garnier* (1825–98) and built 1861–75, set the pattern for cities all over Europe (**14**). Strongly related to it is, among others, the *Burgtheater* in Vienna (**Plate 10**), the *Romanian Athenaeum* in Bucharest (**48**), the Opera Houses of *Odessa* and *L'vov* (p. 64 and **Plate 24**) and the *Theatre* in *Cracow* (**50**). The Paris Opera is sumptuous, imperial and very Baroque. The exterior is three-dimensional and plastic, more Italian than French. The sculpture on the façade by *Jean Baptiste Carpeaux* (1827–75) is noteworthy (**Plate 5**). This sculpture, entitled *La Danse*, was being damaged by air-pollution in 1964. It was therefore replaced by a copy, and the original is now in the Musée d'Orsay. Inside, the foyer, grand staircase and auditorium are superbly luxurious in gilt with crimson velvet, the essence of the period in the wealthy countries of western Europe.

Outside Paris a neo-Baroque layout of great magnificence is the *Palais Longchamps* at *Marseilles* (1862–9) by H. J. Espérandieu (1829–74). The monument constitutes an imposing entrance to the park, set into the hillside, with a central, sculptured cascade, flanked by a sweeping staircase and curving colonnades which lead, at each side, to square, classical blocks (**15**).

French architectural influence grew from the Second Empire onwards. France, together with England, moved into the sphere of influence which

14 *Place de l'Opéra, Paris, 1858–64, Rohault de Fleury and Henri Blondel. The Opera House (centre, Académie Nationale de Musique), 1861–74, J. L. C. Garnier*

Italy had held since the Florentine Renaissance. The *École des Beaux Arts* acted as an educational magnet for students from other European countries and, even more, the United States. The expression '*Beaux Arts*' became synonymous with the architectural precepts of the institution.

France in the nineteenth century, like England, thoroughly restored the monuments of her great medieval heritage. The leading figure in this Gothic restoration, a contemporary of and equivalent to the English *Sir George Gilbert Scott* (pp. 9–10) in his large practice and tireless rebuilding programme, was *Eugène-Emmanuel Viollet-le-Duc* (1814–79). The majority of this work was in the field of reconstruction and repair and, like Scott, he was often overenthusiastic and has, accordingly

been blamed by later generations. His name is most clearly associated with the *Cathedral of Notre Dame* (Vol. 2) and *La Sainte Chapelle* (Vol. 2) both in Paris, the *Abbey Church of S. Denis* (Vol. 2), the *Château of Pierrefonds* (Vol. 2), the hill town of *Mont-S. Michel* (Vol. 2) and the walled town of *Carcassonne* (Vol. 2). Chief among his published works which had considerable influence in his day was his ten-volume *Dictionnaire raisonné de l'Architecture Française du XIe au XVIe Siècle*, published 1854–68. Viollet-le-Duc's own new work was not especially notable and commissions were not numerous. An exception to this was his new church in the Parisian suburb of S. Denis, *S. Denys-de-l'Estrée* (1864–7). This is a large stone-vaulted church, decorative without being over-

15 *Palais Longchamps, Marseilles, 1862–9, H. J. Espérandieu*

*16 Reading Room, Bibliothèque Nationale, Paris,
1862–8, H. P. F. Labrouste*

ornamented, with a wide-pointed, arched nave
arcade above which were lancet clerestory
windows and an eastern five-light lancet window.
Also of interest are his apartment blocks in Paris in
restrained Gothic style.

The *fin-de-siècle* brought a new wave of neo-
Baroque buildings to Paris, when further grand-
scale structures were built. Among these are the
Grand and the *Petit Palais*. Completed at the same
time, but quite different in style, was the great
Church of the Sacré Coeur, set on the hill of
Montmartre, with its approach stairways and
platforms. This church had been begun in 1875 by
Paul Abadie (1812–84) but was not completed until
1919. It is in Romanesque/Byzantine style after the
Church of S. Front at *Périgueux* (Vol. 2), a
controversial building but an arresting one.

As in England, the French became interested in
developing the use of iron and glass in building –
separately, then together – both decoratively and
structurally. Also, as in England, they began to
establish a railway communications system earlier
than elsewhere in Europe and built stations and
related buildings for which ferrovitreous construction proved an ideal method. Of the early stations
the *Gare de L'Est* in Paris by *Duquesney* (1847-52)

was an excellent example, its great iron and glass
lunette surviving later remodelling. Later, at the
end of the century, came the *Paris* station of the
Gare d'Orsay (1898–1900) by Laloux, a more
ornate Baroque-style design in keeping with the
contemporary work in the city. For long this
impressive mansard-roofed structure was empty
and desolate but has recently been restored and
adapted to become a museum of nineteenth-
century art.

Apart from railway stations, French architects
utilized ferrovitreous construction for a variety of
buildings. Especially notable are the two great
libraries of Paris, the earlier *Bibliotèque Sainte-
Geneviève* (1843–50) by *Henri Labrouste*, with its
restrained classical exterior façade and interior
iron structure and, in the later *Bibliotèque Nationale*, the *Reading Room* incorporated into the
earlier building, also by *Labrouste* (1862–8). This
has a remarkable interior, the slender, delicate iron
columns with their tiny Corinthian capitals carry-
ing the roof. This is divided into nine equal
compartments, each covered by a saucer dome
with central oculus which effectively illuminate
the entire interior: a functional and attractive
scheme (**16**).

As in England, French architects used iron extensively as a structural material in church design, especially for Gothic buildings as in, for example, *S. Eugène* in *Paris* (1854–5) and *S. Paul* in *Montluçon* (1863), both by *Boileau*.

The metal was also utilized for commercial structures, for example, the Paris *Halles Centrales* (1853–8) by *Victor Balthard* (demolished 1971) and the *International Paris Expositions* of 1855 and 1878.

The most famous iron monument in Paris is undoubtedly the *Eiffel Tower*, designed for the Paris Exposition of 1889 by *Gustave Eiffel* (1832–1923) to commemorate the start of the French Revolution 100 years ealier. Eiffel was an engineer and the structure an engineering not an architectural feat: at 984 ft (300 m) high this metal tower was then the tallest structure in the world. Eiffel's researches and achievements in this field, including his bridges and other work, led later to the construction of metal buildings clad in stone or concrete.

The Germanic Influence: Germany

The finest work here was produced in the first four decades of the nineteenth century and the major part of this was in the Romantic Classical style. The influence of Professor Durand of the École Polytechnique was considerable. Paradoxically, in view of the Napoleonic Wars, a greater quantity of fine architecture owing much to Durand's influence was erected here than in contemporary France, where, in the first two decades at least, the bulk of designs did not get off the drawing board. Centres of several major cities were rebuilt and laid out with extensive new schemes: Berlin, Munich, Karlsruhe and Dresden, for example.

The Greek Revival form of Romantic Classicism dominated the work of the first 20 years of the century, notably the contribution of Langhans, Gilly and Schinkel in Berlin, and Fischer and von Klenze in Munich.

The most popular source material was the *acropolis* of Athens, especially the Propylaea, and the *Parthenon*; city gateways were based upon the former and memorial monuments upon the latter. The impressive first instance of this is the Greek Doric ceremonial gateway, the *Brandenburg Gate* in *Berlin*, designed 1789–83 by K. G. Langhans. It

was planned as the entrance to the city and the great boulevard Unter den Linden and was based on the Athenian Propylaea. In modern times, it was renowned as the symbol of political division, being part of the wall that until recently separated the two halves of the city (**17**). Influential and contemporary in this field also was *Friedrich Gilly's* (1772–1800) projected *memorial* to Frederick the Great with its 'Parthenon' raised dramatically upon a high podium. *Von Klenze's* (1784–1864) later '*Walhalla*' (1831–2) near *Regensburg*, was even more romantically sited.

The most homogeneous and extensive urban centre replanning was at *Karlsruhe* (1800–26); one of the earliest of such schemes, its very homogeneity stemmed from the fact that the same architect, *Friedrich Weinbrenner* (1766–1826), supervised the complete building operation. The central *Marktplatz* was begun in 1804 on Romantic Classical lines. This was a rectangular space with two blocks of buildings facing each other across an open square, where a pyramid was set in the middle. Central to each facing façade were, on one side, the *City Hall* and, on the other, the *Evangelical Church*, which was fronted by a great projecting Corinthian portico. Weinbrenner also laid out the circular *Rondellplatz* (1805–17), this time with a central obelisk. The two important buildings here were the *Ducal Palace* and *Catholic Church*. Before his death in 1826, Weinbrenner was able to supervise the building of streets of houses to complete a newly designed and constructed Romantic Classical city centre.

The capital city of Bavaria, *Munich*, was extensively replanned in this period, the work designed and supervised by three great architects. Little survives of that by the earliest of these, *Karl von Fischer* (1782–1820), who laid out the *Karolinenplatz* from 1808 and built the *National Theatre* in the Max-Josef-platz 1811-18. The latter was a traditional classical building with Corinthian portico upon a rusticated podium. Apart from later replanning which took place, Munich suffered great damage in the latter months of the Second World War, and extensive rebuilding has taken place since then. Little exists from the original Karolinenplatz; the National Theatre was rebuilt by von Klenze after a fire of 1823, and a necessarily radical restoration took place in the 1960s.

A great deal more survives from the considerably larger contribution to the city by *Leo von*

Klenze (1784–1864). His chief work here was the laying out of the vast *Königsplatz* in Greek Revival style. Von Klenze had studied in Paris under Professor Durand. He was also widely travelled, in Italy and Greece, and had spent a long time studying both Italian Renaissance buildings and ancient Greek remains. The Königsplatz is an immense open square with free-standing buildings on three sides constructed over a long period from 1816–64. The first structure was the sculpture gallery *(Glyptothek)*, a somewhat pedestrian design with Corinthian central portico facing the square flanked by lower, plainly pilastered façades. Opposite this on the other side of the square, is the artefacts gallery (Antikensammlungen), built in 1838–48 to a design by Ziebland (1800–73), a not too dissimilar building but more animated and with an Ionic portico. The building was restored in 1967 after damage incurred in World War II. Strangely, since it was not designed until 1846 and the style was then *démodé*, the central building, the *Propylaeon*, by *von Klenze*, is the most Greek Revival in design. It has a trabeated Greek Doric centrepiece flanked by monumental classical towers (**21**). The originals upon which this 'last fling' of Greek Revivalism were based are clearly the Athenian acropolis Parthenon with doorways from the Erechtheion (Vol. 1).

Also in Munich, but in the Max Josefplatz, *von Klenze* designed the *Königsbau* (1826–33). This extension to the royal palace here was in total contrast to the Grecian Königsplatz. The Königsbau takes its inspiration from early Florentine Renaissance palaces and, in this particular instance, the later-extended Pitti Palace. Here is a completely rusticated long façade, in three tiers, broken only by round-arched doorways and windows, except on the first and second storeys, where the windows are separated by Tuscan pilasters (**18**) as was the case in the Rucellai Palace by Alberti (Vol. 3).

Museums were erected in many cities of Europe in these years and, as a result, a number of excellent examples are in Romantic Classical style, for example, Smirke's British Museum in London. *Von Klenze* was responsible for the art gallery *(Alte Pinakothek)* 1826–33 in *Munich*, but this was based more on Italian Renaissance pattern (restored after war damage in 1957). In 1839 he went to *St Petersburg* to design the *Hermitage Museum*, also classical but no longer Grecian.

During the later years of Romantic Classicism and onwards, largely between 1825 and 1845, the Germans coined the term *Rundbogenstil* (the round-arched style), which encompassed a variety of eclecticism – Italian Renaissance, Romanesque, Byzantine, and Early Christian – and placed the design stress upon the use of an arch, whether appearing as an arcade or as repeated fenestration. To a large extent this stemmed from Professor Durand's standard bay design, which catered for such permutations in his formulae.

Rundbogenstil aptly applied to von Klenze's Königsbau. It was even more apt in reference to Gärtner's contribution to urban planning in *Munich. Friedrich von Gärtner* (1792–1847) was responsible for the long, important thoroughfare in the city called the *Ludwigstrasse* (after his patron), which contained his *University* (1834–40), the *Blindeninstitut* (1834–8), the *State Library* (1831–40) and the *Ludwigskirche* (1829–40). All these structures were designed in some form of *Rundbogenstil;* especially typical, is the façade of the State Library. The church is Italian Romanesque on the exterior, tall twin towers flanking the central gable pierced by its rose window while, below at ground level, a round-arched arcade extends arcross the whole façade (**23**). The interior is Byzantine in quality and atmosphere. The great barrel vaults and walls are painted all over in rich colours and gilt to represent mosaic culminating in an immense painting on the east wall behind the altar. Even the capitals are in Byzantine basket form: a most impressive scheme. At each end of the Ludwigstrasse Gärtner has returned to Roman classicism with his triumphal arch at the upper end – the *Siegestor* (1843–50) – and, at the city end, his replica of the Loggia dei Lanzi in Florence, the *Feldherrenhalle* (1841–4).

The outstanding German architect of the first half of the nineteenth century was *Karl Friedrich von Schinkel* (1781–1841), whose work displayed an originality and simplicity to compare with that of Sir John Soane in England (pp. 4–5). Schinkel's contribution extended over both periods of Romantic Classicism; the earlier Greek Revival phase and the later *Rundbogenstil*. He was a Prussian architect, and the majority of his considerable output crowded into his relatively short architectural career was in Berlin and nearby Potsdam.

Schinkel's career began in 1816 with his guard-

17 *Brandenburg Gate, Berlin, 1789–93,*
K. G. Langhans

18 *Königsbau, Max Josefplatz, Munich, 1826–33,*
Leo von Klenze

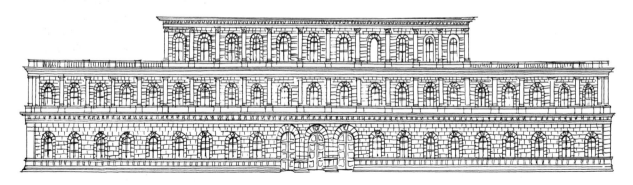

19 *Altes Museum, Berlin, 1824–8, Karl von Schinkel*

house gateway, the *Neue Wache* on the Unter den Linden in *Berlin*. This has a severe Greek temple Doric portico with low sculptured pediment (**20**). In 1817–22 he built the *Berlin Cathedral* (later replaced, p. oo) and, one of his great works in the city, the *Schauspielhaus* (theatre) (1818–21). Still in Greek classical form, this building is original Schinkel. It has a giant Ionic portico set upon imposing entrance steps. Behind, rising again, is the pedimented attic fronting the auditorium. The decoration is restrained, with a plain entablature surrounding the building and, below, simple rectangular window openings.

Schinkel's masterpiece of Greek Revival architecture is his *Altes Museum* in *Berlin* (1824–8). Of deceptively simple appearance this ranks with Soane's work at the Bank of England for originality and purity of line. The museum is fronted by a long Ionic colonnade of 18 columns, behind which four two-storeyed wings form a square and a first floor ambulatory give access to the upper galleries. The domed central area of the museum is not visible on the exterior as it is encased by a rectangular attic, which may be seen to rise behind the colonnaded façade (**19**).

Schinkel showed his versatility later in a variety of works in different materials from his cast-iron Gothic *War Memorial* (1819–21) on the *Kreuzberg* in Berlin, his houses and flats, such as the plain Feilner House of 1829 in Berlin and the *Court Gardener's House* (1829–31) in Potsdam, to his version of *Rundbogenstil* in new churches for the Berlin suburbs. He carried out a great deal of work for the Royal House at Potsdam from 1826, especially in palace design. Of his last works the *Nicolaikirche* in Potsdam was the major commission. He designed this large impressive building in 1829, planning it as a cube surmounted by a hemispherical dome carried on a drum not unlike Wren's S. Paul's Cathedral in London (Vol. 3). The church was finished up to the base of the dome in 1837, but the final completion came only after Schinkel's death (1842–50) and was carried out by one of his pupils, *Ludwig Persius*, who added the corner towers to assist in the pendentive construction. Almost all of Schinkel's buildings were severely damaged in the Second World War and restoration has been slow, though of high standard, as they are all sited in East Berlin and the former Democratic Republic of Germany.

The city of *Hamburg* contained a number of important buildings of early Renaissance interpretations of *Rundbogenstil*, but the majority of these were destroyed or severely damaged in the Second World War. *Gottfried Semper* (1823–79), among other architects, designed a number of houses here in this style but is best known for his work in *Dresden* where he built the *Synagogue* (1838–41), the *Palais Oppenheim* (1845–8), the *Art Gallery* (1847–54) and (best known) the *Opera House*. This was begun in 1837 but had to be rebuilt later by the architect after a fire.

The Italian Renaissance classical form continued to be used as a model by architects of the mid century as at, for example, the *Opera House* in *Hanover* by *Laves* (1845–52) and the three-storey courtyard palace of the *Königsbau* in *Stuttgart* by Leins (1857–60). *Rundbogenstil* was, till the end of the century, to be seen in ferrovitreous and brick construction of railway stations, for example, the *Hanptbahnhof* at *Bremen* (*Hubert Stier* 1886–91).

A quantity of Gothic Revival building was carried out in the second half of the nineteenth century but, as in France, the new structures here were not, in general, of noteworthy quality. One of the better churches was the *Hamburg Petrikirche* (1843–9) by *Alexis Chateauneuf* (1799–1853). This has a slender, simple square brick tower capped by a tall spire, very much in the tradition of the Medieval Hanseatic churches of the Baltic coastal regions, for example, St Mary at Lübeck (Vol. 2) and derived its form from its Medieval predecessor which was destroyed in the fire in the city of 1842 (**22**). It is also a hall church. Probably the most notable new Gothic church in northern Germany (also a replacement for a medieval church lost in the fire of 1842) was that in the same city. The competition for the new design was won by *Sir George Gilbert Scott* and built 1845–63. This was

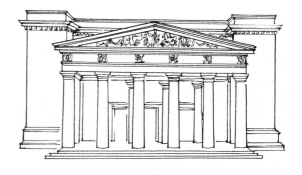

20 Neue Wache, Berlin, 1816, Karl von Schinkel

21 The Propylaeon, Königsplatz, Munich, 1846–63,
Leo von Klenze

22 (left) Petrikirche Hamburg, 1842–9, Alexis de
Châteauneuf and H. Fersenfeldt

23 (right) Ludwigskirche, Munich, 1829–40,
Friedrich von Gärtner

the *Nicolaikirche*, a combination of English and German Gothic elements. It was largely destroyed in the Second World War with only the steeple surviving and now, like Coventry Cathedral in England, is retained as a memorial. The chief secular example is, as befits its later date, of more richly ornamented character. This is the *Rathaus* (town hall) at *Munich* (1867–74) by *von Hauberrisser* (1841–1922). It is in the tradition of the decorative town halls of fifteenth- and sixteenth-century Belgium, such as those in Brussels and Oudenaarde (Vol. 2) (**24**).

As elsewhere there was much restoration of medieval buildings but, also, completion of some notable structures which had never been finished.

The most important was *Cologne Cathedral*, the choir of which had been constructed 1248–1322 (Vol. 2). After this, building began on the transepts and nave, but little had been achieved when construction ceased. During the nineteenth century work recommenced to the original design. This continued between 1824 and 1880 under the supervision of several architects. This was when the great, tall west front, with its characteristic German twin steeples, took shape.

Towards the end of the century the medieval form of architecture preferred in Germany as a basis for church design was that of the late Romanesque, characterized especially in the Rhineland cathedrals such as those at Worms and Speyer (Vol. 2). Typical of new versions of this was the large church built at the head of the Kürfürstendamm in *Berlin* in honour of Kaiser Wilhelm I and the unification of Germany (**25**). The church was severely damaged during the Second World War but the blackened shell was retained as a memorial. Now known simply as the *Gedächtniskirche*, an interesting modern church (1961) has been incorporated into the old one.

24 *Neues Rathaus (town hall), Munich, 1867–74,*
  G. J. von Hauberrisser

25 *Kaiser Wilhelm Gedächtniskirche, Berlin, 1891–5,*
  Franz Schwechten

During the last 30 years of the century many German architects returned to the Baroque and rococo forms of the great days of eighteenth-century architecture. In Bavaria, Ludwig II commissioned palaces and retreats on a scale equal to that of Louis XIV. *Schloss Linderhof*, near Oberammergau (1870–86), designed by *George von Dollmann* (1830–95), is a nineteenth-century interpretation of rococo, heavier and more ornate. The building is not large, its interiors are richly decorated and, outside, there is a wealth of sculpture displayed in a natural setting of fountains, lakes and glades (**Plate 8**).

The establishment in 1871 of Berlin as the imperial capital led to its development and expansion as well as the erection of buildings in the centre of the city, appropriate to its new status. For civic and ecclesiastical purposes a weighty Baroque was considered *de rigueur*. Characteristic was the *Reichstag Building*, won in competition by *Paul Wallot* (1841–1912) and built (1884–94). Set on

fire in 1933 and further damaged during World War II, the building was so immense and solidly constructed as to appear indestructible. The blackened shell has since been restored and cleaned, and the building is now used partly as a museum and partly for political meetings (**Plate 9**). An equally weighty neo-Baroque structure was erected at the other end of the Unter den Linden: the *Cathedral*, rebuilt 1894–1905 by *Julius Raschdorf* (1823–1914) and now restored after war-time damage.

Austria and Hungary

The most important nineteenth-century building occurred in the replanning of the two capitals of the Austro-Hungarian Empire, Vienna and Budapest, under the aegis of Franz Josef. Since he did not accede until 1848, there are few examples of Romantic Classicism. *Luigi Pichl's* (1782–1856) *Diet of Lower Austria* (1837–44) at No. 13 Herrengasse in Vienna is one such building. Another work

Plate 8 Schloss Linderhof, near Oberammergau, 1870–86, Georg von Dollmann

Plate 9 The Reichstag, Berlin, 1880–94, Paul Wallot

of the time is in the German *Rundbogenstil* based on Renaissance forms such as the neighbouring *Landeshauptmannshaft* (1846–8) at No. 11 Herrengasse by *Paul Sprenger* (1798–1854).

The Emperor Franz Josef made plans for his great reconstruction of Vienna in 1849. He intended to build a capital as fine as Napoleon's Second Empire Paris. Certainly Vienna is the only western European capital to rival Paris in its thoroughgoing nineteenth-century restructuring which created broad boulevards, lined with harmonious buildings of good standard, obviously planned and executed under a régime powerful enough to overcome commercial and political opposition and thus attaining homogeneity. Neither the Prince Regent in London nor Kaiser Wilhelm I in Berlin were able to carry out so successfully their ambitious plans.

Vienna, on Franz Josef's accession, was still a fortified, largely medieval city. Its fortifications were destroyed (1857) and the Emperor created his famous *Ringstrasse*, which, with the Danube Canal, completely encircles the medieval city containing S. Stephen's Cathedral (Vol. 2), the old town hall and contemporary buildings. In 1858 *Ludwig Förster* (1797–1863) won the competition

to design the 'Ring' on the line of the old fortifications: this took 30 years to effect. The structures erected around and near the Ring are in keeping with one another but are not uniform, indeed far less so than in Haussmann's Paris. Some, chiefly the earlier ones, were of *Rundbogenstil* type, for example, the Herrengasse *Bank* (1856–83) by *Heinrich von Ferstel* (1828–83). The majority are in High Renaissance style, a little heavy with rusticated lower storeys and pilastered or columned above. Typical are the *Palais Epstein* (1870–3) by the Danish architect *Theophil von Hansen* (1813-91), (**33**) with façades flanking the new town hall and the two great museums in the *Mariatheresienplatz* adjoining the Ring. By *Gottfried Semper* (1803–79) and his partner *Karl von Hasenauer* (1833-94), these two virtually identical buildings, designed for Natural History and Art History, were erected in 1872–81. In each case a central dome arises on an octagonal drum above a long, ornate façade. A statue of the seated Empress provides a focal centre for the square.

Though these are typical, they are neither the most interesting nor the best buildings here. These were subject to a wider variety of eclectic inspiration: Greek Revival, neo-Baroque, Gothic. In a

26 Parliament Building, The Ring, 1873–83,
Theophil von Hansen

27 Neue Hofburg, The Ring, 1881–94,
Karl von Hasenauer

number of instances the same architect would employ different styles for different commissions. One such architect was *von Hansen* designer of the Palais Epstein but also the High Renaissance *Heinrichshof* (1861–3), situated on the Opernring opposite the Opera House but now demolished. Von Hansen is probably best known for his *Parliament House* on the Ring (1873-83), an exceptionally late instance of the use of Greek Revival form; it is a most graceful and impressive structure, long in façade and centred by a pedimented portico (**26**). Another such architect was Von Ferstel, designer of the Herrengasse Bank but also the neo-Gothic *Votivkirche* (1856–79) – a smaller more slender version of Cologne Cathedral (**28**) – but also, later, and just opposite, the *University* (1873–4), a neo-Renaissance building.

The chief neo-Gothic architect of this period was *Friedrich von Schmidt* (1825–91) who had worked for some time on the completion of Cologne Cathedral. In Vienna he was responsible for the lofty, ornamental *Neues Rathaus* (new town hall) (1872–83) on the Ring, a very characteristic building for this date and reminiscent of Sir George Gilbert Scott in England (pp. 9–10) (**29**). Schmidt built many Gothic churches, especially in Vienna. A number of these are brick hall churches on typical German pattern (Vol. 2). More unusual and interesting is his parish church of Fünfhaus in the south-eastern area of the city outskirts. Built 1868–75, this is a large, centrally-planned church, Gothic in its architectural vocabulary, but with a great dome rising over an octagonal interior flanked on the entrance front by two towers making it a blended Baroque/Gothic building of considerable success. On a more Baroque pattern is the Vienna *Opera House* on the Ring (1861–9), designed by *Eduard van der Nüll* (1812–65) and extensively restored after war damage. On a different part of the Ring, opposite the new town hall, is the *Burgtheater*, clearly derived from the Paris Opera house design. This is a later (1874-88) more Baroque structure, designed by *Gottfried Semper*. It has an attractive bow front with shallow dome above (**Plate 10**). One of the last and the largest of these neo-Baroque compositions was the new wing added by Franz Josef to the existing royal palace, the *Hofburg*. Mainly the work of *Karl von Hasenauer*, this was built 1881–94. Though heavy and eclectic, there is nevertheless panache in its sweeping colonnades (**27**). Behind this range, on the opposite façade, the Michaeler elevation was completed finally in 1893 to the original designs of Fisher von Erlach (Vol. 3). The work is boldly Baroque but also clearly nineteenth century in its hardness and heaviness (**32**).

28 Votivkirche, 1856–79, Heinrich von Ferstel

Plate 10 (top right) Burgtheater, Vienna, 1874–88, Gottfried Semper and Karl von Hasenauer

Plate 11 (bottom right) Parliament House, Budapest, 1883–1902, Imre Steindl

29 Neues Rathaus (town hall), 1872–83, Friedrich von Schmidt

The Hungarian capital of *Budapest* was also built up under Franz Josef in the second half of the nineteenth century. Unfortunately the city suffered greatly in the latter part of the Second World War when the German army defended it against the Russian advance. Further damage was done to buildings in the uprising of 1956, but the majority of structures have since been restored.

Mihály Pollack's (1773–1855) *National Museum* (1837–47) is an example of his earlier work on Romantic Classical lines. This has a central Corinthian pedimented portico above a rusticated base. There are flanking towers and side colonnaded wings. The building stands in a garden behind the immense *Parliament Building* (1883–1902) on the riverside. This stems from the neo-Gothic movement, which reached Budapest late in the century. It is partly inspired by Barry's Palace of Westminster in London (p. 3), but has in addition a great central drum and dome, still in Gothic design. It was designed by *Imre Steinl* (1839–1902) and is a strange but successful marriage of styles (**Plate 11**).

In classical style and typical of the later years of the century are the *East Railway Station* façade (**30**) and the great *Heroes Square*, on the edge of the park to the north-east of the city. This is an immense layout, designed by *Schikedanz*, completing the vista at the end of the great *Nepköztár-*

sasag Boulevard, which is flanked by imposing houses where most of the consulates are situated. The Boulevard's most notable building was the *Opera House* built 1879–94 and designed by Hungary's leading architect of the time, *Miklós Ybl* (1824–91). It was based upon Garnier's Paris prototype but, being later, it is in a more heavily neo-Baroque manner. In the centre of the open space of Heroes Square is the *Milennium Monument* commemorating (in 1896) the thousandth anniversary of the occupation of the Danube basin by the Magyars. There is a central column surmounted by the archangel Gabriel and two flanking, curved colonnades, surmounted by horses and chariots and with statues of Hungarian Kings below. In 1945 several reactionary kings, including Franz Josef, were removed and replaced by more suitable proletarian candidates. At the foot of the column are groups of Magyar horsemen, which show great characteristic vitality. Classical build-

31 (top right) S. Stephen's Basilica, begun 1851, dome rebuilt by Ybl, interior completed twentieth century

32 (bottom right) Hofburg, façade to Michaelerplatz, (Michaelertrakt), Vienna. Designed 1729 by Josef Emmanuel Fischer von Erlach but only completed, largely to his designs, in 1893

30 East Railway Station façade, 1881, Julius Rochlitz

EGO SUM VIA VERITAS ET VITA

33 Palais Epstein, The Ring, Vienna, 1870–3,
Theophil von Hansen

ings flank either side of the monument. On the left is the Corinthian colonnaded *Fine Arts Museum* (1900–6) and on the right the *Exhibition Palace of the Fine Arts* (1894). This is in classical temple design with relief and mosaic decoration (*Schikedanz* and *Herzog*).

There are many nineteenth-century churches in Hungary. Two of the large classical examples are *S. Stephen's Basilica* in *Budapest* and *Esztergom Cathedral*. S. Stephen's (**31**) is a traditional, well-proportioned Baroque design on the exterior, a massive, heavy building with temple front, flanking towers and central drum and dome. It is built on Greek cross plan, the vast central dome supported on pendentives and immense piers. The Corinthian Order is used, and the decoration is in marble, gilt, mosaic and painting. It is rich, heavy and ornate. The building was completed by Ybl in 1899.

The *Cathedral* at *Esztergom* is very different. It is also immense but has a wonderful site, high on a hill. Framed against the skyline, it rises directly above the River Danube and dominates the town, instead of being sited in a busy city square full of parked lorries. The exterior is plain and almost totally undecorated. It has an immense Corinthian portico, with Adam-type Composite columns surrounding the drum beneath the dome. The exterior, despite its siting, is a much less satisfactory design than S. Stephen's. It is ill-proportioned and too nakedly undecorated. The interior, in contrast, appears well handled. The dome, which is too small on the exterior, here seems effective, and both it and the drum and pendentives are decorated with paintings and mosaic. The interior is very light with subtle colouring, a sparing use of gilt and blue and grey marbles. There are simple altar paintings based on Titian's work.

Switzerland and Czechoslovakia

There was a tendency for styles in Switzerland to be split along the language divide. French architects designed many buildings in the French-language-speaking towns like Neuchâtel, Geneva and Lausanne, while the German *Rundbogenstil* was followed in many German-speaking areas. Little of the work is of outstanding interest and stylistically was often many years out of date. In Zürich *Winterthur Semper* designed several buildings, including the temple-porticoed *town hall* and the huge *Polytechnic* buildings begun in 1859.

Work in *Czechoslovakia* was eclectic, but livelier and of more interesting design. In the later nineteenth century some imposing structures were evidence of the prosperity. This can be seen in *Prague*, for example, among other large cities. These are generally on neo-Renaissance or neo-Baroque lines, richly ornamented and of good quality workmanship. Typical are the immense *National Museum* (1885–90) by *Joseph Schulz*, standing on the crest of the hill at the top of Wenceslaus Square, which includes the Pantheon used for the lying-in-state of the city's great men, and the more elegant *National Theatre* (1881–3) by Joseph Zítek on the banks of the River Vltava (**34**). This is decorated by many artists of the period.

34 The National Theatre, Prague, 1881–3, Josef Zítek

Southern Europe:
Italy

By 1800, Italian dominance of the world of art and architecture had come to an end, and there are no great names in nineteenth-century Italian architecture. France was leading European design at the turn of the century and soon after the impetus of new ideas and thought began to come from England and Germany. The Italians produced work quite comparable to other western nations and, indeed, created far fewer monstrosities to blight their cities than did other countries, but they had been pre-eminent for so long, their work had been so superb, that they themselves deprecated their nineteenth-century efforts more than foreigners did. Italian architects felt the standards to be poor and thought little of having to follow on foreign lines.

Because of this deprecatory view, Italian nineteenth-century work has long been undervalued and it is only now being appreciated for its genuine worth. Designs were almost all classical as Italy's classical heritage was overwhelmingly strong; there was no Gothic Revival here by indigenous architects. Among the works of the early part of the century, some interiors are particularly fine. At the *Royal Palace of Caserta*, some of the state rooms first built by Luigi Vanvitelli (Vol. 3) were redesigned. Of especial quality are the *Sala di Marte* and *Sala di Astra*, carried out by *Antonio di Simone* in 1807. This work is not just decorative but monumental in the serious, classical manner in the immense interiors, with coupled Ionic pilasters alternating with high-relief sculptured panels extending from floor to entablature. Deeply coved, sculptured ceilings echo the scheme above.

Also at Caserta, but later, comes the *Throne Room* designed in 1839–45 by *Gaetono Genovese* (1795–1860). This interior, rich and sumptuous, is craftsmanship of high quality. This architect was also responsible for enlarging the *Royal Palace* in *Naples* between 1837 and 1844, adapting the long quayside façade and redecorating the interiors in a sumptuous fashion (**35**). The beautiful ornate interior of the famous Opera House of *La Scala* in *Milan* was superbly decorated. Both these interiors are in white and gold. Other notable theatres include the Neapolitan *San Carlo Opera House* and the Venetian *La Fenice*. In *Naples* the opera house was rebuilt in 1816–17 by *Antonio Niccolini* (1772–

1850). At this time he redecorated the interior of his earlier building and returned to it again in 1841. The *Venice Opera House* had been rebuilt in the eighteenth century but its elegant neo-rococo interior dates from 1836 when the brothers *Meduna* restored it after a fire.

In one field of work the Italians excelled in the nineteenth century; that of town planning and civic schemes. In the first half of the century extensive layouts were completed in Turin, Trieste and Naples and in the second half in Rome. The work in *Turin* was the most far-reaching and, being of an early date, of the highest architectural standard and craftsmanship. The seventeenth- and eighteenth-century tradition of planning by streets and squares was continued (Vol. 3), and the city centre was expanded along lines already begun. Turin architecture always had a French influence owing to its nearness to the French border and its links with that country. The great schemes of the *Piazza Vittorio Veneto* and the *Piazza Carlo Felice* illustrate this. The former, designed by *Giuseppe Frizzi* (1797–1831), is an immense open space extending from the arcaded Via Po to the river, its vista being terminated by the *Church of Gran Madre di Dio*, built 1818–21 by *Fernando Bonsignore* (1767–1843) to commemorate the re-establishment of the Savoy monarchy to its capital at the end of the Napoleonic occupation (**37**). The church, based on the Rome Pantheon, is not outstanding, but the homogeneity of the Piazza, in which it is included, is notable. On the other side of the city, the Via Roma divides into the two branches of the Piazza Carlo Felice and ends at the T-junction of the *Corso Emmanuele II*, its vista blocked by the fine glass-and-iron façade of the *Porta Nuova Railway Station*. The Piazza is from a scheme of the 1820s and 1830s, and is also homogeneous, with decorative, elegant, well-proportioned façades (**36**).

In the great piazza near the harbour in *Naples* stands the *Church of S. Francesco di Paolo* (1816–24) by Pietro Bianchi (1787–1849). An imposing church, it is doubly eclectic, the body being a Rome Pantheon and the curving side colonnades based on Bernini's St Peter's. It is a successful, large-scale design (**38**).

After the fall of Napoleon, the Pope returned to *Rome* and authorized the resumption of work on interrupted urban projects as well as the undertaking of new ones. The *Piazza del Popolo* scheme

35 *The Royal Palace, Naples. Façade above the quay. Re-modelled and enlarged 1837–44, Gaetono Genovese*

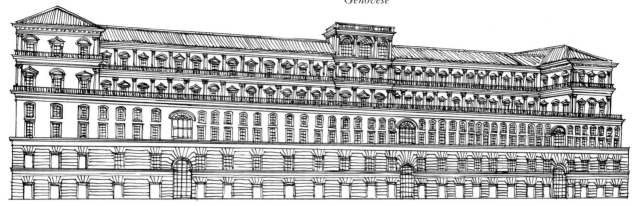

was completed, and a new coffered barrel-vaulted wing was added to the Vatican Museum – the *Braccio Nuovo* – which provided a superb sculpture gallery with natural overhead lighting, designed by *Raffaelle Stern* (1752–1833). The gallery was completed in 1822 after Stern's death by *Pasquali Belli* (1752–1833). A vitally important task of reconstruction was undertaken in 1825 and took over 30 years to finish under the supervision of a succession of architects. This was the rebuilding of the early Christian Church of *S. Paolo-fuori-le-Mura*, disastrously damaged in the fire of 1823 (Vol. 1). This large fourth-century building was faithfully reproduced, though the interpretation, handling and materials were typically nineteenth century.

After the unification of Italy in 1861, Rome became the capital and King Victor Emmanuel, like the Kaiser in Berlin, tried to give to his capital city suitably imposing architectural layouts. Berlin did not fully succeed and neither did Rome. The latter had, of course, been a great city in too many past ages – in Ancient Rome, in the Middle Ages, in the days of the Renaissance and Baroque. Victor Emmanuel in the nineteenth century could not hope to compete in any way with these past achievements; the days of great architecture were over. A number of great boulevards were laid out

36 *Porta Nuova Railway Station façade, Turin, Piazza Carlo Felice, 1866–8. Architect: Carlo Ceppi. Engineer: Alessandro Mazzuchetti*

in emulation of Haussmann's Paris. These include the *Via Nazionale* and the *Via XX Settembre*. In the former, two great buildings are particularly notable: the *Banca d'Italia* (1889–92) by *Gaetono Koch* (1849–1910) and *Pio Piacentini's* (1846–1928) *Palazzo delle Belle Arti* of 1878–82, both carefully designed Renaissance structures less weighty and overdecorated than was usual at this date. Most original and successful in this part of the city is Koch's *Piazza Esedra* (1880–5 and now *Piazza Repubblica*), terminating at the head of the Via Nazionale in twin arcaded quadrants and forming a backcloth to *Guerrieri's* Baroque-style sculptured fountain (**39**). The name of the piazza derived from its hemispherical form and the fact that it was built on the site of an *exedra* from the Roman Baths of Diocletian and thus faces the Church of S. Maria degli Angeli, which was

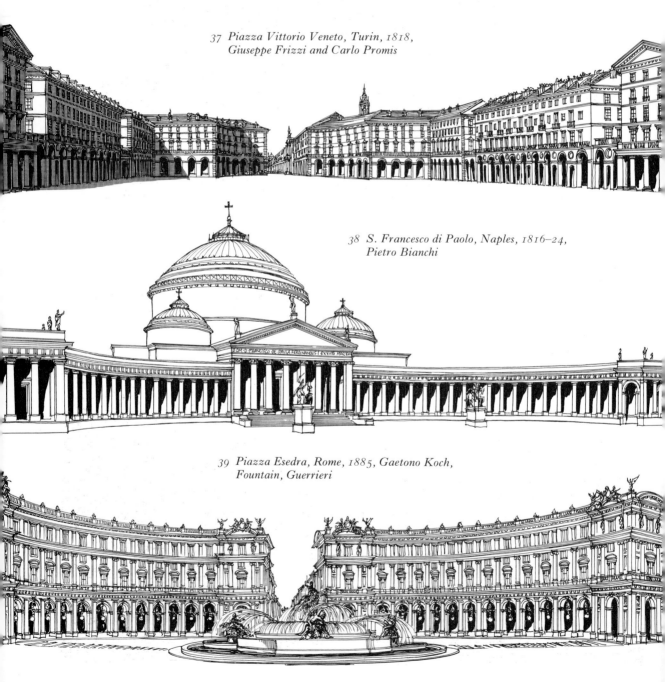

*37 Piazza Vittorio Veneto, Turin, 1818,
Giuseppe Frizzi and Carlo Promis*

*38 S. Francesco di Paolo, Naples, 1816–24,
Pietro Bianchi*

*39 Piazza Esedra, Rome, 1885, Gaetono Koch,
Fountain, Guerrieri*

40 *Monument to Victor Emmanuel II 1885–1911.*
    Many architects, including Sacconi, Koch,
    Piacentini, Manfredi and Brasini

41 *Canale Grande layout with Church of Antonio di*
    Padova at end of vista, Trieste, 1826–49,
    Peter von Nobile

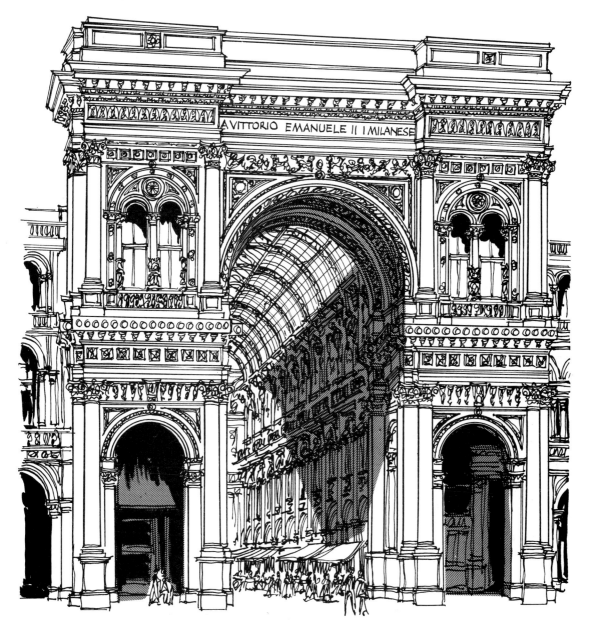

A VITTORIO EMANUELE II I MILANESI

42 (opposite) Interior of the Galleria Vittorio
Emmanuele II in Milan. Iron and glass structure,
1865–77, Giuseppe Mengoni

43 Street façade of the galleria

converted from the caldarium and tepidarium of
the baths by Michelangelo in 1563 (Vol. 1).
Characteristic of the late neo-Baroque phase is the
massive pile on the banks of the River Tiber, the
Palace of Justice by *Giuseppe Calderini* (1837–
1916) built 1888–1910.

The great *monument* to *Victor Emmanuel* in
Rome, impossible to ignore, is that dazzlingly

white marble edifice dominating the Piazza Venezia. In 1884 *Count Giuseppe Sacconi* (1854-1905)
won the competition for this memorial, but work
continued until 1922 under the supervision of most
of the leading architects of the day. This monument, like the Albert Memorial in London, is now
accepted as an integral part of the city of Rome,
scorned by the intelligentsia but a magnet for

tourists of all nations, Italians included. It represents the epitome of the 1880s in all European nations. It is imperial, richly sculptured and decorated, dramatic and larger than life. Dedicated to king and country, it stands for sentiment and sacrifice, a true monument of its age (**40**).

Italy, like other European nations, restored and completed her medieval cathedrals in this century. The two chief examples were *Milan Cathedral*, where the façade was finally finished early in the century, and *Florence*, where the façade was at last built in 1887 by *Emilio de Fabris*. The latter achieves its objective of carefully matching the medieval marble veneers, colours and decoration, but it is still nineteenth century in feeling.

Italy made an important contribution to architectural design in iron and glass through its railway stations and galleries. The *Turin Porta Nuova* railway station of 1866–8 by the architect *Carlo Ceppi* and engineer *Alessandro Mazzuchetti*, is a late instance of *Rundbogenstil*, its great façade central lunette flanked by round-arched arcades with windows above (**36**).

The finest surviving ferrovitreous gallery structure in Europe of the late nineteenth century is undoubtedly the *Galleria Vittorio Emmanuele II* in *Milan* (**42**, **43**), which extends from the Piazza del Duomo to the Piazza della Scala, an immense cruciform structure covered in glass panels in iron frames. It was built by an English firm, and with English professional advice, under the Italian architect *Giuseppe Mengoni* (1829–77). The decoration and sculpture is of the period, mostly in iron, painted and in good, if restored, condition. The arcade still fulfils its original function, as the meeting place where the people of Milan stroll, sit in the cafés and look in the shops. It is the Roman forum of its day, providing protection from rain and sun.

Other Italian galleries survive in *Genoa* – the *Galleria Mazzini* (1871) and in *Naples*, the *Galleria Umberto I* (1887–90).

The Iberian Peninsula

Little of outstanding interest came from either *Portugal* or *Spain* in much of this century. Typical of the best work early in the century, is the *Praça do Comercio* district in *Lisbon* (**Plate 14**); this is the huge central square, open on one side to the estuary of the Tagus. The centre of the city was slowly rebuilt in squares and streets after the earthquake of 1755 and retains its late-eighteenth-century style.

In *Madrid* a number of classical buildings were erected during the century, such as the *Palace of the Congress* (1843–50) and the city gateway, the *Glorieta Puerta de Toledo* (1817). The immense *Cathedral, Nuestra Señora de la Almudena* which was begun in 1880 by *Marquès Francisco de Cubas*, is still unfinished. The neo-classical exterior, next to the royal palace, has twin towers on the façade,

Plate 12 (opposite) Entrance, the Episcopal Palace, Astorga, 1887–93, Antonio Gaudí y Cornet

Plate 13 Detail of portal sculpture. Church of the Holy Family

THE LIBRARY
GUILDFORD COLLEGE
of Further and Higher Education

joined by a two-storey colonnade, Ionic superimposed on Doric. Later building incorporated some Romanesque and Gothic work, which blends satisfactorily with the whole.

Typical of neo-Gothic design in Spain is the *Cathedral* of *San Sebastian*, begun in 1888. It is a Latin cruciform church and has a German-type tall tower and perforated steeple of the Ulm or Freiburg type. Inside is a tall nave arcade with slender piers and early-Gothic foliated capitals. Above is a blind triforium and clerestory windows. The choir is apsidal and contains some fine glass.

The outstanding figure of Spanish architecture in the nineteenth century and, indeed the most original architect of the period in Europe, was *Antonio Gaudì y Cornet* (1852–1926). His name is generally coupled with the movement of Art Nouveau, but much of his work was carried out in the nineteenth century before the movement commenced, and even his twentieth century work is so individual that it cannot be filed neatly under a

general label. His career stems from the 1870s and he soon turned away from Neo-classicism, developing, for some years, a style on neo-Gothic lines. He was a Catalan and most of his contribution is to be found in and around *Barcelona*. He built palaces and houses and restored a number of Medieval monuments such as *Palma Cathedral* and the *Monastery of Montserrat*. In medieval style, but essentially Gaudì, is his *Bishop's Palace* at *Astorga* (1887–93), adjoining the medieval Cathedral. This has Gothic towers, battlements and fenestration, but the parabolic curve of the arches of the portal indicate the master's original touch. This feature can be found in much of his work (**Plate 12**).

The personal quality of Gaudì's building in this century can be seen clearly on the palace and park in Barcelona named after Don Eusebio Güell and the fantastic cathedral-temple of the Holy Family. The *Palacio Güell* (1885-9) is on the street Conde del Asalto just off the main Rambla Capuchino. It is a six-storeyed stone front, restrained and simple

Plate 14 Gateway detail. Praça do Comercio, Lisbon, early nineteenth century

*Plate 15 Parque Güell, Barcelona, 1885–9,
Antonio Gaudì y Cornet*

but unmistakably by Gaudì in its two entrances with characteristic, parabolic-arched doorways and decorative iron grilles. The *Parque Güell*, where Gaudì worked up to 1914, now the city's public park, is situated on a hill on the outskirts of the town. It contains a church, a house, arbours, sculpture and playgrounds. The motifs are chiefly natural ones – caves, rocks, plants, animals – but the architectural derivation is Gothic apart from the classical supports for the children's playground. Here, he used Doric columns, but so vast that they resemble a cross between Paestum temples and the Nile palaces. The church, the

grottoes and the garden layout are in coloured ceramic faced with inset stones. This is a fairytale garden with the marzipan and gingerbread house of Grimm's stories (**Plate 15**).

The temple dedicated to the Holy Family is still slowly and painfully being added to in the city of Barcelona. The *Templo Expiatorio de la Sagrada Familia* was designed by *Francisco del Villar* in neo-Gothic style and begun in 1882. In November 1883 the work was entrusted to his assistant *Gaudì*, who devoted himself to it during the rest of his life. By 1893 he had completed the crypt and the outer walls of the chevet, according to Villar's designs.

44 *Church of the Holy Family (Templo Expiatorio de
la Sagrada Familia), Barcelona. Begun 1882,
Antonio Gaudì y Cornet*

This part can be seen in the right hand half of the drawing in Fig. **44**.

After this beginning Gaudì developed his own design, and the part built largely before 1914 is the façade to one of the transepts, which includes the triple doorway and four towers shown on the left of Fig. **44**. Here is the personal Gaudì, all curves and three-dimensional plasticity, and his treatment is quite different from that of any other architect. When he had been working at Montserrat, he was fascinated by the formation of the mountain peaks, rising vertically above the shelf on which the monastery stands, high above Barcelona. Anyone who has seen this mountain formation, resembling vertical, rounded pillars of solidified molten lava, will at once recognize the same molten-stone effect in Gaudì's porticoes, where stalactite-like deposits hang from each pointed arch; the sculpture has the same semi-liquid quality, each drip caught as in a snapshot, before it falls. There is the same instant quality of arrested movement that is seen in Bernini's work (**Plate 13**).

The Sagrada Familia was continued, after a break for the First World War, in 1919, but stopped at the architect's death in 1926. Since then the monument has remained for years a fragment (though an immense one). Work is now fully in progress again, but whether such a vast enterprise will ever attract sufficient funds to be completed must be in doubt. It is to be hoped that the Sagrada Familia will be finished, however. It is a unique, non-eclectic design, the greatest ecclesiastical structure since the eighteenth century. The building finished so far, though appearing large (the towers are 330 ft (100 m) high), is still only a small portion of the whole. It represents one transept façade and the outer choir chevet walling. Still remaining to be built are the nave and other transept with similar towers, the choir *cimborio* and the great crossing group, the *cimborio*, whose tower should rise to about 560 ft (170 m), higher than the tallest medieval church in Europe: Ulm Minster, at 529 ft (162 m).

The Low Countries: Belgium

As in France, the early years were represented chiefly by buildings in the Romantic Classical style. Typical is the *Théâtre de la Monnaie* in Brussels, begun by the French architect *Damesme*

in 1819. It was altered and enlarged later but retained its carefully designed temple portico. However, after the middle of the century, boulevards and squares were being laid out in the capital on the lines of the Parisian Second Empire. In general, though, the work is heavier and the detail coarser. Typical is the *Boulevard Anspach*, with its iron balconies and mansard roofs. This is now largely losing its character, with alterations to individual premises.

The two chief examples of civic building in these years are the Exchange and the Palais de Justice. The *Exchange* (1868–73), by *L. P. Suys* (1823–87), stands in its own square half way along the Boulevard Anspach. It is in neo-Baroque style and has a heavy, ornate portico with approach steps and flanking lions. There is a wealth of sculpture typical of this date. The *Palace of Justice* (**45**) is also heavy but is more original in conception. It was designed by *Joseph Poelaert* (1817-79) and built 1866-83. It has much of the feeling of Vanbrugh's work in its strong massing and three-dimensional weightiness. Standing on the highest point of this part of the city, it dominates the area as the blocks pile up to the tall dome. It is the most original building of its date in the country.

Belgium also produced some interesting structures in iron and glass. A surviving example in Brussels is the *Galérie de la Reine* (formerly the *Galérie S. Hubert*) built in 1847 by *J. P. Cluysenaer*. This is an early city shopping gallery and has delicate detail and good, subtle proportions. Doric pilasters line the walls of the ground arcade. Above are two stages of classical fenestration, and the gallery is roofed in a semicircular vault of glass panels in iron frames. The sculptural decoration is restrained and in a classical Greek pattern. Nearer the end of the century department stores of iron and glass were being constructed that anticipated the Art Nouveau style (pp. 73–4). A decorative but rather heavy example was the *Old England Department Store* in *Brussels*, situated near the Place Royale. It was designed in the 1890s by *Paul Saintenoy* (1832-92).

45 *Palace of Justice, Brussels, 1866–83, Joseph Poelaert*

46 *The Exchange, Amsterdam, 1897–1903,*
Hendrik Berlage, rebuilt after fire of 1833

Holland

There is little of note to record for the first half of the century here; Romantic Classicism seemed to have almost passed Holland by. Where it was employed, as in the *Haarlemer Poort* in *Amsterdam*, built 1840 by *Zocher*, the traditional Dutch brickwork was hidden under a layer of stucco as in Nash's Regent's Park terraces in England (p. 4). Similar was the *Academy of Fine Arts* in *The Hague*, built 1839 by *Reijers* but now demolished.

By the 1860s, a number of architects were creating prominent buildings of the neo-Gothic or heavy Second Empire Renaissance style. Of the latter type of design is the work of *Cornelis Outshoorn* (1810–75). A typical example is the large *Amstel Hotel*, its four storeys and dormered mansard roofs lining the river bank in *Amsterdam*. Designing in equally heavy-handed manner, but in a neo-Gothic style, was the Scott or the Viollet-le-Duc of Holland, *Petrus Josephus Hubertus Cuijpers* (1827–1921). Two large civic contributions of this architect are the *Rijksmuseum* (1877–85) and the *Central Station* (1881–9) both in *Amsterdam*.

From the exterior, these buildings are so similar that it is difficult to know which is for trains and which for paintings. Both have long, dark brick façades, with gables and steep roofs broken by dormer windows. Each has a centrepiece with flanking, gabled towers, a central gable and main doorway and, at the ends of the façades, terminal gabled pavilions. Only the museum, however, on closer inspection, is appropriately ornamented with panels of relief sculpture and ceramic scenes (**Plates 16, 18**).

Cuijpers, like his contemporaries in England and France, also designed a number of churches and these, too, bear great resemblance to one another. The *Vondelkerk* in *Amsterdam*, like his *Maria Magdalenkerk* nearby (1887), is similar to numerous examples produced in England at a similar date. The Dutch examples are in brick, with striped or polychrome decoration and the emphasis on height in sharp, hard turrets, spires and arches (**Plate 17**).

At the very end of the century there was a change of style. Brick remained the usual material (as it had been since Hanseatic days in Holland), but a

Plate 16 The Central Station, Amsterdam, 1881–9, P. J. H. Cuijpers

Plate 17 Vondelkerk, Amsterdam, 1870,
Petrus Josephus Hubertus Cuijpers

Plate 18 The Rijksmuseum, Amsterdam, 1877–85,
Cuijpers

lead was taken (as in England, pp. 13–14) in simplifying the design and in creating a more original line and detail. The leading architect of this movement, which was centred in Amsterdam, was *Hendrik Petrus Berlage* (1856–1934), who continued his work in the early twentieth century, developing Dutch prototypes for the modern school of architecture. His two pace-setting buildings of the 1890s were the *Exchange* (1897–1903) and the *Diamond Workers' Trade Union Building* (1899–1900). Both are built of brick with stone decoration and dressings, both have large rectangular window openings divided by mullions and transoms, both have plain, square towers and, in doorways, stress the round arch; ornament is chunky and non-eclectic. These large, bold structures were greatly influential in Holland (**46**, **Plate 20**).

Another architect who worked on similar lines was *Willem Kromhaut* (1864–1940). He is best known for his *Hotel Americain* also in Amsterdam (1898–1900), of brick and forward-looking in design and treatment. This is a large building on a corner site, the corner marked by a tall, chunky clock tower. Roof dormers have stepped gables and decoration – a throwback to seventeenth-century Amsterdam – but much of the decoration is Gothic inspired (**Plate 19**).

Plate 19 The American Hotel, Amsterdam, 1898–1900, Kromhaut and Jansen

Plate 20 Headquarters Diamond Workers' Trade Union Building, Amsterdam, 1899–1900, Hendrik Berlage

East Europe

Balkan countries had been restricted in developing their own architectural expression for centuries by the overlordship of the Ottoman Empire. In the nineteenth century, one by one these nations achieved their independence and began to build up their chief cities. From the late 1830s, civic building was re-started in *Athens*. The Hansen family, of Danish origin, who carried out so much Romantic Classical work in Europe, built here in this period. Theophil von Hansen (architect of the Parliament House in Vienna, (p. 30), and his older brother, *H. C. Hansen* (1803–83), created some fine buildings in the university area. Using academically correct, impressive but weighty Greek Revival in the Ionic Order, the older brother was responsible for the *University* (1837–42), Theophil

for the *Academy* (1859–87) (**Plate 21**) and the *National Library* (1860–92). In Italian Renaissance style nearby is *von Klenze's Roman Catholic Cathedral* (1854–63).

The best building in Athens, dating from this time, is the royal palace, now used as the *Parliament House*, at the head of the main Syntagma Square. This is simple, with clean, classical lines and an elegant Greek Doric portico, inspired, one would imagine, by the Parthenon at the other end of the road. This building, surprisingly enough, is by *Gärtner*, the architect of the Ludwigstrasse in Munich (p. 23). It contrasts sharply with his Bavarian style elsewhere (**Plate 22**). In the rest of the century, streets in Athens became lined with typical classical façades of the day, as they did in the rest of Europe.

Even less building took place in the country now

Plate 21 (above) The Academy, Athens, 1859–87,
          Theophil von Hansen

Plate 22 (below) The Old Royal Palace (later
          Parliament House), Athens, 1837–41,
          Friedrich von Gärtner

known as *Yugoslavia*. In the nineteenth century the northern part still belonged to the Austro-Hungarian Empire and so formed part of the building programme there, while the southern part of the nation, then Serbia, was under Turkish rule till after mid century. Typical of the work at the end of the century is the *University of Belgrade*, which is a traditional Renaissance design of its period.

Bulgaria remained under Turkish domination till the later nineteenth century though the Church gained its freedom in 1870. Among the great *monasteries* of the country *Rila* (Vol. 1) is one of the most famous. Set in a fine mountain landscape, it was founded in the tenth century, but the church was destroyed by fire in 1833. Later in the century it was rebuilt and the whole monastery restored and extended. The polysided courtyard is surrounded by arcaded galleries, which contained cells. These galleries are painted in striped horizontal lines. After the fire a further storey was added, and a new *church* was set in one corner of the courtyard. It is a five-domed basilica in Byzantine style, with an arcaded narthex on three sides, all covered by saucer domes. The interior is painted all over; it is in excellent condition and the standard of craftsmanship is high. Inside the church there are three large central domes on tall, fenestrated drums. It is a simple, three-aisled interior with marble columns but is painted on all surfaces, including the drums and cupolas of the domes. The chancel screen is a fantastic piece of decorative craftwork. The present church is much larger than the one it replaces. The exterior of the monastery is like a fortress with solid, very high walls rising out of a mountain stream. Tiny windows pierce this vastness (**48**). Rila Monastery is now a museum; no monks remain.

Modern *Romania* is a large country, but until the middle of the nineteenth century was composed of small provinces much of whose lands were controlled by the Austro-Hungarian Empire or by the Turks. Independence from the latter came in the 1870s. There are a number of classical build-

47 The Romanian Athenaeum (Concert Hall), Bucharest

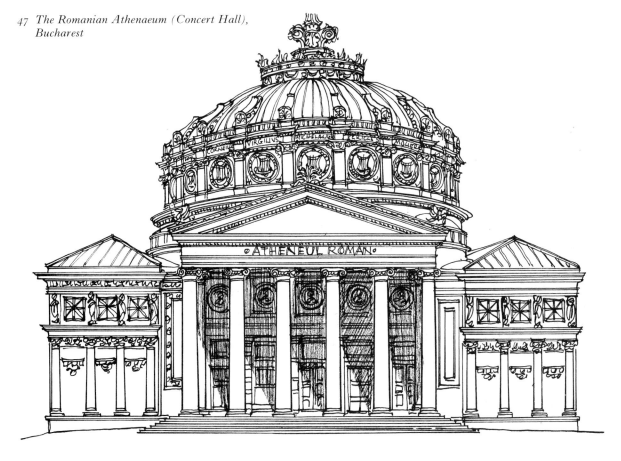

48 Rila Monastery, Bulgaria. Founded tenth century

49 The Savings Deposit Bank, Bucharest

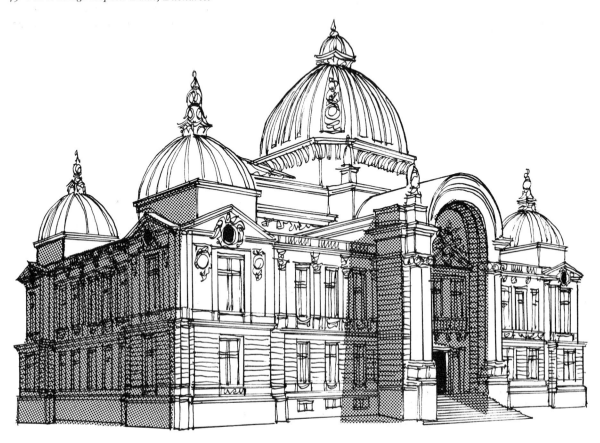

ings in *Bucharest*, dating from different periods in the nineteenth century. One of the best is the *Romanian Athenaeum* (**47**) in the centre of the city, inspiration for which has clearly stemmed from Paris. Indeed, the Rumanians call their capital the 'Paris of the Balkans' – an extravagant claim in spite of some fine boulevards. Among the more exceptional structures are the *Palace of Justice*, the *Centre for Economic Development*, the *General Post Office* and the *Central Bank* (**49**). Sadly, much of this and earlier heritage has been destroyed in present-day Bucharest.

In towns such as *Sibiu* and *Cluj* there are also some good Neo-classical buildings in the central streets, as well as some neo-Gothic ones. In *Sinaia*, the *Castle Peles*, the royal palace built in 1873, is a romantic turreted pile set in hilly parkland. It is reminiscent of romantic German or Swiss six-teenth-century castles and, not surprisingly, the architect, *Wilhelm Doderer*, was *Viennese*.

In the nineteenth century church building was revived in the Byzantine tradition, much as neo-Gothic was established in England. The *Greek Orthodox Cathedral* in *Constantza* (1884–95) is a large example, as is the *Domnita Balasa Church* in *Bucharest* (1881–5).

Poland

Nineteenth-century European architecture is pre-dominantly found in cities. In Poland a great proportion of this building was lost during the Second World War, as the major cities suffered more than in probably any other country. The war began by Hitler's invasion of Poland, and the cities of *Wroclaw* and *Warsaw* were – amid an almost total state of destruction – among the last to find peace in 1945. The country was a buffer between the retreating German army and the advancing Soviet forces and only *Cracow* of the major cities survived fairly intact. It is, therefore, from a few surviving examples that nineteenth-century Polish architecture can be judged, although a great proportion of the finer buildings have been restored.

Designs in *Cracow* are strongly influenced by the Austro-Hungarian Empire directives and cities like *Gdansk* on the Baltic coast by Prussian ideas. The *Municipal Theatre* in *Cracow* (1891–3) by *Zawiejski* is another attractive variant on the Paris Opera House (**50**). There is also the elegant neo-rococo *Stadnicki Palace* in Grodzka Street, with a pleasant façade and doorway. The *Museum*

50 The Municipal Theatre, Cracow, Poland, 1893, Zawiejski

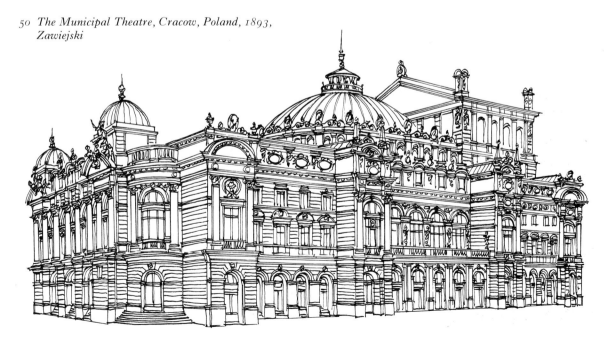

of Silesia in *Wroclaw* is a large structure along typical late-nineteenth-century Renaissance lines. Standing on the banks of the River Oder, this vast block was damaged but is now restored. It is of neo-Renaissance style, monumentally conceived and well executed.

Russia

The first half of the nineteenth century in Russia produced architecture of a design and quality which compares favourably with any in Western Europe. Much of this was created under Tsar Alexander I, who reigned from 1801–25 and was an enlightened patron of the arts, *au fait* with the modes of his day and a man of taste. In the first half of his reign he encouraged Romantic Classicism based on the Greek model, while later work, towards 1825, was more on the lines of Imperial Rome. Like all Russian architecture, the structures are large in scale, many part of extensive civic schemes and set in immense squares and boulevards which offset the building size.

As under the patronage of Peter, Elizabeth and Catherine, foreign architects were still employed, but Russian architects too were now making their full contribution to the beautifying of their cities, and here *St Petersburg* (now *Leningrad*) was, as

51 *Cathedral of the Virgin of Kazan, Leningrad, 1801–11, A. N. Voronikhin*

52 *General Staff Arches, Winter Palace Square, Leningrad, 1819–29, K. I. Rossi*

53 State Department Store GUM, Red Square, Moscow, 1889–93, A. N. Pomerantsev

ever, the prime recipient. Three architects contributed in the main in the years 1801–15: Voronikhin, de Thomon and Zakharov. *Andrei Nikiforovich Voronikhin* (1760–1814) was born a serf but, on showing promise as an artist, was sent by his master to study at the *St Petersburg Academy* and later undertook the Grand Tour in Paris and Rome. He returned to St Petersburg in 1790 and, after a few years, began work on his large commission, the *Cathedral of the Virgin of Kazan* (**51**). This is an immense building, based on St Peter's in Rome, with a domed church fronted by a great portico and with forward-curving Corinthian colonnades on each side. Terminating these are *Orlovski*'s statues of *Barclay de Tolly* and *Marshal Kutuzov*. It is a finely proportioned, imposing cathedral, but monumentally cold, rather in the same manner as the Paris Pantheon. The interior is richly ornate Baroque, with coffered barrel vaults supported by walls with Corinthian order entablatures. It is difficult to see below this level because of the exhibits; the building is now laid out as a museum of the history of religion and atheism and it is now called the 'Temple of Atheism'. An instance of Voronikhin's severer Greek styles can be seen in his *Institute of Mines* in the city, which he built in 1803–7, based upon the Temple of Poseidon at Paestum. This has the characteristically sturdy Doric columns of the early-Greek period and some fine sculptured groups.

Thomas de Thomon (1754–1813) was born in France but settled in Russia in 1790. His outstanding work in St Petersburg is the *Exchange* (Birzha) (1810-16), which has a Doric portico, also closely deriving from the Paestum temples.

The buildings of *Adrian Dmitrievich Zakharov* (1761–1811) are much more Russian. He trained in St Petersburg, then spent some years in Paris and Italy, but his style has all the breadth and hugeness and the ability to handle great masses and contrasts in chiaroscuro that characterizes the best Russian architecture. This manner is not eclecticism but a national interpretation of the design of his day. His chief work in St Petersburg is the *Admiralty* group

*Plate 23 (above) The Opera House Odessa, 1884–6,
Felner and Gelmer*

*Plate 24 (left) New Admiralty, Leningrad, 1812.
Sculptor: Shchedrin*

of buildings, where he had to reconstruct older parts, retaining the landmark on the southern side of the River Neva, the tall steeple and certain features of the previous buildings, yet at the same time greatly extending the group. The façade facing the Neva has a Doric colonnade and square entrance pavilion blocks. On the southern elevation is the tall entrance tower, its square, Ionic-colonnaded base and above the sculptured figures supporting the lofty steeple. Flanking the entrance below are the draped female figure groups (1812, *Shchedrin*) (**Plates 24, 26**).

A hiatus in building was caused by the Napoleonic invasion but, after the final retreat from Moscow, a new era of construction began under different architects: Stasov, Rossi and Montferrand. *Vasili Petrovich Stasov* (1769–1848) was a Russian architect who also studied and worked in western Europe. He began his architectural career

in Russia in 1808, working for the Tsar on the St Petersburg palaces and at *Tsarkoe Selo* (since 1937 re-named Pushkin after the poet who had studied there at the lycée). He also designed a number of churches. His work was mainly on Greek lines such as the *Moscow Triumphal Arch* in St Petersburg (1833–8).

Karl Ivanovich Rossi (1775–1849) had a different background. Of Italian descent, he was, however, Russian born. His contribution to St Petersburg was in extensive civic schemes, based on Imperial Roman prototypes. He designed the beautifully delineated and finished *Alexandra* (now Pushkin) *Theatre* (1827–32) in Ostrovsky Square. Leading from the rear of the theatre, he laid out *Rossi Street* in the same period. This is a classical terrace reminiscent of Nash or Wood in England. A giant order of coupled Ionic columns extends along the whole length of the long façade, broken only at the terminal pavilions. Below the order are simple arches containing windows, connected by rusticated walling.

A larger scheme was his *Senate* and *Synod* (1829–34), a long line of buildings near the Admiralty, adjacent to the Neva and looking out on to the equestrian statue by Falconet of *Peter the Great*, erected by Catherine. These buildings housed the supreme judiciary and ecclesiastical representatives. Rossi's design is in one long elevation comprising two identical façades joined by a central triumphal arch. The Corinthian Order in columns is used over the whole length of the elevation, above a rusticated lower storey. The proportions and handling are good and the interest is maintained along a very lengthy façade.

Rossi's most ambitious project, and his masterpiece, is his layout for the gigantic square opposite to the Winter Palace. This is a tremendously long façade of simple, unadorned fenestrated treatment, broken by an immense central, concavely-curving sweep. In the centre of this area (which houses the buildings for the *General Staff*) is an equally large-scale triumphal arch, complete with surmounting chariot and six horses (**52**). Such classical groups, as their name, quadriga, indicates, had four horses. The vastness of the country encouraged Russian architects to design on a larger scale than in Western Europe. This great façade, monumentally and imperially handled, offsets admirably the fine Baroque of Rastrelli's Winter Palace opposite (Vol. 3).

The achievement of *Auguste Ricard de Montferrand* (1786–1858), a French architect, was the building of *S. Isaac's Cathedral* in *St Petersburg* (1817–57). He won the competition for this commission in 1817, but the cathedral was many years in the building, with consequent deterioration in craftsmanship and design during the period. Though French, Montferrand has produced a very Russian building, immensely large and monumental, in robust classical style. It is on a Greek cross plan, with a large central dome on Corinthian colonnaded drum and small cupolas set round it. The façades have weighty Corinthian porticoes, pedimented and sculptured. The exterior has been recently restored and cleaned, and the gilt domes gleam in the pale northern sunshine. It is a solemn structure, lacking in warmth but gaining greatly from the richness of its materials, especially the granite columns with their gilt capitals and bases.

There is also a quantity of sculpture typical of the mid-century date (**Plate 25**).

The best architecture of the period 1800–30 was certainly in St Petersburg. But other cities were also being developed and laid out with civic schemes in Neo-classical style. Interesting work of this type includes *Odessa* where, for example, buildings round the *Square of the Commune*, mainly by *Boffo*, have elegant façades. Typical is the *Archaeological Museum* – now the *Workers' Soviet* – which has a well-proportioned Corinthian colonnaded front. Along the *Black Sea front* are terrace buildings which have much in common with contemporary work in Brighton and Hove in England. Numbers 7–8, for example (1827–8, designed by *Melnikov*), have plain, classically fenestrated façades broken by a curving crescent with Ionic pilastered front. The statue by *Martos* (1826) of Richelieu stands at the central intersection of the curve.

The dominance of classicism in the official line in architecture continued unbroken in the period up to 1850. This was evidenced particularly in the buildings of German and Russo-German architects, for whose work the Tsar had a preference. The chief of these was *Konstantin Andreevich Ton* (1794–1881). He designed the *Grand Kremlin Palace* in *Moscow* (1838–49), a Russo-Renaissance building, classical in structure but with decorated windows and columns. It shows the common decline from early-nineteenth-century standards (**Plate 27**). The *Dutch Church* on the Nevski Prospekt in *St Petersburg* by *Jacquot* (1837) is more robustly and correctly classical. This is clearly modelled on the Mausoleum of Diocletian in the Palace at Split.

In the 1860s eclecticism came fully to Russia and, in addition to various classical themes, all the earlier styles were tried out too. These were not based on western-European medieval structures but on Russian ones. Next door to one another in *Red Square* in Moscow are two typical examples, the Russian equivalents of work by Scott in England or Cuijpers in Holland: the *Lenin Museum* (originally the city hall), 1892, by *P. N. Chichagov* and the *History Museum* (1874–83) by the Anglo-Russian architect *V. O. Sherwood*. Both of these are very large, dark brick, overdecorated structures. They incorporate all the traditional medieval and Byzantine Russian architectural motifs – tent roofs, *kokoshniki*, octagonal towers and pinna-

*Plate 25 St Isaac's Cathedral, Leningrad, 1817–57,
    Ricard de Montferran*

Plate 26 The New Admiralty, Leningrad, 1806–15,
  A. D. Zakharov

cles, ornate window surrounds and wall panelling – but this is all assembled together in a heavy, uninspired manner and with little comprehension of the medieval type of massing and design.

On the other side of the Square (an immensely wide street rather than a square, which was formerly called Market Square because of the stalls in and around it) is the fantastic State Department Store, *GUM*, an immensely long façade opposite the Kremlin walls and adjoining the *Cathedral* of *S. Basil*. The exterior has similar characteristics to the museums but is handled better and with more imagination. The interior is most interesting and a classic of its type in iron and glass, like the galleries of the period in western Europe. GUM has three parallel, barrel-vaulted galleries, each about 1000 ft (300 m) in length, with balconies and walkways at different heights, all serving shops. There are then iron connecting walkways from one section to another. The interior is like the nave and aisles of a church, only the aisles are nearly as wide and as high as the nave. In the centre is a fountain and a very tall lamp, hanging from above, almost down

to it. One can walk round the centrepiece at gallery passageway levels, covered by the iron and glass domed roof above. There are literally hundreds of shops and stalls in GUM, selling a wide variety of goods (**53**).

In ecclesiastical building the neo-Byzantine style of about the sixteenth century was prevalent in the 1880s. In St Petersburg, *S. Saviour's Church in the Spilled Blood* was built 1883–1907 by *A. A. Parland* on the site of the assassination of the Tsar Alexander II. It is modelled on the Cathedral of S. Basil in Moscow, but its highly ornate façades and towers are overdone and the elegance and beautiful form of the prototype are missing. In Kiev the *Cathedral of St Vladimir* (1882) is a simpler example, taking its pattern from the Byzantine churches of the city. The interior is particularly fine, decorated on all surfaces with painted and marble veneer and paintings with gilt backgrounds in Byzantine style. The plan is cruciform, with barrel-vaulted arms, a tall drum and dome over the crossing and subsidiary smaller ones around. The piers are square and solid and there is a high gallery. With the wide narthex, the whole interior is very much in Russian and eastern Byzantine style rather than in western.

Of the eclectic classical structures of the later years of the century, *L'vov University* (1880s), originally in Poland, is a good example. The *Bolshoi Theatre* in Moscow, rebuilt 1886 by *Cavos*, and the *L'vov* and *Odessa Opera Houses* are in neo-Baroque style. The Odessa example is especially impressive; it is closely modelled on the Paris Opera. It was designed by *Felner and Gelmer* in 1884–6 (**Plate 23**). It has a fine situation and, newly cleaned, sparkles in the sun. The interior, exceptional acoustically, is a rich and fine example of late-nineteenth-century décor. There are four rows of balconies, in gilt and cream, with red velvet seating and curtaining. The four-centred proscenium arch is ornamented in the spandrels by white sculptured figures. The magnificent ceiling has a circular centrepiece and is painted to depict scenes from Shakespeare's plays. A glass and gilt chandelier in the style of the English Regency hangs from the centre.

Scandinavia: Denmark

So far as indigenous architects were concerned, Denmark produced the best work, especially in Copenhagen. In the first half of the century many buildings were designed in Romantic Classical and Neo-classical style by architects such as Hansen and Bindesbøll. Development was by streets and terraces, but the chief monuments are civic and ecclesiastical.

Christian Frederik Hansen (1756–1845) was the prime classical architect in the early years. His main contribution was in the *Cathedral* and the *Palace of Justice* in *Copenhagen*. The great fire in the city in 1795 caused extensive damage, as did the English bombardment of 1807. Hansen rebuilt the *Cathedral, Vôr Frue Kirke*, 1811–29, using the old walls. The exterior is plain, with apsidal east end and a tall, square western tower rises above the Doric façade portico. The interior is most impressive (**54**). There is a caissoned, barrel-vaulted ceiling throughout and a plain screen in front of the

Plate 27 Grand Kremlin Palace, Moscow, 1838–49, K. A. Ton

organ (west end) with Doric colonnades above and simple arches below. This pattern of colonnaded gallery above an arched nave arcade leading to aisles is repeated all round the church, except at the east end where a great triumphal arch fronts the apse; this is decorated below the cornice with a frieze depicting Christ on the way to Golgotha. The altarpiece, set on a curving stylobate, contains, in a niche, *Bertel Thorvaldsen's* (1768–1844) figure of Christ. This and the other marble statues of the 12 Apostles standing round the church, as well as much of the remaining sculptural decoration are by this famous Danish sculptor. The work was done in Rome between 1820–40.

Much of Hansen's work derived from ancient Rome but in his *Raad-og-Domhus* (1803–15), which was built as a combined Town Hall and Court House but now survives only as the Law Courts, his inspiration was French Romantic Classicism. This is a plain, monumental building with simple Ionic portico. Hansen also rebuilt the *Christiansborg Palace* in Copenhagen, again using the walls of the older structure. This was his most important commission but unfortunately it was, in its turn, burnt down in 1884 and the present immense structure, housing the Parliament, the Supreme Court and the Foreign Office, was built by *Jørgensen* in 1907–16.

From the 1830s Danish architecture tended to follow the German lead, very much influenced by Schinkel (pp. 23–5). Leading architect in the mid-century was Gottlieb Bindesbøll (1800–56), a pupil of Hansen. A man of his age, he built eclectically, in neo-Gothic, such as his *Church at Hobro* (1850), and in German *Rundbogenstil*, as in his *Agricultural School* (1856–8) in *Copenhagen*. His masterpiece, which is original not eclectic, is the *Thorvaldsen Museum* in *Copenhagen* (1839–48), which was built to house the collections and works of the sculptor, as well as to provide a suitable setting for his tomb. The tomb is set in a central court which, like the rest of the building, is severely simple, with something of Greek form but more of Egyptian. The astylar façade has Egyptian-styled doorway openings. Round the exterior are murals by Jørgen Sonne, depicting the story of the bringing of Thorvaldsen's sculpture from Rome to Copenhagen.

After this eclecticism was prevalent in Denmark for the rest of the century. Some of the work was strongly influenced by Germany, seen in *Rundbo-genstil* and neo-Byzantine form. Other examples show the effect of Second Empire France. Many architects designed in more than one style, changing their approach according to commission. The *University of Copenhagen* (1835) is a typical work by *Peder Malling*. This is classical, but with a neo-Gothic flavour to the gables and dormers. It is in the same square as the cathedral, and next door to it is Herholdt's neo-Gothic *University Library* of 1856–61. This is in red brick and very typical of Danish neo-Gothic work.

J. D. Herholdt (1818–1902) was the most important architect in Denmark in the 1850–70 period. Much of his work was in the *Rundbogenstil*, as, for example, his *Danish National Bank* in *Copenhagen* (1866–70). He also turned his hand to more traditional neo-Gothic on Italian pattern, as in his *Town Hall* at *Odense* (1880–3). This has a crenellated parapet after the medieval type common in Ferrara and Verona and a frontispiece with clock above the doorway which is Florentine in origin.

A number of architects were designing in the heavy neo-Renaissance and Baroque work of the later years of the century. *Vilhelm Petersen* and *Ferdinand Jensen* used this style for the building of apartment blocks and offices such as *63–5 Bredgade* in Copenhagen (1886–7), while *Jens Vilhelm Dahlerup* built the *State Museum for the Fine Arts* (Glyptotek 1892–7) and the *Royal Theatre* (1872–4) in the city. These are both typical products of their age, heavy and unimaginative, but well constructed and large scale.

The leading architect of the period 1875–1900 in Denmark was *Ferdinand Medahl* (1827–1908). He was Professor at the Copenhagen Academy from 1864 and its Director for over 30 years. His work in the reconstruction of *Frederiksborg Castle* in 1861–75, after its severe damage by fire in 1859, is typical. It is competent and imposing but very heavy, hard and unimaginative. His most outstanding work was the *Frederik's Kirke* or the *Marble Church* in Copenhagen. This was finally built 1876–94, having been designed by Jardin and left as a fragment since the eighteenth century (Vol. 3). The exterior is very fine. The immense drum and dome, clearly modelled on St Peter's in Rome, rather over-dominate the church; and this is more apparent in the interior, which is completely circular, with a circular ambulatory round the nave. The interior dome is flatter and painted in

54 Copenhagen Cathedral, 1810–29, C. F. Hansen.
Marble sculpture by Thorvaldsen

panels. It is in the inside of the church that the fact that the building was largely constructed in the later nineteenth century, instead of the mid-eighteenth, is so apparent; it lacks warmth, life and character.

As in some other European countries, the beginnings of a new national architectural style, reverting to simplicity and away from overt eclecticism, began to appear after 1890. The leader of this movement in Denmark was *Martin Nyrop* (1849–1923). His *Town Hall* in Copenhagen (1892–1905) is his chief work, built in brick on similar lines to Berlage's style in Amsterdam (p. 52). In both cases the architects were reverting to the traditional building material used simply and clearly, without stucco covering or over-decoration, to reinstitute a national style.

Sweden

Architecture in the first half of the nineteenth century in Sweden was undistinguished. There were no outstanding architects designing in the field of Neo- or Romantic-classicism, as elsewhere, and financial means were not available to indulge large civic schemes or public buildings of note. Classical architecture was designed and built that was adequate and competent but no more.

Typical were works like the *University Library* at *Uppsala* by *Karl F. Sundvall* (1754–1831) and the *Skeppsholm Church* in *Stockhlom* (1824–42) by *Frederik Blom* (1781–1853). This is an octagonal building with shallow dome and lantern above; inside, the church is circular.

From the later 1840s a Gothic Revival was begun. The dull, derivative classical designs of the recent years were abandoned, especially in ecclesiastical work, castles and museums, in favour of medieval inspiration. Sweden produced its own competent, energetic restorer and recreator of the medieval heritage – *Helgo Zettervall* (1831–1907). Zettervall was as enthusiastic as Viollet-le-Duc in France or Scott in England to restore the great cathedrals and churches of his native land to their former glories and, like his colleagues in these other countries, passionately believed that it was better to return the entire building to its original design and style rather than tolerate Renaissance, Baroque, or even late Gothic intrusions, however fine quality work they might be. Like his colleagues, his intentions were of the best, his work good, capable and correct; without his contribution, much of Sweden's medieval heritage would by now have become lost. His hand was, however, a heavy one, especially on the fine *cathedrals* of *Uppsala, Lund, Linköping* and *Skara* (Vol. 2).

Zettervall was versatile and his own contribution (apart from restoration work) varied from the Neo-classic *University House* in Lund to the delicate tall *Church* of *Oskar Frederik* in Göteborg (Gothenburg). This is an elegant but typical example of Gothic Revivalism of the 1870s, built in deep red and black polychrome brickwork with green metal roofs and slender spires and gables. The interior is also lofty and slender (**55**) with delicate ribbed vaults over nave and aisles. Clustered, slim columns with small foliated capitals support the arches and vault springing. Like others of his age and belief, Zettervall had no objections to the spurious use of materials. Here, metal columns support the gallery, and he often substituted cement for stone.

Quite different from Revivalist Gothic but finely designed and functional is the *Fish Hall* at *Göteborg*, a simple, northern interpretation of the style.

In the last 20 years of the century, in Sweden as elsewhere in Europe, eclecticism ran riot, and all previous styles were re-introduced and experimented with. Typical of its period and in classical-vein is the *Central Railway Station* in *Stockholm* by *Edelsvärd*; a long, monumental façade with Ionic pilasters. In less sombre and richer style is *Anderberg's Opera House* in Gustav Adolf's Square also in Stockholm (1898). An enthusiastic quality example is the Baroque *Church of Gustav Vasa* in the capital, designed by *Agi Lindegren* (1858–1927) at the end of the century. This is a large, opulent church on a classic central Greek cross plan, with tall drum encircled by coupled Doric columns and with dome and lantern above. Inside, the decoration is of fine quality Baroque · design with painted cupola and pendentives and stucco ornament between. Doric pilasters and piers are used throughout the church. The different standard of craftsmanship between this highly competent, late-nineteenth-century work and that which it imitates is seen clearly here when it is compared with the beautiful altar, made by Burchardt Precht in 1731 for Uppsala Cathedral, from where it was removed when Zettervall restored the cathedral to its medieval origins. The eighteenth-century altar-

55 *Oskar Frederik's Church, Göteborg, 1870s,
Helgo Zettervall*

piece is magnificent, rich and ornate, with its Composite columns with gilt capitals and entablatures. Life-size figure sculpture is set in groups at the sides and above.

Also at the end of the century there emerged in Sweden, as in England and Denmark, a simpler, plainer type of architecture, still eclectic but of astringent quality. The leading Swedish architect in this work was *Isak Gustav Clason* (1856–1930). One of his earlier works (1886) was the large block at No. 31 Strandvägen in Stockholm, at the edge of the harbour, called *Bünsow House* and dedicated to Frederik Bünsow, whose portrait plaque appears over the main doorway. Built in polychrome brick and stone, it is a well-designed structure in early-French-Renaissance style. It is plain for its time, the ornament being restricted to the portals and gables. Another work by Clason is the *Nordiska* (northern) *Museum in Stockholm* (1890–1904). Based on the Danish palace design of Frederiksberg, this is a Dutch gabled building with central steeple and corner turrets. It also has much in common with English Jacobean work with its brick façades and stone facings. It is an elegant structure, a notable landmark across the waters of the lake.

Norway

Until the early nineteenth century, Danish influence on Norwegian architecture was extensive, due to the political union between the two countries. In 1814 this union was dissolved, and the newly independent country of Norway began to establish an architectural tradition, built up in the early years by architects from different lands: Germany, England, Holland as well as the other Scandinavian countries.

Oslo, till 1924 called Christiana, was small and lacking the large civic structures and street layout suitable for a capital city. Under King Karl Johan the years 1814–44 saw the establishment of such features. The Danish born architect *H. D. F. Linstow* was responsible for planning the centre of the capital, with the *royal palace* at one end of the long boulevard, Karl Johansgate, and the *University* and *Parliament Buildings* further down. The royal palace is situated on an eminence in parkland at the top of the vista. Built 1835–48, it is a rectangular, classical building with Ionic portico. It is simple, well proportioned and finely sited. In front is the equestrian statue of the King.

Linstow's contribution was the street layout and the palace. *C. H. Grosch*, also born in Denmark, was responsible for the University Buildings (**56**),

the Doric *Exchange* and the *Market Hall*. The first two of these are also classical buildings, a little heavier than the palace but of good quality, design and workmanship. The great German architect Schinkel (pp. 23–5) advised on the designs for the University buildings, which are Grosch's best work here. They comprise three separate blocks, the central one having an imposing Ionic portico.

By the mid century, Norwegian architecture had followed the general western European pattern of eclecticism. Grosch designed the Market Hall, near the cathedral, in red brick in neo-Romanesque style, heavy in treatment and solemn in design. Also Romanesque, almost *Rundbogenstil*, is the Parliament Building, further down the Karl Johansgate. Designed by the Swedish architect *E. V. Langlet*, it was built in 1866 in yellow brick. It is a stolid building whose most interesting feature is the central, circular hall, flanked by projecting wings (**57**).

Apart from the capital, much of the building in Norway throughout the nineteenth century was still in the traditional building material of wood. This was especially true in the construction of houses and churches. Towards the end of the century the 'dragon style' was evolved, which was based on the medieval stave church designs with their characteristic finials (Vol. 2). The style was popular as it was founded on a national type of structure, not a foreign import, like classical building. An interesting example of this work is the *Frognerseteren Restaurant*, built in 1890 by *Holm Munthe*. This has a magnificent site, 9 miles (14 km) from Oslo. Standing 1,387 ft (424 m) above the city and the fjord, it is reached by a mountain

56 The University, Oslo, begun 1840, Christian Heinrich Grosch

57 Parliament House, Oslo, 1866, E. V. Langlet

railway, which passes by the University at Blindern. The restaurant is in good condition, though the building of a terrace and some additional structures have interfered with its original clean lines.

The *Kvikne Hotel* at *Balestrand*, far up the Sognfjord, is another typical Norwegian timber structure of the 1890s. This is not in 'dragon style' but is characteristic in its fretwork wooden gables and supporting posts and balconies. It is a large building, set at the water's edge and dwarfed only by the high mountains closing in behind.

Finland

The quality of classical architecture built here in the first 40 years of the nineteenth century is far finer than in any of the other Scandinavian lands and compares favourably with that in any European country at this time, even Schinkel's and von Klenze's Germany, Napoleon's Paris and Nash's London terraces. In 1809, Finland's centuries-old ties with Sweden were broken as the country became part of the Russian Empire. Until this time Turku (Abô) had been the capital.

In 1812, the Tsar Alexander I decided to set up a new Finnish capital city at *Helsinki*, a site nearer to Russia and further from Swedish influence. At that time, Helsinki was a small fishing town of only 4,000 inhabitants living in wooden buildings. Alexander decided on an imposing city, laid out on

classical lines, with all the important civic structures to be designed specially in one homogenous layout. *Carl Ludwig Engel* (1778–1840), the German architect and fellow student with Schinkel, who had studied and worked in Italy, Berlin and S. Petersburg, was put in charge of the operation. He came to Finland, stayed there for a quarter of a century (the rest of his life) and carried out the Tsar's wishes. Helsinki was made into a fine capital city, magnificently laid out on monumental lines, the whole scheme and individual buildings a triumph of Romantic Classicism, with the structures in keeping with each other but varied and not monotonously similar. The city has been added to ever since but the original layouts are unaltered, well cared for and unforgettably impressive.

The chief of these, designed by Engel, is the great *Senate Square*, 560 by 330 ft (171 by 100 m), and near its centre the bronze monument to the *Tsar Alexander II,* erected in 1894. The square is dominated by the vast *Lutheran Cathedral of S. Nicholas* (**59**). Built on a great podium, approached by an immense flight of steps and flanked at the corners by classical pavilions, it is a centrally designed church on a Greek cross plan. Completely symmetrical, with a Corinthian portico on each of the four sides and with central drum and dome over the crossing, it is classical with Byzantine overtones. The interior is light, all in white and light stone colour, and is entirely classical. The immense, Corinthian crossing piers support the four semi-circular arches and pendentives with a shallow, plain interior dome without lantern. There are four apses, each with its Ionic colonnade, ambulatory behind and a hemispherical dome above. There is an elegant, simple pulpit with gilt classical decoration; the restrained altar is in keeping.

Engel designed classical buildings on other elevations of the square. The *Senate House* (now the *Council of State Building*) occupies the eastern side (**58**), the main *University Building* (1828–32) the western, with the domed *University Library* next to it, further north. The University Building is a simple, classical block, not dissimilar to the Senate House but with Ionic portico. The adjacent library has no portico, but Corinthian columns and pilasters across the front. Inside are three reading rooms; the central one is under the dome which is visible on the exterior. Though damaged in the Second World War, it is now restored and has a fine interior. It is a rectangular room with a colonnade of 28 Corinthian columns supporting a gallery. The ceiling is domed with lunettes on the four sides. The decoration is all painted: caissons in the dome and figure compositions in the lunettes.

The Senate Square slopes gradually towards the Market Square and the *South Harbour*. Here, there is a long line of fine buildings fronting the harbour, mainly classical in design but dating from different decades in the nineteenth century. Facing the buildings, one's back to the harbour, from left to right they comprise the *City Hall*, 1833, by *Engel*, a large building with Corinthian pilasters in the central portico and end pavilions; a small classical building, 1815, by *Pehr Granstedt*; the *Swedish Embassy*, also classical though astylar, 1922, by *Torben Grut*; the *Supreme Court*, rusticated classical, 1883, by *E. A. Sjöström*; and the *President's Palace*, 1813, by *Pehr Granstedt*. This was built as the Helsinki palace for the Tsar and has a central, Ionic portico. This homogeneous, curving elevation round the harbour's edge is of one theme but has vitality and interest springing from its varied dates of construction. A taller structure, on higher ground beyond the palace, is in complete contrast. The classical buildings are white and pastel shades, while this building, the *Orthodox Cathedral*, is in deep-red brick, Russian Byzantine in style, built in 1868 by *Gornostajeff*. The interior is surprisingly light considering the heavy Byzantine décor in gilt and colour.

Apart from the creation of the capital city, many other buildings were erected in Finland in these years, in classical style and of high quality in design and structure. In 1810, a national body for administering and constructing buildings was set up. Its first Controller of Public Works was the Italian architect *Carlo Francesco Bassi* (1772–1840). The few works by him that survive include the *Old Church* at *Tampere* (1824). Largely of wood painted white, it is picturesquely sited, like so many of Finland's buildings, in a group of trees in the centre of the city. It has a separate bell tower and is a simple domed church with plain portico.

In *Turku*, the old capital, *Bassi* designed the *Abö Akademie* (the Swedish-language University Building), which is near to the cathedral. It was

58 Senate House, Senate Square, Helsinki, 1818–22, Carl Ludwig Engel

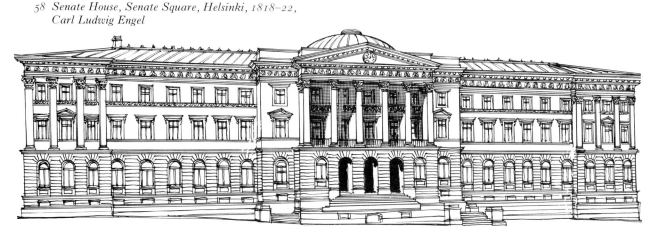

built in 1832–3 and is a rectangular, classical block with a two storey Doric portico. *Carl Christoffer Gjörwell* designed the *Old University Building*, not far away, in 1802–15, with Bassi's co-operation. Turku's classical heritage is less complete than Helsinki's due to the removal of its capital status, but *Engel*, who succeeded Bassi as Controller, laid out a new town here on the opposite side of the River Aura from the medieval city constructed round the cathedral. This was done after the fire of Turku in 1827. The centre is the large market square, the *Kauppatori*. On the north side is the low building of the *Orthodox Church*, with its immense dome and sturdy, Doric portico (1846) and on the west, the *Swedish Theatre* (1838), which has a façade ornamented by Corinthian pilasters.

In *Hamina*, since 1945 near the border with the Soviet Union, the small town centre possesses some beautiful classical buildings (Vol. 3). *Engel* built the circular, domed *Orthodox Church* (1837), though the separate campanile in mixed classical and Russian Byzantine style was by *Visconti*. The *Medieval Church* nearby was restored by Engel in 1828 in simple classical manner. In *Hämeenlinna*, the classical church by *L. J. Desprez* (1798) still stands in the town centre. Surrounded by trees, it is in good condition, though the interior has been completely modernized. The *Prefecture* nearby is also a classical building, built 1833–6.

In the second half of the nineteenth century, Finland also turned to eclecticism, building in classical, Romanesque and neo-Gothic manner. Typical of the *fin de siècle* are *Gustav Nyström's*

buildings in *Helsinki*; the *House of Estates* (1891) and the *State Archives Building* (1890). These are both high-quality classical architecture, well designed and proportioned with good detail and sculpture. In *Hamina*, the *Military Academy* (1898) is another excellent example, this time in the Doric Order.

Georg Theodor Chiewitz worked more in Medieval style. In *Loviisa*, his *Town Hall* is on simple, Romanesque lines (1856), reminiscent of Italian small town halls such as that of Montepulciano. His *church* nearby is in neo-Gothic vein (1865), in deep red brick. It is a large building of good quality, belonging to the same spirit as the Gothic Revival of England and Germany, on cruciform plan with a tall, eastern steeple. Chiewitz's best known work is the *House of Nobles* in *Helsinki*, near the Senate Square. Built in 1861, this is red brick and stone in Gothic Revival style. The exterior is solemn and pedestrian; the interior has an impressive stairway and assembly hall. Also in Helsinki, very typical of the period, is the heavily ornamented *office building* now used by the Forestry Board. Designed by *Carl Theodor Hoijer* in 1889, it is in neo-Renaissance style.

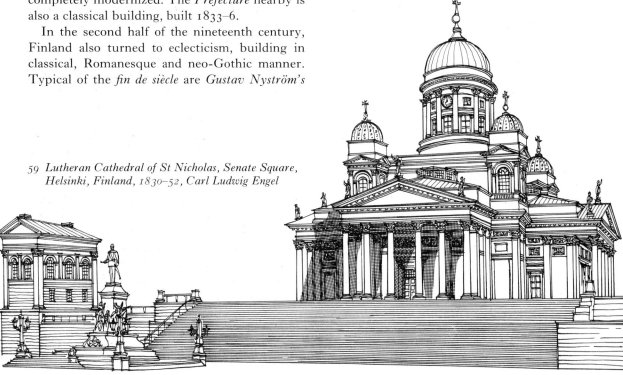

59 *Lutheran Cathedral of St Nicholas, Senate Square, Helsinki, Finland, 1830–52, Carl Ludwig Engel*

II
The Twentieth Century

Introduction:
Art Nouveau

Until 1900, architecture in Europe had been based upon two fundamental styles: classical and Gothic (medieval). The ancient cultures of Greece and Rome had evolved the classical pattern; Byzantine and Romanesque forms were partially derived from them. Then there had developed in northern Europe the medieval style which we call Gothic. The Renaissance rediscovered the classical world and Baroque, rococo and Romantic Classicism reinterpreted the theme until, finally, during the nineteenth century, came an eclecticism of these forms, successively and almost indiscriminately.

The twentieth century is different. Modern architecture makes use of new methods of construction, materials and, therefore, different proportions: the traditional yardstick could be abandoned. This has made the architect freer – although he has not always used this freedom wisely or, indeed, often exploited it at all – to design in a totally different manner from that circumscribed by the traditions of the past. In the United States, as long ago as the 1870s architects were experimenting with multi-storey buildings using steel framing to build high and fast. In Europe, where traditionally a huge, low-cost labour force continued to be available, where cities were old and established and where the population increase had been less rapid, the need to build quickly – using modern methods of construction – was not required until after the First World War.

As a result, in the years 1900–20, there existed in parallel four basic architectural trends. There was Art Nouveau, showing the desire of designers for something new; secondly, and most commonly, there survived a continuation movement (though in simplified form) of traditional classical and Gothic forms; thirdly, there was a plainer, less eclectic approach though still using traditional materials and proportions; and, lastly, there emerged early prototypes of modern architecture.

Art Nouveau was an aesthetic, romantic, ephemeral movement which showed itself in many European countries between the late 1880s and 1910 but which had burnt itself out by 1914. It was a movement engendered by those who were searching for a new mode of artistic expression that would take them away from the re-vamping of styles which had been the chief expression of the nineteenth century and, at the same time, would lead to a resurgence of quality craftwork and away from the pressures of a technological age.

Art Nouveau was a decorative rather than an architectural movement. In architecture it was concerned more with surface decoration than with plastic structure. Though short-lived and limited in scope, it is important historically in architecture as an early attempt to break away from eclecticism. It was not entirely successful in this but manifested a deeply felt striving to do so. It was an escape for architects who sought new forms of design yet shied away from the current trend towards industrialization. They preferred the world of the individual, the craftsman, the cottage industry. Art Nouveau was an extension of the ideas of Morris and Ruskin (pp. 9, 14). Despite the search for new ideas in design, the movement was based upon a return to craftsmanship, geared towards a smaller population as in pre-industrial times: it could not last. The First World War finally broke down the illusions and post–1918 architects were either eclectics or moderns.

The term Art Nouveau (as the style was later called in England in succession to the 'Modern Style'), derives from the name of Siegfried Bing's shop – Maison de l'Art Nouveau – which opened in Paris in 1895 to sell merchandise of a modern, that is, non-derivative, style. Countries adopted different names for the movement, calling it after individual designers or journals or using descriptive terms. In Belgium it was termed *Coup de fouet* (whiplash) after the flowing lines of the designs. Germany and Austria called it *Jugendstil* after the Munich journal *Jugend*, France the *Style Guimard* after the architect Henri Guimard who designed the ornamental ironwork of the Paris Métro entrances in 1899, though the French also used the descriptive term *Style Nouille* (noodle or vermicelli style). The Spanish talked of *Modernismo* and the Italians *Lo stile floreale* or *Lo stile Liberty* after the Regent Street store, which was famous at the time for selling textiles with Art Nouveau designs.

Art Nouveau had begun as a decorative movement in book illustration, textiles, glassware and furniture. Predominant motifs were undulating plant forms, flames, moving waves and flowing hair. Abstract and geometric motifs were also used but evidenced the same quality of line and movement. Decoration then extended to the use of faïence, coloured glass, terracotta and veneers. In architecture iron and plain glass were favourite materials as well as stained glass and stucco. Typical interiors were *Victor Horta's Hôtel Tassel* in Brussels (1892–3) and *August Endell's Studio Elvira* in Munich (1897). Otto Wagner in Vienna was introducing the ornamental style into his Stadtbahn stations (as Guimard was doing in Paris) and his block of flats, the Majolika Haus, was decorated across the façade in floral designs as was the ironwork of the balconies and grilles.

Modern Architecture

Modern architecture is a term universally applied to a style which was born and slowly developed in a number of countries in the early years of the twentieth century and which has culminated in the current building form to be found world-wide, constructed of glass, steel and concrete on the module pattern. Other names have been applied to this type of architecture – international, rational, functional, for example – but no more comprehensive or apposite name has been suggested to describe these differing structures which appear to have no link with past styles.

Not all building since the First World War can be termed modern architecture. Indeed, until after 1950 only a minority of work could be so classified. The bulk of construction up to this time was of traditional, eclectic design and, in Europe, it was only a handful of pioneers who created modern architecture in the inter-war years.

The term 'international style', was coined in the 1930s to express the fact that this modern building type transcended frontiers and was being adopted spontaneously and simultaneously on both sides of the Atlantic, throughout Europe and beyond. But this was not just because it spread as an architectural style but because, more fundamentally, the social structure of society in so many countries had a need for the type of buildings which it produced and at a cost and speed which such constructional methods made possible.

The idea, though, that internationalism in architecture meant the same type of buildings being put up everywhere was, by the 1950s, found to be unsound. National trends were making themselves apparent, based, as always, on climate, available resources, individual mode of living and economic necessity. Although modern architecture everywhere utilized similar materials and means of construction, national differences arose. Those countries with an advanced steel industry – the United States, Germany and Britain, for example – used steel-frame construction based on the rectangular block format which was then glass curtain-walled (see p. 81) or concrete faced. In Italy and Spain, on the other hand, where for several decades after the First World War steel was less readily available, there was greater emphasis on the use of ferroconcrete, a type of material suited to parabolic arches and vaults. Also, before the development of solar glass control, such curtain walling was unsuited to countries with a hot sunny climate. Here also, the traditional desire for colour led to external mural decoration and ceramic facing, while in northern Europe a feature was made of raw concrete as a desirable prevailing mode.

Modern architecture did not, however, appear fully formed in the early years of the twentieth century. Despite the deep desire of architects and designers for a change of building style, new forms were, in most countries before the Second World War, still on traditional lines though of a simplified character. Traditional materials were still being used. In Holland and Scandinavia, for instance, brick continued to be the chief material employed, with leading architects adapting the centuries-old tradition of this material into the modern idiom. Hendrik Berlage was a Dutch leader in this movement as was Jensen Klint in Denmark and Sigfrid Ericsson in Sweden. A more personal interpretation could be seen in the same period in Lars Sonck's great granite structures in Finland. Even in the 1920s and 1930s a conservative clinging to the traditional proportions and forms of building in a plain, barely ornamented interpretation was manifest in most European countries, most notably in Britain in the work of such fine architects as Lutyens.

Finally, it was pressure engendered by two other vital factors that created the catalyst for a complete stylistic break with the past. The first of these was the population explosion which had taken place in Europe in the later nineteenth century, which, together with the effects of the Industrial Revolution, created an irresistable expectation of a higher standard of living so making urgently necessary an increased rate of building for all purposes. The second, later, factor was the extensive destruction caused by two world wars, which necessitated the rebuilding of whole towns as well as individual sites. Such urgency greatly hastened the technical development of new and improved materials, making it possible to erect structures on a large scale more cheaply by mass-production methods. The combination of these factors brought about a transformation in twentieth-century building which has killed for ever an architectural industry founded upon individual craftsmanship.

Modern architecture is quite different from both Art Nouveau and simplified traditionalism in its aims and principles. A very few men were experimenting with such ideas before 1918 and a new generation joined them in the inter-war years, developing the possibilities of a new range of materials and means of utilizing them constructionally. The chief materials of such modern architecture were concrete, steel and glass.

It was the Romans who had developed the use of concrete for structural purposes and their addition of *pozzolana* to the mix, thus incorporating alumina and silica, produced an exceptionally hard, durable concrete that made possible the massive vaulted structures of their basilicas and baths (Vol. I). After the collapse of the western part of the Empire in the fifth century the greater part of this technical knowledge was lost for some 1,300 years, and the use of concrete as a structural material was not revived on an extensive scale until the late eighteenth century.

It was the development of concrete *reinforced* with iron, and later steel, which initiated its wide scale use as a structural material. The Romans had carried out only limited experimentation with metal reinforcement, in their case bronze, and

their normal concrete walling was of massive thickness. Experiments with iron in the later eighteenth century showed this to be a material exceptionally suited to the purpose of reinforcement because it possesses about the same coefficients of thermal expansion and contraction as concrete over a normal range of temperatures and so provides a tensile strength that plain concrete lacks. An early use of reinforced concrete was by Rondelet in the piers supporting the dome of the Panthéon in Paris (Vol. 3).

During the nineteenth century experimentation was continued in a number of countries, but the French were the chief pioneers in Europe, notably in the work of *François Coignet* (1814–88) and *François Hennébique* (1842–1921). The next development was in *pre-stressing* concrete, which again enormously increased the potential of the material. The purpose of pre-stressing is to make more efficient and economic use of materials. It makes possible the creation of slender elegant forms, curved or straight, which are at the same time immensely strong. The theory is that the metal reinforcement (wire cables threaded through ducts) should be stretched before the concrete is poured into position and the pull maintained until the concrete is hard and strong.

Pre-stressing, to be successful, requires high-quality concrete and high-tensile steel. Early experimentation in the late nineteenth century was unsatisfactory because such materials were not then available. It was the French engineer *Eugène Freyssinet* (1879–1962) who pioneered pre-stressed reinforced concrete. As an army engineer he experimented with building bridges in the material and, later, after 1918, formed his own company to develop his ideas. These proved highly successful and brought him fame when, in 1934, he succeeded in saving the *Ocean Terminal* at *Le Havre* from sinking into the mud and being covered by the sea by building new foundations of pre-stressed concrete.

Freyssinet had pioneered the industrial use of the material in his great parabolic-vaulted airship hangar at Orly in 1916. Before the First World War *Auguste Perret* (1874–1954) was using concrete to build apartment blocks in Paris and, later, his most famous work, the *Church of Notre Dame* at *Le Raincy*. Concrete proved an ideal material for the Expressionist architecture of the 1920s, being capable of being formed into sculptural-type structures of all kinds. This theme was adopted particularly in Germany, as in the interior of the *Grosses Schauspielhaus* by Hans Poelzig (1869–1956) in Berlin (1919). The material was widely utilized by modern architects of the inter-war years in areas as far apart as Loos in Austria, Terragni in Italy, Le Corbusier in France and Melnikov in the Soviet Union.

Post-War Building

After the Second World War steel was at first in limited supply, and architects turned to pre-stressed reinforced concrete. With increased experience of these techniques, it was realized that the structural possibilities were virtually unlimited. It became a desirable material because the needs of an individual project could be calculated exactly in terms of reinforcement and strength of concrete. Further, it could be cast into any form and so gave a freedom of design to architects which they had not previously possessed and which was particularly suited to modern styles.

Outstanding among the exponents of the material was the engineer *Pier Luigi Nervi* (1891–1979) in Italy, who produced a wide range of curved and vaulted structures such as his *Palazzetto dello Sport* built for the Rome Olympics in 1960 and, in quite a different sphere, the work of the architect *Le Corbusier* (1887–1966), who created such totally diverse designs as the low-cost *Unité d'Habitation* and the *Church* at *Ronchamp*.

During the 1950s and 1960s it became fashionable to build in unfaced concrete, a material called in Britain 'brutalism', a term coined from the French *béton brut* meaning concrete left in its natural state and used in its most overt, naked form handled in strong masses. Such so-called 'honesty of material' was extolled as a virtue, particularly in Britain, and it is largely due to the erection all over Europe of vast quantities of buildings in this material and for diverse purposes, which have aged and weathered badly, that reaction in the 1970s against raw concrete was so strong and widespread.

An important spin-off in modern architecture from steel-framed construction has been high-rise building, a type of structure that came late to Europe, mainly after 1945. The skyscraper was conceived and named in the United States, where, as early as the 1880s, conditions were ripe for this type of architectural development. In the big

cities, notably Chicago and New York, steeply rising land values provided the incentive to build high, and the structural means to do so had become available.

In the United States the desire to build high for commercial and office needs was frustrated for several decades for two important reasons: by the requirement of transporting the occupants from floor to floor and by the problems of load-bearing walls. As early as 1849 seven-storey buildings were being erected, but, until the development of the passenger lift, this was the limit.

The hoist for raising and lowering goods had been in use for centuries but it was not considered safe for passengers in case the rope broke. It was *Elisha Graves Otis* (1811–61) who adapted the hoist for passenger use. In 1852 he devised a safety mechanism consisting of spring-controlled pawls, which, if the rope gave way, would engage ratcheted guide rails fitted into the sides of the lift shaft and so hold the cage in position. In 1854 in New York Otis personally demonstrated this device, and within a few years passenger lifts were being installed in office blocks and taller buildings resulted.

The next essential development to enable buildings to rise above about ten storeys was the steel-framed structure. Until the early 1880s tall buildings up to this height were still being erected on traditional load-bearing lines but, to rise still higher, required impractically thick walls at base in order to carry the load above. It was the emergence of the load-bearing metal framework, structurally independent of the external walling, which made the true skyscraper possible. An early landmark in this development was the *Home Insurance Building* in *Chicago* built in 1883–5 by *William LeBaron Jenney* (1832–1907). In this he devised an iron-and-steel framework of columns, lintels and girders. The building was quickly followed by the fully developed steel skeleton construction of the *Tacoma Building* by *Holabird* and *Roche* in the same city where the walls were mere cladding.

From the early years of the twentieth century European architects began to build higher, but, until after 1945, did not attempt to follow the American example of the tall structures there of the 1920s and 1930s: the *Empire State Building* of 1930–2 in *New York*, for example, rises through 85 storeys. Much of the early European multi-storey building was more traditional, some eight to ten storeys, the form of the steel structure being concealed by the cladding of traditional design as in the Ritz Hotel in London of 1906. Later work in the 1920s and 1930s was higher and plainer but generally clad in stone. London University's *Senate House* (1933-7) is typical, though examples in Germany, for instance, Fritz Höger's *Chilehaus* in Hamburg is much more strikingly original.

Since the Second World War all over the world high-rise building has become prevalent, not just for commerical needs but for housing too. Shortage and high cost of land have created an incentive for this type of construction, and, especially, in the 1950s and 1960s, the tower block has been adopted by architects and planners as an ideal new design for working and living with its economy of space and open-plan landscaping. In city centres tower blocks have been constructed on podia, the surrounding public space laid out as 'piazzas', which, in northern Europe, have tended to be windswept for much of the year. Such schemes were then developed to include necessary car parking. Technical advances in building materials and construction have made such structural methods more practical, for example, the substitution of welding for riveting, the increased employment of on-site plant and wide-scale prefabrication.

The style of high-rise building varies to a certain extent from country to country depending by and large upon materials available, climatic conditions and the overall political system. Especially characteristic of the Soviet Union, for instance, was the traditionally grand scale of the projects. During the years 1945 to the early 1960s, the Stalinist form of classical architecture was imposed upon high-rise building, creating innumerable skyscraper 'wedding cakes' here and all over Eastern Europe. Only after 1965 did the 'international form' begin to emerge here.

This international form – the pattern set in the United States by such structures as the *United Nations Headquarters Building* of 1947-50 in *New York* by *Wallace K. Harrison* – was for a steel-framed glass curtain-walled tall box. As early as 1918 San Francisco, *Willis Polk* in his *Halladie Building* in San Francisco had introduced the curtain wall of steel and glass, which, hanging in front of the building's construction framework, was separated from the structure. After 1945 architects all over Europe began to emulate the famous American examples being erected in cities such as New York, including the *Lever Building*, (1950–2) by *Skidmore, Owings and Merrill* and the *Seagram Building* (1955–8) by *Mies van der Rohe* and *Philip Johnson*.

With an increased use of factory-made units in the building industry, standardization, the essential concomitant of the prefabricated method, became more fully effective. The standardizing of separate building parts had been vital from the earliest experimentation, but a system to establish an overall three-dimensional unit was urgently needed. This system, known as *modular design*, ensures the accurate fitting of all building parts of whatever material, wherever and by whomsoever manufactured. The *Modular Society* was formed in Britain in 1953 to promote such a system of uniformity. Its members were drawn from all concerned in the building industry, from architects to clients and craftsmen. The work of the society was later taken over by the *British Standards Institution*. Le Corbusier had put forward a system of proportion in 1951, based upon the male human figure, to be used in building; he called it *Le Modulor*.

From the beginning of the twentieth century a variety of schemes have been experimented with and fully developed for providing a better standard of housing than had been evident in the previous century, required by a still-growing population and one which was becoming increasingly urban. In a number of countries, for example, Britain, Sweden, France and Finland, the new town approach was favoured, where a new site on rural land was chosen where could be created a self-supporting community and not an extension of an existing conurbation. Industry would be developed in an area adjacent to the town and all facilities, such as banking, office accommodation, police and fire services, libraries, schools, universities, hospitals and shops, were provided on site. A different approach was the *dormitory suburb*, creating only housing adjacent to an existing town. Yet another variant was the *satellite town* in which a new site was selected not too far from an existing large town. Many facilities would be provided here but the town would be dependent upon the larger centre of population for costly facilities such as universities and hospitals.

In many city centres after the Second World War high-rise municipal estates were erected.

These 'vertical garden cities' were hailed in the 1950s and 1960s as an ideal answer to the problem of housing a large number of people as quickly as possible on the smallest area of land yet providing open space around the tower blocks.

When put forward in his various ideal urban schemes in the 1920s by Le Corbusier, the architect envisaged large areas of open space, landscaped into parkland with lakes and facilities for sport and recreation around a limited number of blocks.

In his *Ville Contemporaine (A Contemporary City for Three Million Inhabitants)* of 1922, for example, Le Corbusier had followed the classical town plan ideal, a grid format with two highways acting as the main axes of the plan and crossing one another on east/west and north/south lines. In the city centre at this point were to be erected 24 60-storey glazed skyscrapers, cruciform in plan, for business and administration. Around this centre would be a 'green' area containing lower 12-storey luxury living blocks. Between this part and the outer ring of low-level accommodation with communal gardens would be the extensive parkland and re-creational region.

In the post-war period, in attempting to cope with the immense problems of rebuilding shattered city centres, the relative proportion of open space to high-rise blocks was drastically altered and the recreational green areas reduced.

Post-modern Design

Towards the end of the 1960s, disillusion was setting in for the client, to a certain extent for the architect but, most of all, for the public. The great ideals of the founders of modern architecture – Le Corbusier and Gropius, Terragni and Mies van der Rohe, Lissitsky and Oud – were shown, in the event, to be less satisfactory than had been confidently projected. Particularly in civic planning and in housing, the intentions had been excellent; to provide a better standard and a richer quality of life than ever before. Perhaps too much had been hoped for but, probably, the chief reason for the disillusion was the vast quantity of building that had been carried out since 1945, so creating a soulless monotony. This feeling of sameness was accentuated by the dominant material of such building, concrete, which weathered to a drab greyness streaked with rain marks.

Disillusion was at its most deeply felt in high-rise building, most particularly when used for housing. The open spaces surrounding the base of such blocks become ill-kept and vandalized. These areas of land were too small to be of value to the occupants of the blocks, while the means of access encouraged crime and personal attack. The social implications inherent in this type of urban living had not been appreciated; the loneliness of elderly people immured 20 storeys above ground level and the difficulties presented to mothers of young children, especially when the lifts were out of order, as they often were. It was not only a social problem but also a constructional one. New building techniques had been adopted without due periods of trial because of the need for haste in erection. Many builders cut corners in putting up the structures, not bothering to follow the architects plans in materials and fittings. In Britain, the decline in such home building was triggered especially by the dramatic collapse of the system-built block of *Ronan Point* in the London borough of *Newham* (1968). Similar collapses occurred in several European countries, and, by the early 1980s, the full scale of the need for rebuilding and reinforcing the many system-built town blocks had become apparent as investigation revealed more results of inadequate site inspection when building such blocks. Demolition then began to be widespread.

It is not only the high-rise structures of which people have tired but it is these – whether for civic, office or domestic – which have been mostly criticized, if only for the inhuman scale of such buildings and the incongruity of their height in comparison with earlier neighbours. This has led, as the pendulum of taste and opinion has swung, to a resistance to further modern building and a tenacious refusal on the part of a myriad of pressure groups of all kinds to oppose demolition of any building, however banal and ugly, erected prior to 1900 – and what a quantity of ugly building was perpetrated during the nineteenth century. Architects and planners have, correspondingly, taken fright and played safe, so creating a more human scale of building but often providing, through its innocuousness, an even duller contribution.

The greatest problem for city planners in the twentieth century is, arguably, that of the internal combustion engine. The need for motorized traffic to be able to negotiate the streets quickly and easily towards its destination has to be weighed against the rights and welfare of the local population. The problem has been solved most often in favour of the former. Pressure has, therefore, built up for some form of separation of traffic from people. The idea was hardly new but the urgency was. Leonardo da Vinci had postulated it in the fifteenth century and illustrated his ideas on such segregation in some detail. In the first few years of the twentieth century both *Antonio Sant'Elia* (1888–1916) in Italy and *Tony Garnier* (1869–1948) in France had designed ideal towns in which industrial areas were divided from leisure ones and traffic from pedestrians. In the United States, just after the First World War, a pilot scheme was actually built in *Radburn, New Jersey*, but it was not until after the Second World War that traffic pressure forced a serious consideration of this as a satisfactory solution to everyday urban movement problems.

Despite such pressures and the urgent need for something to be done, resistance from commercial interests was fierce, and bitter opposition was mounted against any attempt to limit vehicular access to their premises. This was especially so in England and France, but in Germany and Holland, where so many city centres had been devastated by bombing, objections were more muted and the opportunity to rebuild differently was, in so many instances, grasped. By the 1960s the city centres of such places as Essen, Düsseldorf, Hanover and Hamburg were peaceful and pedestrianized. The famous prototype of the city pedestrian precinct was in the devastated centre of Rotterdam where the *Lijnbaan* was laid out in 1953–4. By the 1970s, city authorities in many countries were appreciating the advantages of such schemes and followed suit as in, for example, Munich and Verona.

In the last 20 years other important features of many schemes for urban renewal have been established, giving maintenance of comfortable, ambient air temperatures and convenience of access: this has been achieved by taking advantage of modern technology. In design, undercover shopping, car parking and entertainment facilities as well as museums and churches may be linked by moving walkways, escalators and pedestrianized streets, a mini-city created to give comfort and ease when patronizing a range of services. Such schemes are particularly welcome in cities which experience extremes of winter and summer temperatures, for example, the re-designed *Place Ville-Marie* in *Montreal*, Canada (1967, *Pei and Cobb*). Other north American schemes include *New York's Lincoln Center* (1966, *Johnson, Harrison* and *Abramovitz*) and *Chicago's John Hancock Center* (1967–9). The *City of London* developed the central area of the *Barbican* (1959–82) to the designs of *Chamberlain, Powell* and *Bon*, creating a residential neighbourhood, an arts and conference centre, a library, school, restaurants and museum. The *Pompidou Centre* in *Paris* (1976, *Piano* and *Rogers*) has been a resounding success (p. 127).

In the late 1960s also technical advances were making available an improved range of materials which markedly affected some architectural design. The distaste aroused by the drab weathering on new concrete buildings led to the cladding of such façades – at least on prestige structures – by ceramic tiling, which greatly improved the appearance.

A notable technical advance was in the field of plastics, materials that had been used extensively internally but had not previously been sufficiently strong for constructional purposes. The development of GRP (glass reinforced polyester) made such structural use possible. The material could be moulded into large wall and roof panels in a range of colours. As with other technical advances, GRP encouraged architects of the so-called late-modern period into what is commonly referred to as *high-tech architecture*. GRP cladding of this type lends itself in its shiny form to a 'wet-look' style. Characteristic is James Stirling's *Olivetti Training Centre* (1969–73). Research into alloyed steels and into aluminium have led to the metal framework theme of the 'exterior plumbing type' – a kind of architectural meccano – such as Richard Rogers' *Lloyds of London* building (1986). In great engineering projects, however, reinforced concrete has no rival, and the *Thames Barrier* in London, opened in 1984, is a notable example (**Plate 34**).

Most notable advances have been made in the field of flat glass manufacture, in particular the development of the *float glass* process by Pilkington. In this process the molten glass floats in a continuous ribbon along a bath of molten tin, leaving the furnace at a temperature of 1500 °C and held at 1000 °C by a chemically controlled atmosphere until the surfaces have become flat and parallel. The ribbon of glass thus cools sufficiently to be removed without the surface being marked so thus making unnecessary the traditional grinding and polishing processes to restore the translucency of the glass. Over this temperature range the tin remains molten yet is sufficiently dense to support the glass. Float glass has made possible larger panes of glass with a pristine quality transparency.

The special problems inherent in using glass for curtain walling – the difficulty of adequately sealing together the panes, the chill factor of the material and, conversely, the heat problem from direct sunshine as well as the sensitivity of the occupants of a building to being on view to passers-by – have now largely been solved. Silicone sealants are truly waterproof. Double glazed units with nitrogen filling the space between the sheets have dealt with the chill factor. Sun reflecting coating has reduced the glare, and air-conditioning controls the cooling of the interior atmosphere. One-way and coloured glass have made it possible to sheath the whole building, giving the occupants both an airy atmosphere and privacy. Recent buildings may now be totally clad in dark-coloured glass, on curved as well as flat planes, as in *Norman Foster's Willis Faber* headquarters building (1972). Changing weather conditions can completely alter the appearance of such structures from reflecting the exterior world (a possible traffic hazard) to becoming almost invisible. At night, illuminated from within, the interior comes to life.

Recent research at Imperial College of Science in London has developed a method of making double glazed sheets in which the colour and transparency may be adjusted for various lighting and weather conditions. This electro-chromic glass contains lithium and tungsten trioxide compounds sandwiched between the sheets. Using an electric method a mixture of the two compounds is achieved by the application of a small positive voltage so bringing about a colour change which remains after the current is switched off. A return to the original clarity is achieved by reversing the voltage.

These developments in concrete, metals, plastics and glass have inspired not only a high-tech form of architecture but also a new wave of expressionism, evidenced in the shell roofs of hyperbolic paraboloid type such as *Kenzo Tange*'s work in *Tokyo* (*St Mary's Cathedral*, 1964, for example).

Another phase of architectural design and civic planning has been referred to, for want of a better term, as *post-modern*. Just as with the earlier phases of the 1960s and early 1970s, this is in reaction to modern architecture, that form evolved by such men as Le Corbusier, Gropius and Mies van der Rohe as an excessively plain functionalism using modern materials to build a better and different world.

Post-modernism looks toward a richer, less stark architectural form, more decorative and more varied in the materials used. It also looks towards re-establishment of a human scale in architecture and, in many instances, displays a nostalgic yearning towards the past, especially the classical past.

Schemes such as *Charles Moore's Piazza d'Italia* in *New Orleans* (1976–9) and *Ricardo Bofill's Palace of Abraxas* (1978–82), a gigantic multi-storey, romantic, low-cost housing scheme on the peripheral motorway encircling Paris, are interesting and original examples of this. Much less original, indeed banal, is the uninspired classical eclecticism, reminiscent of the vacuous forms of the 1930s, increasingly being accepted for civic schemes by authorities afraid to face criticism for an outmoded 'modern' town block scheme.

Western Europe: Germany

The history of the twentieth century in Europe has been turbulent. This has been clearly reflected in its architecture, where fashion has fluctuated violently from ornate eclecticism, through severe functionalism, to a dominance of civil engineering module construction. Nowhere in Europe is this more apparent than in Germany, which began the century a newly-forged proud nation only to suffer, after two world wars, once again a division of its peoples. From 1945 to 1990 this division resulted in the architecture of the two Germanys taking a different path. The essential German characteristics of energy, industry, determination and a wealth of talent are, however, to be seen in both parts of the country. It was these qualities which made Germany into the leading nation in new architectural ideas for so great a part of the twentieth century.

It is not easy today for a student to follow the development of German architecture *in situ* because of the extreme devastation of so many German cities in the Second World War. Most of the damage was in the northern industrial areas and, naturally, it was in these cities, which were built up in the industrialization programme of 1900–39, that the new architectural ideas were promulgated and came to fruition. The internationally famous buildings in Art Nouveau, Functionalist and Expressionist form, as well as those which stemmed from the Bauhaus ideas, have largely disappeared; only a few remain. The architects who experimented and built in these styles either emigrated in the early 1930s or stayed at home, designing in Fascist Neo-classicism as directed or remained commission-less.

The Germans began to design in the Art Nouveau manner in 1896. One of the first and notable examples was the *Studio Elvira* in *Munich* (1897–8), the work of *August Endell* (1871–1925). The simple stucco façade was ornamented with a centrally-placed bold abstract relief, the design of eastern derivation. Another example, this time of ferrovitreous type of design, was *Alfred Messel's* (1853–1909) *Wertheim department store* in the Leipzigerstrasse in *Berlin* (1896). Messel later went on to industrial commissions, including his work for AEG.

The most important formative years for modern architecture in Europe were those between 1918 and 1939. The work varied from country to country but the leading architects were all united in their rejection of both eclecticism and ornament as a reaction against nineteenth-century building. In consequence, their work tended to be starkly uncompromising. Primarily they were concerned with the proper use of material and with architectural structure.

It was a paradox of these years that so many of the original thinkers and designers of the modern style, those men who also possessed the courage to defy the established architectural traditions, were nationals of countries which submitted to totalitarian government; a type of government which rendered it impossible for such architects to retain integrity in their work. This happened in both the Soviet Union, and Italy, but the greatest loss of architectural talent through emigration was in Germany.

Entirely new ideas in architecture were being experimented with by a number of designers in Germany even before 1914. The most famous name in this field is that of *Walter Gropius* (1883–1969), who began his architectural career in 1908, after training at the Technische Hochschule in Munich, then travelling in Europe for a year. One of his early works was the *Fagus Factory*, making shoe lasts, at *Alfeld-an-der-Leine* (**60**). Although today this building appears ordinary, in 1911 it was a revolutionary prototype, heralding the glass curtain-walling systems so prevalent after 1950. It is one of the few of Gropius' buildings to have survived in Germany.

In 1919 Gropius was appointed to head the Art College at Weimar. Two institutions were amalgamated in this, the Grand Ducal School of Applied Arts and the Grand Ducal Academy of Arts. Under Gropius the new institution became the *Staatliches Bauhaus*. Here he was able to put into practice his strongly-held ideas. He was so successful that this small college, which trained only a few hundred students in the limited years of its existence, became architecturally world famous, a Mecca which attracted architects, artists and students from all over Europe, seeing here something new which would free them from the straitjacket of designing in medieval or classical idiom. This applied to all the visual arts. Artists of such stature as Paul Klee from Switzerland and Vassili Kandinsky from Russia were two who joined his orbit.

Gropius' idea was to set up an institution where students in all the arts and crafts could study and learn one from another. He abhorred the artificial barriers which existed between artists and craftsmen and between artists in different media; he believed that all artists should be craftsmen anyway. He saw them all as interdependent. He felt that the manual dexterity in the craft was as vital and necessary as the mental contribution of the designer. The phrase so often heard to denote lack of academic ability but compensating artistic dexterity, 'he is good with his hands', would have found no favour with Gropius. He knew only too well that the skill of the craftsman is as fundamentally directed by the brain as that of the original designer. So, every Bauhaus student, whatever his field of work or talent, took the same workshop training. He saw and studied what was necessary for the complete design. When qualified he was able to comprehend and oversee all the aesthetic and constructional processes needed in his field.

All this, of course, was nothing new. It had been practised by the architects of the Italian Renais-

60 *The Fagus Factory, Alfeld-an-der-Leine, 1911–14,*
   Walter Gropius and Adolf Meyer

61 *AEG Turbine Factory, Berlin, 1909–10,*
   Peter Behrens

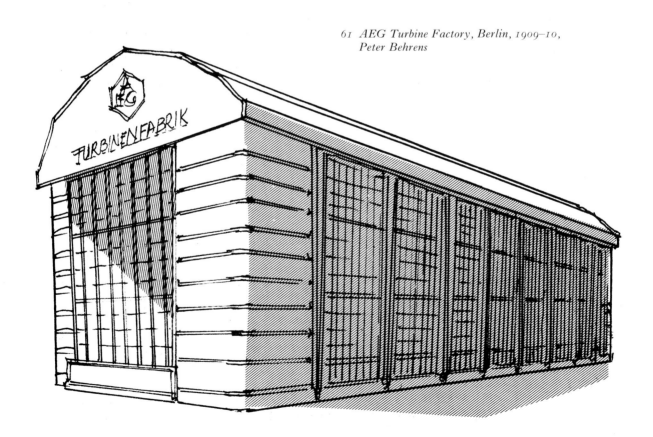

sance and Baroque periods, for example, and by eighteenth-century designers such as Robert Adam, who not only worked out every detail of a building but also fully understood the arts and crafts, as well as the building science, which went into it. During the nineteenth century these down-to-earth ideals and practices had been somewhat lost. Gropius and his staff re-established them, aiming at collaborative design in a building. It is unfortunate that in their efforts to break the shackles that had tied architects for hundreds of years to the medieval/classical design pattern, they went to extremes in reaction. Bauhaus building is today sometimes felt to be inhuman, mechanical. Its plainness is too obvious. It lacks warmth and colour. These qualities were far from the aims of the builders, but they were held in the grip of an intensity of desire to build something new, something functional, clean and stripped of tawdry decoration.

In the 1920s there were many different movements and all tended towards extremes. All were reactions both to what had preceded them and to one another. The architectural styles of the period did not last long, but the effect of these movements was like a pebble dropped into a pool of water. The widening circles of ripples spread all over Europe and beyond and, after 1945, had a widespread and permanent effect. Architecture could never again be as it was before 1914. The tradition was finally broken. A measure of the influence engendered by the Bauhaus was clear in the intensity of reaction to it – for and against. Its opposers included architectural reactionaries in the 1920s, the Nazis in the 1930s, who described the work as art-Bolshevism, and the Russians, who, at the same time, thought it bourgeois.

In 1925 Gropius was invited to leave Weimar and move to Dessau to re-establish the Bauhaus there in new premises. The buildings created for the Bauhaus themselves became prototypes for the new architecture, of which the glass-boxed studio block was the most famous (**70**). Gropius left the Bauhaus in 1928, after which it was transferred to Berlin, and continued his own work, which for some years had been largely in the field of low-cost housing estates for industrial workers. Much of this was in *Dessau* (now in East Germany) and also at *Karlsruhe*. His best-known work in this field was in *Berlin* in *Siemensstadt*, from 1929, an immense estate housing the workers from the Siemens Co.

This was the prototype on which estates all over Europe were modelled. It is a mixed development of tall slab blocks interspersed with long lines of terrace building in three and four storeys. The estate survives, and Gropius' work as well as that of his colleagues like Sharoun can be seen in streets like *Goebelstrasse* and *Jungfernheidweg*.

Gropius' views on architecture became so unpopular under Nazi rule that he left Germany in 1934 and settled in England (p. 117). Finding himself underemployed, he moved on to the United States in 1937, where he accepted the post of Professor of Architecture at Harvard University. There his influence was chiefly in the educational field.

A few years before Gropius was building the *Fagus Factory* (**60**), *Peter Behrens* (1868–1940) was developing the combined use of steel, glass and concrete in his industrial work. In the late nineteenth century he had been a painter and then a designer using Art Nouveau themes but his interest in architecture was aroused in the first years of the twentieth century and a turning point in his career was his appointment in 1907 to be architect and consultant to *AEG*, the Berlin electrical company. His *Turbine Factory* in the city (1909), which survives, was a breakthrough in design. Built in concrete, steel and glass, this is a truly modern functional building (**61**). In 1910 two more factories followed in Berlin then, in 1913, the great *AEG* plant at *Riga*, now in the Soviet Union. He became in demand for industrial work but also designed office schemes on more traditional lines such as that for the *Mannesmann Steel Works* at *Düsseldorf* (1911-12, destroyed). His later extensive complex for *IG Farben* at *Höchst* (1920–4) reflected the current Expressionist mode (pp. 85–6). In England, Behrens is known for his house in *Northampton*, *New Ways* (1925-6), which reflected the international modern style current on the Continent at the time but still an innovation in England. Behrens numbered among his pupils in the years before the First World War some of the most famous of later modern architects: Gropius, Mies van der Rohe, Le Corbusier.

A third, highly-talented and original architect was *Ludwig Mies van der Rohe* (1888–1969), who developed his full potential later in life, especially after he had left Germany. He was less influential than Gropius in the 1920s. His chief work at this time was the *Weissenhof housing estate* at *Stuttgart* (which still exists), where he was General Director

62 *Stuttgart Railway Station, 1914–27, Paul Bonatz and F. E. Scholer*

from 1927. Other architects, like Behrens, also worked here, but Mies van der Rohe's contribution is the most interesting and advanced.

In 1930 he became Director of the Bauhaus in Berlin. After the Bauhaus was closed in 1933, he was unemployed under a hostile government, so, like Gropius, he settled in the United States. Here, he found immense opportunities to develop his architectural style, which was primarily the employment of steel and glass in severely plain curtain-walled, often high-rise structures, and his many and varied buildings had a great influence on architects both there and in Europe. His work is always finely proportioned and elegant. Typical is his *Lake Shore Drive* luxury, apartment blocks in Chicago (1952). Like Gropius, some of his last works were for Europe, notably the *New National Gallery* in *West Berlin* (1965–68) (**63**) and his design for a *Piazza Tower* in the City of London near the Bank of England. This design was the subject of Peter Palombo's controversial plan for the development of 'Mansion House Square' which was recently refused by the Minister of the Environment.

There were several, but related, movements developing within the main trend of modern

63 *New National Gallery, West Berlin, 1965–8, Ludwig Mies van der Rohe*

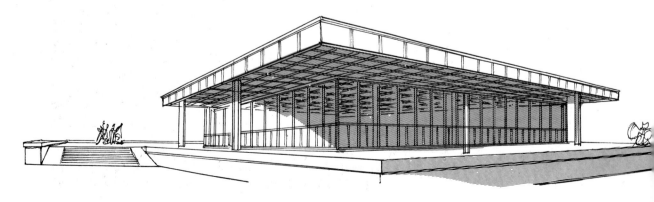

architecture just after the First World War. One of these, which was particuarly taken up in Germany, was *Expressionism*, an architectural form prevalent in the early 1920s. This style, derived from contemporary art, was one in which dramatic forms, and especially curves (such as parabolic arches), predominated. One example was Behrens' *IG Farben* complex at *Höchst*.

The most notable and individualistic architect in the German Expressionist movement was *Hans Poelzig* (1869–1936), a Berliner and a teacher and practising architect. After teaching for some years at the Breslau Academy, in 1916 he became city architect at *Dresden* where he designed a number of very Expressionist buildings in which a Baroque feeling was strongly evident: a *concert hall* and *Town Hall* in particular. However, the structure for which Poelzig is best known and which will always be associated with his name is the *Grosses*

Schauspielhaus in *Berlin* (1919, badly damaged in the Second World War), a city to which he returned at this time. Poelzig remodelled the great theatre, using modern materials to create a fabulous interior capable of seating 5,000 spectators. In this vast interior, above the circular stage rises a cavernous stalactited dome, the Arabic-seeming stalactites used for acoustic purposes (**Plate 28**).

In the 1920s Poelzig went on to design cinemas – a field for which Expressionism was especially suited – including the *Capitol Cinema* in *Berlin* and the *Deli* in *Breslau*. For his later, industrial commissions he had perforce to come into line and design in traditional modern manner. One of his last works in this vein was the immense *Headquarters Building* for *IG Farben* in *Frankfurt* (1930). Poelzig died in 1936, spared the choice of emigration or working for National Socialism.

Expressionism lingered on into the early 1930s

Plate 28 Grosses Schauspielhaus, Berlin, 1919, Hans Poelzig

64 Chilehaus, Hamburg, 1923, Fritz Höger

in church building. Characteristic but also highly individual was the *Kreuzkirche* in *Berlin – Wilmersdorf* (built 1930 by *Paulus*). A brick church, it has an immense towering façade, like the fortified 'Westwerk' of some Romanesque churches in Germany (Vol. 2), and a purple ceramic-faced sculptured porch. The interior is eight-sided on elliptical plan the parabolic arch dominating the whole design. The leading church architect in the Expressionist vein was *Domenikus Böhm* (1880–1955), who was building Roman Catholic churches in this style between 1923 and 1933. He used brick and concrete, the parabolic arched form always apparent especially in interior vaulting. Each church was different and most original as may be

seen by comparing the Memorial Church at *Neu-Ulm* (1923) with *Christ König* at *Bischofsheim* (1926) and, probably his best design, *S. Engelbert* at *Cologne-Riehl* (1931–3) (**68**). This last church is on a circular plan, the exterior brick walls in parabolic-arched faces, each with a small circular window set near the top of the arch. The bell tower stands separated in Italian manner. The centrally-planned interior is constructed in complex yet clean lines of parabolic arches blending into one another. Being in the suburbs of Cologne the Church survived the war almost unscathed; one of the few Expressionist buildings to do so.

Expressionist architecture also influenced tall building design. Few skyscrapers were built in

Europe in the inter-war years but some of limited height appeared in the 1920s in Germany. *Fritz Höger's (1877–1949) Chilehaus, Hamburg, (1923)* was one of these. In this most striking building (which still survives), erected on an awkwardly-shaped corner site, the architect has made use of the difficulties imposed upon him. He designed the structure with a double curve on one side which rises to a sharp prow-like point at the corner, giving an irregular, unsymmetrical yet Expressionist silhouette. Further accentuating this appearance, the top three storeys are set back from the main façades. The brick building, with its emphasis on vertical lines, echoing the steel structure within, strongly indicates the influence of Sullivan's 1890s skyscraper designs in the US (**64**).

In his early work *Erich Mendelsohn (1867–1953)* also designed Expressionist architecture. He envisaged bold sculptural forms, dramatically expressed in light and shade, which he created with the use of ferroconcrete, steel and glass. Most characteristic of his early Expressionism was his *Einstein Tower* at *Potsdam*, a physical laboratory and observatory purpose-built in 1921 for Professor Einstein's research work. As its shape suggested, it was intended to be constructed in poured concrete but in the event, because of technical difficulties, it became a steel and brick structure faced with stucco to resemble concrete (**65**). Equally dramatic were Mendelsohn's *Schocken department stores* at *Stuttgart* (1925) and *Chemnitz* (1928), this time in curves of glass, steel and concrete (**66**). His later *Columbus Haus* in *Berlin* (1929–31) was a more traditional modern building, tall and functional. Built in the Potsdamer Platz in the city it has disappeared from this devastated, once-famous square.

In 1933 Mendelsohn moved to England where he went into partnership with another emigré, the Russian-born Serge Chermayeff (p. 117). However Mendelsohn did not stay long in England. He went on to Palestine where he worked for some time and finally, in 1941, settled in the United States.

The fame of these outstanding men tends to overshadow the work of other pre-war architects in Germany, several of whom produced talented and original work. As elsewhere, the years before 1914 saw the designing of eclectic buildings on Romantic Classicism lines. The *Town Hall* at *Berlin-Charlottenburg* is a chunky example (1905, by *Reinhardt-Sessenguth*). There were also several

instances of more forward-looking modern work, such as *Bonatz's (1877–1951) Stuttgart Railway Station* (**62**); a bold design in large plain ashlar blocks. Some interesting churches were built, such as the *Gustav Adolfkirche* in Berlin (1934) by *Bartning* (**67**). This characteristic church has a vertical accent in angular stages and is built in brick and concrete.

Until 1933 German architecture had been vigorously capable of expansion and development. The government of the Third Reich under Adolf Hitler ended this stage of affairs. From then on until after 1945, modern architecture was not permitted; the official expression in architecture was Neo-classicism of a heavy, monumental, uninspiring type.

After 1945 Germany was in a bad economic state and many of her cities lay in ruins. Until the early 1950s only essential structures were put up, using poor materials. With American aid the economy was started up again and a large building programme was initiated. Because of the urgent need for city buildings of all types, there was no time for the planning or reorganization of towns. Buildings were erected on the old sites and traffic problems became acute.

Housing was given low priority and, when begun, the programme continued along pre-war lines. The *Hansaviertel* of *West Berlin* is a typical example. It has a fine site in the Tiergarten and, thanks to the prestige of the Interbau Exhibition scheme of 1957 which initiated it, it possesses some fine blocks of flats designed by internationally

65 *Einstein Tower, Neubabelsberg, Potsdam, 1921, Erich Mendelsohn*

famous architects, including Le Corbusier, Alvar Aalto and Walter Gropius. However, it is all haphazard, with no basic planning scheme. The most interesting church here caused some controversy when first built. It is the *Kaiser Friedrich Gedächtnis Kirche*, designed by *Ludwig Lemmer*. The grey exterior is drab and has weathered poorly, though the see-through bell-tower still has an ethereal quality viewed through the Tiergarten trees. The interior is pleasant, its walls of wood slats and attractively coloured in abstract paint and mosaic designs. One large wall is mainly of coloured glass in greys, greens and blues.

The best architecture in the 1950s was in government building, civic architecture and offices. The designs were severely rectangular in glass curtain-wall or concrete blocks. Steel and module construction set this pattern, as in the

United States and England. Typical of the better examples are the *Thyssenhaus Hochhaus* (1956–60) by *Hentrich* and *Petschnigg* and the *Mannesmann Hochhaus* (1956–8) by *Schneider-Esteban*, both in *Düsseldorf*. There are a number of city-centre schemes in the traditional pattern of the period, like the *Europa Platz* at the head of the Kurfürstendamm in *West Berlin* (1963–5) by Hentrich and Petschnigg and the more interesting *Ernst Reuter Platz* also in the city.

In the 1960s West German architecture became more varied and of better quality in building. The tall glass box was still being constructed, but more architects were, where the opportunity permitted, designing in more interesting and unusual styles. Some 'brutalist' buildings were being put up in great concrete cubes and masses, showing the same desire as in England for the 'honesty' of exposed

66 Schocken Department Store, Chemnitz, 1928, Erich Mendelsohn

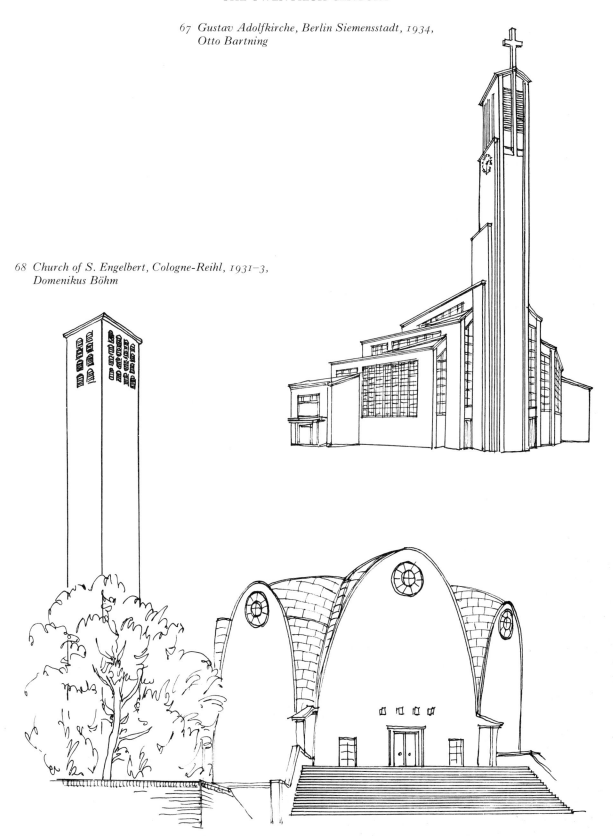

67 *Gustav Adolfkirche, Berlin Siemensstadt, 1934,*
Otto Bartning

68 *Church of S. Engelbert, Cologne-Reihl, 1931–3,*
Domenikus Böhm

concrete. West German architects took the theme further and produced some more original and exciting variants, using a greater selection of materials, surfacings and facings to provide contrast and interest. A good example is *Gottfried Böhm's town hall* at *Bensberg* (**71**). Set on top of a hill above the town, the new building is amalgamated in one scheme with the old castle, blending admirably.

Architects were gradually tending away from the rectangular box and hard right angles. This is particularly seen in the many theatres and concert halls built all over West Germany. Examples include the *Beethovenhalle* at *Bonn* (1959, *Wolske*) and the nearby town theatre, the *city theatre* at *Münster* by *Deilmann* and the *theatre* at *Düsseldorf*, 1967–9 by *Bernhard Pfau*. This last design takes furthest the breakaway from rectangular boxing, with its undulating curving façade.

Churches also provided a greater opportunity for variety in form and treatment. There are many interesting examples, but four, in particular, illustrate this. In *West Berlin*, the *Sühne Christi Church*

in Siemensstadt has an original interior. Built 1962–4 by *Hansrudolf Plarre*, it is an octagonal plan and has brick walls inside, decorated by cavity brick facings. Above, the roof is of metal struts, criss-crossing one another with metal spheres at the intersections, in the manner of the structure of a crystal. Nearby is the *Church of Maria Regina Martyrum*, built 1961–3 by *Schädel* and *Ebert* in memory of Catholic Martyrs who died in the years 1933–45. It is a severe, concrete church with a separate bell tower and large, open atrium in front of the church, round which are some avant-garde sculptured 'Stations of the Cross' by *Hajek* and a metal relief of *Joseph, Mary and Christ* on a donkey. Downstairs is the memorial chapel and, above, is the main church, severe and very plain. There are no windows; the light comes from the ceiling between the beams.

Helmut Striffler's Church of the Atonement at the site of the previous concentration camp at *Dachau* was built 1965–7. It is long and low, finely-shaped and proportioned 'brutalism'. In contrast is *Baumewerd's Church of the Holy Ghost* at *Emmerich*.

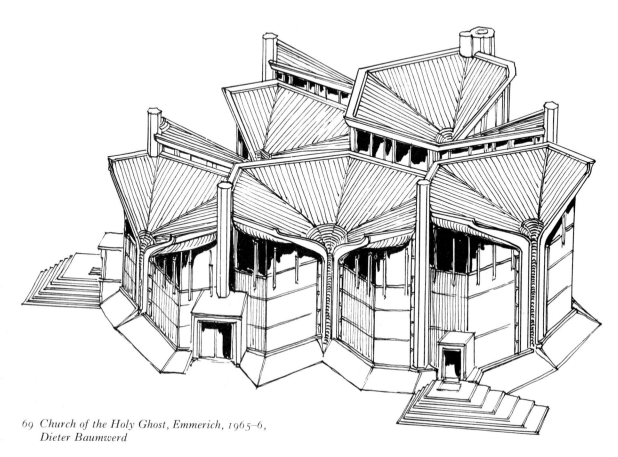

69 *Church of the Holy Ghost, Emmerich, 1965–6, Dieter Baumwerd*

70 The Bauhaus, Dessau, 1926, Walter Gropius

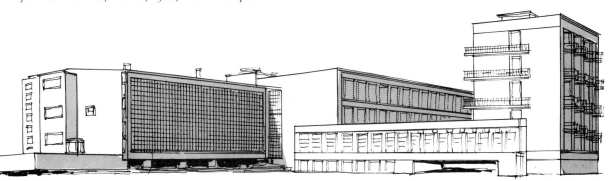

Built in boarded concrete, the lighting and spatial forms are unusually designed, with changing planes and angles. The interior walls are faced with abstract patterned glass. The planed concrete pillars are capped in spreading lotus forms, opening up into the roof. This formation can be seen in a view of the exterior shown from above (**69**). The altar cross, in blood-red metal, made from burnt and devastated war materials, is a symbol of our age.

A minority of talented architects who had been young in the Nazi era, remained in their homeland and, in the 1950s and 1960s, became noted senior men in their profession. Of these, two in particular established a link in architectural excellence from the pre-war days till now. One, *Hans Sharoun* (1893–1972), studied and worked chiefly in Berlin as a young man. He contributed to the *Weissenhof Estate, Stuttgart*, under Mies van der Rohe in the 1920s and extensively to *Siemensstadt, Berlin*, in the 1930s. He was allowed little latitude under the Third Reich and designed few buildings. In 1945 he was appointed to lead the Department for Building and Reconstruction in West Berlin.

71 The Town Hall (adjoining the old castle), Bensberg, 1967, Gottfried Böhm

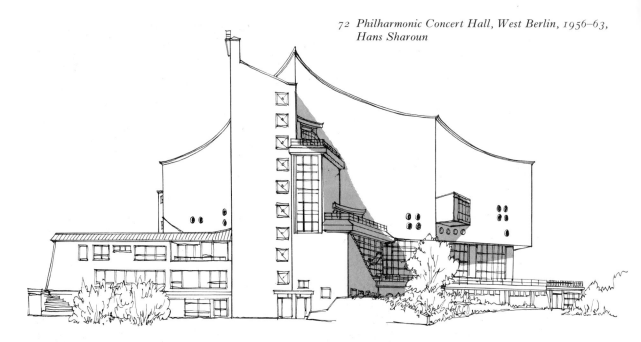

72 Philharmonic Concert Hall, West Berlin, 1956–63, Hans Sharoun

Among his numerous contributions there since then are the *American Memorial Library* and the *Philharmonic Concert Hall*, built almost on the 'wall' near the Brandenburger Tor (**72**). The pattern for a return to Expressionism, signs of which can be seen in the Philharmonic Concert Hall, was set in Berlin a few years earlier with the building of the *Congress Hall* (1957), designed by the American architect *Hugh Stubbins Jnr*. With typical quirky humour the Berliners dubbed it the 'pregnant oyster'.

The other important architect is *Egon Eiermann* (1904–1970), among whose post-war contributions are a number of interesting churches. Germany lost so much of its earlier architectural heritage during the Second World War that there was the greater inducement to restore and adapt what remained. A common practice in ecclesiastical building has been to retain the surviving tower and add a new church to it. Some of these schemes are not successful marriages: for example, the *Church of St Rochus* in *Düsseldorf* or the *Christikirche* in *Bochum*. The most dramatic of these conceptions is Eiermann's *Kaiser Wilhelm Gedächtnis Kirche* in the Europa Platz in *West Berlin*. The old church of 1891–5 by Schwechten was a large, heavy design characteristic of the current revival of German Romanesque style (p. 27). It was decided after 1945 to retain the blackened and truncated tower as a war memorial

for West Berlin. In 1955–63 Eiermann made the tower safe and weatherproof, restored its barrel-vaulted interior mosaics and sculptured panels and added, on one side, an octagonal bell tower and, on the other, an octagonal church, both in plain, honeycombed concrete – a brutal and emotional change of style. The interior of the new church is most effective, the honeycomb pattern showing as myriads of tiny glass windows, in square panes, on all eight sides of the building, in rich colourings of which deep blue predominates. There is a simple altar table, above which is a modern metal sculpture of Christ crucified; it is very large and has no cross. Opposite the altar, above the entrance door, is a fine organ and a platform gallery, suspended over the doorway, to accommodate a whole orchestra and choir.

The development of the *Democratic Republic of Germany* since 1945, under the aegis of Moscow, was different, but the energy, talent and capacity for thorough workmanship were equally apparent

Plate 29 (top right) Zur Heiligsten Dreifaltigkeitskirche, Wien-Mauer, 1976, Fritz Wortruba and Fritz G. Mayr

Plate 30 (bottom right) Staatsgalerie, Stuttgart, 1977–84, Stirling and Wilford

here as in the western half of the country. In East Germany, work was held back till after 1960 and little building was done, apart from one or two show schemes like *Stalinallee* (now *Karl Marx Allee*) in *East Berlin*. These were in the official Soviet style as seen in Kiev and Moscow (p. 147) – a sterile, provincial version of modern classicism.

In the 1960s the rebuilding of cities was begun, notably East Berlin, Leipzig, Dresden, Frankfurt-an-der-Oder and Karl Marx Stadt (Chemnitz before 1945). Here, the buildings are dull, in rectangular blocks, unenterprisingly designed round large squares or wide boulevards left open for mass parades. The *Unter den Linden* and *Alexander Platz* in *East Berlin* are typical. Here, as in Leipzig and Dresden, the restoration of the great buildings of the past is being carried out to a characteristically German high standard, but work has been slow compared to western achievements. Also, in Berlin especially, the whole of the original centre of the city, containing therefore all the fine buildings, is now East Berlin. It was devastated, with a consequent need for wholesale restoration and rebuilding.

Since the late 1960s more modern designs have appeared and also more enterprising ideas. The heavy hand of the planners was less apparent. Hotels in western style were built to attract the tourist from Western Europe, the *Hotel Berolina* in *Berlin* for example. Even so, standardization was still much stronger than further west, resulting in much greater urban monotony.

The trend from the 1970s onwards in Germany reflected, as elsewhere, the breaking of ties with the modern school of architecture to which so many architects had contributed in the inter-war and immediate post-war years. The divergence from the modern theme, the seeking for greater variety of form and decoration, the abandonment of tall buildings of non-human scale and the attachment to open plan living had been explored by architects such as the Finnish Alvar Aalto (p. 142) and the Americans Louis I. Kahn, Robert Venturi and Charles Moore. Characteristic of this post-modern outlook in Germany is *Oswald Mathias Ungers* (b. 1926) whose new *Museum of Architecture* in *Frankfurt-am-Main* (1981–4) was built within the gutted ruins of a nineteenth-century villa, and on an intimate scale, also appropriate to the older outer shell, his *Badische Regional Library at Karlsruhe* (1980–4).

Austria

In the years before 1918 the Austria of the great Austro-Hungarian Empire was an important European leader in the field of art and architecture. Franz Josef had celebrated his 50 years as Emperor in 1898. His great town planning achievement of the Ringstrasse in Vienna (pp. 29–32) was complete: a monument to nineteenth-century eclecticism. By 1900 younger architects were stirring in reaction to this pattern and were looking forward to a more modern twentieth-century future.

That august Viennese institution, the Academy of Fine Arts, had largely established this nineteenth-century pattern. In 1897 several of the younger, talented artists resigned from the Academy in protest at its artistic conservatism to set up a society of their own that would eschew eclecticism. These artists were followed by architects led by *Otto Wagner*. This mass resignation became known as the *Sezession*.

The architectural *Sezessionists* led the way towards a twentieth-century style which developed to become Austria's contribution to modern architecture. In the early years, the designs were at first in the Austrian *Jugendstil* (Art Nouveau) manner and later in a style termed Sezessionist. The modern approach was established towards 1920.

Otto Wagner (1841–1918) was the leader and the oldest of a group of four architects who were the main moving spirit behind this fundamental change in architectural design. Some of Wagner's apartment blocks in Vienna, particularly the so-called *Majolika Haus* (1898), were decorated in floral Jugendstil manner. The Majolika Haus was faced with elaborate coloured ceramic ornamentation of this same type, repeated in the ironwork of balconies and grilles. Also of Art Nouveau derivation was the decorative ironwork on some of his Vienna stadtbahn stations. Wagner had been appointed advisor to the Transport Commission in Vienna so was involved with the construction of stations, bridges and viaducts for this urban railway system. The *Karlsplatz Station* (1899–1901) is the most notable example of his work in this field (**74**).

Wagner's contribution in the second decade of the century abandoned decorative Jugendstil and moved towards unornamented façades and a more functional approach. This can be seen in his workers' flats in Vienna, for example, *40 Neustift-*

73 *The Steiner House, Vienna, 1910, Adolf Loos*

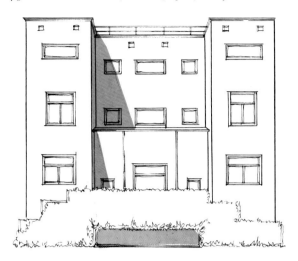

74 *Karlsplatz Station Vienna, 1899–1901, Otto Wagner*

gasse and *4 Doblergasse* (1910-11), but more importantly in his best building in the city, the *Postal Savings Bank* (*Postparkasse*), built in two stages, 1904–6 and 1910–11. The exterior is clad in granite. The interior, in particular, is very modern. The main counter hall is a plain glass-covered courtyard constructed of ferroconcrete, glass and aluminium, the roof carried on slender metal piers and the walls clad in marble (**76**).

Wagner's influence was widespread and important both by his architecture and from his teaching as professor at the Vienna Academy. Two others of the four leading architects of the Sezessionist movement worked for some time in his office – Olbrich and Hoffmann. *Joseph Maria Olbrich* (1867–1908) worked on some of the Vienna stadtbahn stations with Wagner, notably that of the *Westbahnhof*. His best known building is the *Sezessionist Exhibition Hall* in the *Karlsplatz* in the city (1898). It is a modern structure but draws its decorative motifs from many stylistic influences, including Egypt, Assyria and India. It is surmounted by an unusual golden foliated sphere (**75**).

The work of *Josef Hoffmann* (1870–1956) of the 1890s was clearly influenced by the English Arts and Crafts movement as well as Voysey and Mackintosh. In 1903, after a visit to Britain where he saw *Ashbee*'s *workshops* in the *East End* of London, Hoffmann helped to set up the *Wiener Werkstätte*, which produced especially designer furniture and decorative metalwork. Of his archi-

tecture, Hoffmann is best known for a large house which he designed for Adolf Stoclet, a Belgian millionaire, in *Brussels* (1905–11), the *Palais Stoclet*. This is a plain, very modern building, clad and finished in superb quality materials, especially marbles and woods. The interior decor is original and striking. Most notable is the dining room frieze designed by the artist Gustav Klimt, carried out on white marble with gold, silver and enamel decoration, its inspiration derived from a blend of ancient Egyptian, oriental and Byzantine sources (**100**).

75 *The Sezessionist Exhibition Hall, Vienna, 1898, Josef Maria Olbrich*

The fourth notable member of the Viennese school of this time was the first truly modern architect here: *Adolf Loos* (1870–1933). Born in Brno, Loos followed his father's profession as stonemason before coming to Dresden in 1890 to study architecture. From his studies there in Germany Loos went to the United States in 1893, where he spent three years in several cities, notably New York, Chicago and Philadelphia. Loos became an *aficionado* of American architecture and the American way of life; he was especially impressed by the work of the great American architect Louis Sullivan. On returning to Vienna in 1896 he found the designs of the Sezessionists too limited and derivative for his taste and broke away to design in a plainer, more functional form though using traditional materials. Up to 1914 his designs were chiefly interiors for cafes, bars, shops and apartments. Decoration was minimal and linear, the shapes geometric and modern, the materials of high quality – marble, glass, metal and wood. His most famous interior was the *Kärntner Bar* in *Vienna* (1907).

In the second decade of the century Loos began to develop his modern architectural style, using reinforced concrete in house design. He rejected ornament, especially on the exteriors; his fenestration was excessively plain and his house shapes cubic. His *Steiner House* of 1910 in *Vienna* was a characteristic example (**73**). He went on to build houses in Paris, Montreux, Brno and Plzen, most of these built after he had left Vienna for Paris where he settled in 1922 and most of which do not survive. The American influence of Frank Lloyd Wright could be seen in several such houses.

After 1919, the great Austro-Hungarian empire was disbanded. Austria became a small, not wealthy country, and her architectural influence correspondingly diminished. Since 1945, architecture there has not, in the main, produced outstanding originality or quality and has generally followed the pattern of other smaller countries. Typical of the better work is the *Church of the Holy Blood* at *Salzburg-Parsch*, by *Holzbauer*. The exterior is uninteresting. The more successful interior is divided into two parts; one is large and

76 Postal Savings Bank, Vienna, 1904–6, Otto Wagner

light with a gable roof, part wood and part glass, and a simple altar under this. The other section is much lower, supported on ribbed columns under a groined roof, like the ancient crypt design of the early-Romanesque period. A stained-glass window on either side of this area gives a lower light, in rich hues, in contrast to the brightness of the main part of the church.

Since the early 1970s a younger generation of architects has created some interesting and more original work on post-modern lines. *Robert Krier* (b. 1938) was born in Luxembourg then settled in Austria in 1975. Since then he has established a reputation as an urban planner and architect, laying out housing schemes on a human scale, some three to four storeys in height and with intimate interior courtyards, for example, *Ritterstrasse* (1980) and *Wilmersdorf* (1984) in *Berlin* and, in *Vienna, Hirschstettenerstrasse* (1982). *Hans Hollein* (b. 1934) is a Viennese but has designed and built in many other countries as well: Italy, France, Spain, Germany and the United States. He is particularly known for his reconstruction work at the *Town Hall of Perchtoldsdorf* (1975–6) and his *Austrian Tourist Bureau Central Office* in *Vienna* (1976–9), his *Museum of Energy in Essen* (1981), his *National Museum of Egyptian Civilisation in Cairo* (1983) and, most notably, his *Museum of Modern Art* in *Mönchengladbach* (near Düsseldorf, 1975 and 1984).

Switzerland

After lagging behind in the field of architectural design in the nineteenth century, Swiss architects began to take advantage of modern architectural thought in the early 1920s. The work of Le Corbusier, himself Swiss, and that of the Bauhaus impressed younger Swiss architects greatly, and several of them began to develop original themes in the new materials of concrete, glass and steel. *Robert Maillart* (1872–1940) was chiefly noted for his structural approach in the civil engineering problems of using concrete and metal for bridges and blocks of buildings. *Hannes Meyer* (1889–1954), Director of the Bauhaus for a time, produced some early examples of functional design. Many architects developed advanced methods of town planning and layout of housing estates. The *Zürich* scheme of *Neubühl* (1930–2) is one of these, where the architects *Paul Artaria* and *Hans*

Schmidt introduced standardization of units and carefully sited the buildings to create open space between.

The new style was brought to the design of churches and in this field *Karl Moser* (1860–1936) was the leader. He was the Swiss equivalent of Auguste Perret in France, and his *Church of S. Anthony in Basle* (1926-31) has much in common with Perret's example at Le Raincy. The Basle church is also in concrete, with large areas of glass panelling and a tall tower, more original than Perret's and one which was widely emulated in both Switzerland and Germany. Inside it is less glowingly lit and is heavier in treatment, but the reticulated, parabolic vaulted ceiling, supported on the uncompromisingly square-sectioned reinforced concrete pillars, is monumentally impressive (**78**). The windows are in rectangular panels of coloured glass with figure groups depicted in them. There is a simple, bronze pulpit covered by a plain, flat canopy; the side panels are sculptured in low relief.

There are two examples of this type of church in *Lucerne* by pupils of Moser: *S. Charles* by *Fritz Metzger* and *S. Joseph* by *Otto Dreyer*. The Church of S. Charles stands on the edge of the River Reuss, not far from its exit from Lake Lucerne. The exterior is in concrete, severe, with a two-storeyed columned porch fronting the river bank. At the side is the familiar lofty, square-sectioned tower, and at the rear the church ends in an apsidal curve, the plain concrete broken only by the window which extends all round the upper part of the building. The interior is unusual and spacious. It comprises one vast open space with flat concrete ceiling supported by concrete columns faced with strips of dark, polished marble; gaps are left between these strips effectively representing classical fluting. There are no capitals, bases or entases, however. The columns extend all round the church, giving aisles and ambulatory. Above, in the walls, is the long, continuous band of window panes in coloured glass of abstract designs, creating a rich glow to the interior when the sun is shining. The pulpit is of wood with sculptured metal panels (**80**).

The *Church of S. Joseph* has a separate campanile, Italian style, and this, like the similar church at Altstetten on the outskirts of Zürich, 1938–41, has a perforated design all over it and a clock and belfry in the top part. The interior is very simple.

77 *En Bergère, International HQ of Nestlé, Vevey, 1956–64, Jean Tschimi*

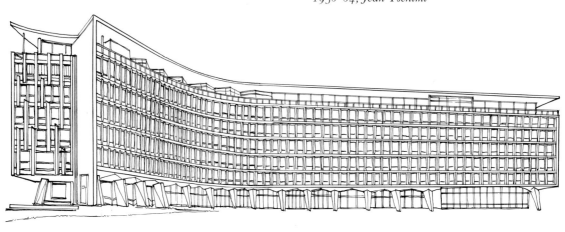

78 *Church of S. Anthony, Basle, 1926–31, Karl Moser*

There is an almost flat ceiling and plain walls with simple, stocky columns. The stark altar table has a draped baldacchino over it and the wall behind is draped also. The colouring is all in grey curtaining, black, unpolished stone and light wood. It is an effective interior but more neutral and less dramatic than the other examples.

In the immediate post-war years, Switzerland constructed far fewer buildings than other countries, since her cities had not been devastated in the war. By the early 1960s Swiss architects began again to show initiative in modern building and designs for churches, apartment and office blocks, illustrating interest and originality. It is notable that French Switzerland, (birth-place of Le Corbusier) and, even more, Italian Switzerland, have fallen behind in this respect. There are many unusual church schemes; two of the more outstanding are the Catholic churches at Buchs and at Lichtensteig. The *Buchs Church* (*Brütsch*, 1966–8) has a plain exterior with tall tower: a more up-to-date version of Moser. The interior is, on the other

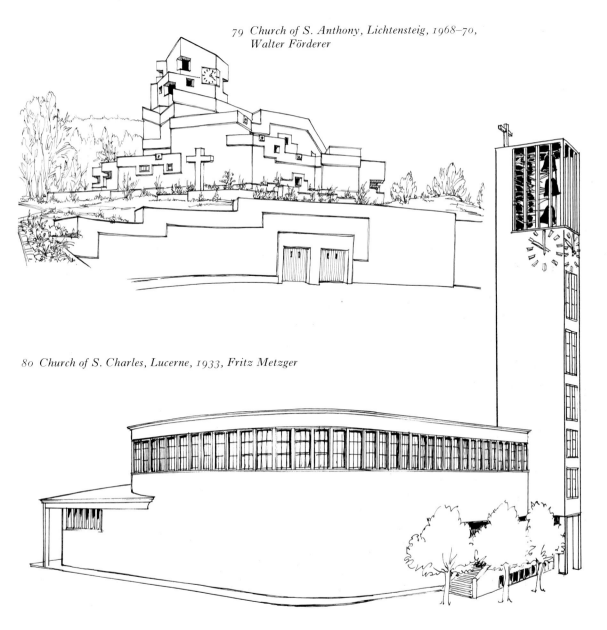

79 *Church of S. Anthony, Lichtensteig, 1968–70, Walter Förderer*

80 *Church of S. Charles, Lucerne, 1933, Fritz Metzger*

hand, finely handled, spatially. The church is entered near the bell tower via a sloping passage, along which are set stone and bronze sculptural 'Stations of the Cross', and this connects to the church, in a separate building. The interior is in boarded concrete and wood, plain, but outstanding in the carefully-angled planes and the handling of both natural and artificial lighting, indirect and reminiscent of Le Corbusier's convent at Eveux-sur-l'Arbresle (p. 125). There is some modern sculpture of unusual design and high quality in the interior, placed carefully as part of the architecture and not merely decoration.

The *Church of S. Anthony* (**79**) at *Lichtensteig*, built 1968–70 by *Walter Förderer*, is sited on a hill at the edge of the small town, pleasantly landscaped behind, with gardens and a cemetery. The building is constructed in stepped blocks in concrete, a design imaginatively handled as these masses approach the original form of the tower. The interior is all of straight lines in light coloured wood. Under the tower is a traditional form of wood structure, its beams radiating from a wheel set asymmetrically; artificial lighting is incorporated in the beams. The altar stands beneath, plain and in traditional materials.

Förderer has designed a number of schemes in Switzerland, developing his ideas on multi-purpose building of church combined with discussion rooms (like the scheme at Sussex University Meeting House, by Spence, p. 120), also, with theatre, concert hall and lecture theatre, providing a multi-purpose structure where people can exchange ideas and experience. His ecclesiastical community scheme at Hérémence, near Sion, is of this type. He is also noted for his *Swiss Graduate School of Economics and Administration* at *St Gallen* (1960–3).

In other fields of work, the terraced flats at *Zug*, set in to the steep hillside, are an interesting development, built 1957–60 by *Stucky* and *Meuli*. The 1960s' tower block scheme in *Zürich* (*Zur Palme*) by *Haefeli, Moser* and *Steiger*, containing offices and shops round a piazza, is typical of the better designs of this type. It is of boarded concrete on the lower part and steel and glass above. The *Nestlé's International HQ* building is attractively situated, fronted by lawns spreading down to the shores of *Lake Geneva* at Vevey (**77**). It is on similar plan to the Y-shaped UNESCO Building in Paris.

Despite the large number of hotels that Switzerland already possesses, the demands of the vital tourist trade have caused the building of new ones. At Interlaken, for instance, the *Hotel Bernerhof* is a pleasant example, combining in its design and treatment the traditional Swiss intimate, mountain hotel style with modern materials. It is on a suitable scale in dark red-brown and white rubble finish, sympathetic in feeling to this town. This is in contrast to the nearby '*Hochhaus*' in concrete, the new *Hotel Metropole*, which intrudes upon this attractive setting.

Italy

Art Nouveau, or *lo stile Liberty*, was introduced into Italian architecture in the early years of the twentieth century. *Basile, d'Aronco, Cattaneo* and *Sommaruga* were architects who built in this mode. *Giuseppe Sommaruga*'s (1867–1917) apartment block in the *Corso Venezia* in Milan (1903) still exists. It is typical of the extrovert Italian approach to Art Nouveau. The doorway and lower windows appear to be hewn from the living rock, the decorative window panels swirl and curve and the second-floor of pairs *putti* cling precariously to their window frames (**82**). Also characteristic is the *Palazzo Mattei, 50 Corso Montevecchio* in Turin.

If Italy was not one of the major exponents of Art Nouveau, she did produce some of the earliest and most talented protagonists in modern architecture. Even before the First World War, *Antonio Sant'Elia* (1880–1916) was creating his designs for cities years ahead of his time. He was a visionary of future architecture, fascinated by the romantic aspects of technology, especially in the United States, and planned whole cities for Italy. His *Città Nuova*, projected in 1914, was exhibited in Milan. It envisaged skyscrapers, pedestrian precincts and traffic moving on overhead roadways at two or three different levels. He was a socialist and developed these schemes as part of his suggestions for an ideal society. Tragically, his talents were cut short in 1916 when he was killed in action. His drawings and designs survive and have strongly influenced later work.

In the early 1920s it was *Giuseppe Terragni* (1904–43) who led Italy's modern school of thought. His life too was abbreviated, this time by the Second World War, and his working years were few between his graduation from Milan

THE LIBRARY
GUILDFORD COLLEGE
of Further and Higher Education

81 *Apartment block for the Società Novocomum, Como,*
1927–8, Giuseppe Terragni

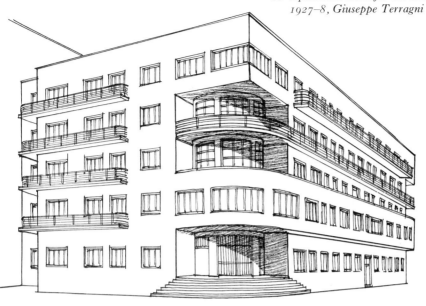

82 *Casa Castiglione, Milan (Art Nouveau), 1903,*
Giuseppe Sommaruga

83 *Library, Città Universitaria, Rome,* c. *1935,*
Mario Ridolfo

84 *Central Railway Station, Milan, begun 1931,*
Eugenio Montuori

85 *Staircase, Florence Stadium, 1930–2,*
Pier Luigi Nervi

Polytechnic in 1926 and his call-up in 1939. This was long enough for him to produce a number of original buildings, which brought him international acclaim and became prototypes in Europe. In 1926 with Gio Ponti he helped to found the *'gruppo sette'*, seven architects who joined the *'Movimento Italiano per l'Architettura Razionale'*. They enunciated a new architectural theme, searching for clarity, order, honesty in use of materials and an end to eclecticism. They were all young and were inspired by the Bauhaus project in Germany (p. 81) and the work of Frank Lloyd Wright in the United States.

Terragni's chief buildings include the *Casa del Fascio* (now *Casa del Popolo*) (1932–6) and his *apartment house* (**81**), both in *Como*, and the *Casa Rustici*, block of flats in the *Corso Sempione* in Milan (1934–5). These are all simple, unornamented structures.

Giuseppe Pagano (1896–1945) also fought and died in the Second World War. He was of Austro-Hungarian descent, born Pogatschnig in Parenzo (now Poreč) and changed his name in 1915. Many of his architectural commissions were for academic buildings, notably his *Istituto Fisico* (Physics faculty building) at the *University of Rome* (1930–5). The Città Universitaria here is a large campus laid out in the 1930s. The entrance propylaeum is a plain rectangular block in white stone unlike most of the faculty buildings, which, like that for Physics, are in red brick. Characteristic of the 1930s buildings here is the *Library*, built *c*. 1935 by *Mario Ridolfo* (**83**). Even plainer, and more functionalist is *Pagano's Università Commerciale Bocconi* in *Milan* (1938–41).

Most Italian architects did not emigrate to escape fascism in their country as the Germans had done. They were exceptionally versatile, designing as required in the 1930s then, after 1945, adapted to the more varied opportunities open to them in the post-war world. *Giovanni Michelucci* (b. 1891), for example, was much praised for his long, low *railway station* façade of *S. Maria Novella* in *Florence* (1933–6) then, in 1957–8, designed the quite different *Savings Bank* in the same city (**88**). In 1962 he was responsible for the *Church of S. Giovanni* built on the *Autostrada del Sole* near Florence. Constructed with coarse rubble block walls and roofed with copper, this is an original design, tent-like and plastic, which is dedicated to the memory of those who lost their lives in the difficult construction of this famous motorway through the mountains between Bologna and

86 Via Roma, Turin, 1938, Marcello Piacentini

87 *Palazzetto dello Sport, Rome, 1957,*
Annibale Vitellozzi and Pier Luigi Nervi

88 *Savings Bank, Florence, 1957–8,*
Giovanni Michelucci

89 *Central Railway Station (Termini),*
Rome, Piazza del Cinquecento,
1947–51, Eugenio Montuori also
Calini, Castellazzi, Fatigati,
Pintonello, Vitellozzi

Florence. *Eugenio Montuori* (b. 1907) was another such man, creating under Mussolini the ornately plastic *Central Railway Station in Milan* (1931) (**84**) then, with others, bringing to completion in 1947–51, the much acclaimed, entirely modern *Central Railway Station (Termini) in Rome* (**89**). *Gio Ponti* (1891–1979) who, with Terragni, was one of the founding modern architects of Italy, designing the *Faculty of Mathematics Building* at *Rome University* in 1934, was renowned for his slender, elegant Milan skyscraper of 1955, the *Pirelli Building* (**91**)

Totalitarian governments rarely advocate new designs or change in the arts. Mussolini was no exception. He saw himself as the head of a new Italian state that would revive the glories of the Roman Empire. The only suitable architectural expression for such a power was, of course, Roman classicism, albeit in modern dress: hence Montuori's Milan station. His enforcement of his desires was much less stringent than Hitler's – otherwise structures like Michelucci's Florence station would not have been built – but architects seeking and accepting government patronage were expected to produce works that were fundamentally classical. The leading architect of the traditional classical school was *Marcello Piacentini* (1881–1961), whose work, despite its eclecticism, possessed vision and vitality. In *Bergamo* he built the new town – the *Città Bassa* – at the foot of the medieval hill city in 1922–4. He supported fascism and so became the natural selection as principal architect for the Mussolini administration. He was responsible for much of Mussolini's vast project for a new capital outside Rome – the *Terza Roma* – and built a number of new towns south of the city. Most of this construction was badly damaged in the Second World War, but surviving is his completion of the *Via Roma in Turin* (1938), between the Piazza San Carlo and the Piazza Carlo Felice, which continues the great eighteenth- and nineteenth-century town planning schemes in a classical manner though in twentieth-century dress (**86**).

In 1945 the need for reconstruction was urgent in a country whose cities had been so badly damaged. A quantity of building was put up, of poor quality and in dull, block design, as fast as it could be completed. This was necessary but, in the 1950s, it was realized that future slums were being created. The pace of building slowed and much

better standards of design and structure were encouraged and enforced.

From the late 1950s the Italian contribution to original and interesting modern architecture has been considerable. Traditional Italian craftsmanship has been modified to unit and mass-production methods, using coloured marbles, granite and mosaic partly for decoration and facing. At this time there was more variety in colour and shape than in the modern work of most European countries. A greater use of curves, both linear and three-dimensional, was usual, and the brilliant colours traditional to Italy's building over the centuries, so aptly complementary to the sunshine, were to be seen.

Italy has also been a leading nation in developing the most ubiquitous of modern materials, available to all countries whatever their natural resources – reinforced concrete. Partly for economic reasons this has been preferred to steel, and the results have shown a greater variety of design. Over emphasis on steel leads to rectangular tower blocks as in the United States, England and Germany. Italian derivations from concrete have produced an infinite range of self-supporting roofs, vaults and shell coverings to all types of buildings.

The most important figure in the development of reinforced concrete is the engineer *Pier Luigi Nervi* (1891–1978). He early established a reputation for this work in 1930 in his *stadium* at *Florence* (**85**) and his later *hangars* at *Orvieto* and *Orbetello*. Since then he continued creating original, beautiful concrete structures of infinite variety of which the *Palazzetto dello Sport* (**87**) is typical. Among his other structures are the *hall* at the *Lido di Roma, Ostia*, the *terme* at *Chianciano*, the other Olympic constructions in Rome – the *Palazzo dello Sport* and the *Stadium* – and the *Exhibition Hall* in *Turin*. In 1960 Nervi returned to Turin to build his imaginative *Palace of Labour* for the centenary celebrations of Garibaldi and Victor Emmanuel in the city. This vast hall, like the English Crystal Palace of a century earlier (p. oo), had to be built quickly and to be suitable for later adaptation. It was, therefore, constructed partly in steel. The metal columns have palm leaf capitals reminiscent of ancient Nile palaces (**90**).

Nervi's aim was to create functional buildings that at the same time act by their aesthetic qualities as an effective educational influence. Functionalism, for Nervi, never became 'brutalism'. In

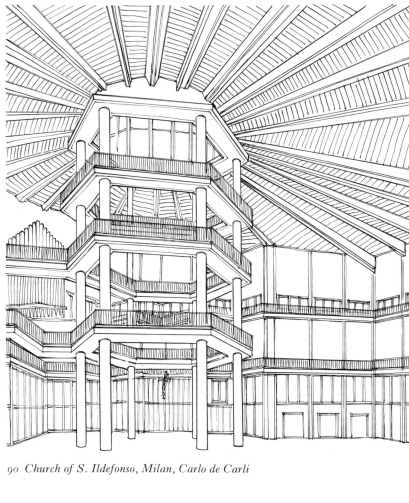

90 *Church of S. Ildefonso, Milan, Carlo de Carli*

consequence, his work is admired by the lay public
as well as by the architects.

Italy built its share of glass, steel and concrete
skyscrapers, hotels, offices, civic centres and buildings for education in the post-war years. Among
the best of these was the *Olivetti Building* in *Milan*
(1954, *Bernasconi*) and the *Faculty of Architecture
Building* at *Milan Polytechnic* (*Bruno, Morasutti*
and *Mangiarotti*). Among the new churches, the
designs of a number were derived from Italian
Renaissance and Baroque prototypes, for example,
Il Redentore in *Turin (Musso)* is reminiscent of
Guarini's Sindone Chapel in the city (Vol. 3) and
S. Ildefonso in *Milan* (1955, *Carlo di Carli*) seems
to be inspired by the nearby Bramante rebuilding
of S. Maria delle Grazie (Vol. 3) (**90**).

In the post-modern phase this affinity with the
Baroque past continued as in *Paolo Portoghesi's*

91 *Pirelli Tower, Milan, 1955–9, Gio Ponti*

(b. 1931) *Casa Papanice* in Rome (1970) where the concave form alternates with the convex as in Borromini's church walling (Vol. 3). Portoghesi was consultant architect for the restoration of the town of *Salerno* (1972) where he had earlier (1968) built the *Church of the Holy Family*. *Aldo Rossi* (b. 1931), on the other hand, is leader of the architectural group entitled *La Tendenza*, a neo-rationalist society, that tends to look back with nostalgia to a severe modernism which might have been apposite in Mussolini's time. Rossi was the architect for the *Hayden Gallery* at the *Massachussetts Institute of Technology* in Cambridge, United States (1980).

Holland

From the beginning of the twentieth century there developed a national modern architecture in Holland which, if not as original as that of architects like Gropius, Mies van der Rohe or Le Corbusier, was unusual, completely non-eclectic and ingenious in its adaptation of the traditional Dutch building material of brick to the modern idiom.

The leader of this national school of the late nineteenth century was *Hendrik Berlage* (p. 52). After his outstanding civic structures of the *fin de siècle*, he launched, in the early twentieth century,

92 Palace of Labour, Turin, 1960–1, Pier Luigi Nervi

Plate 31 Eigen Haard Estate (Spaandammerplantsoen), 1917, Michael de Klerk

Plate 32 De Dageraard Estate 1918–23, Kramer and de Klerk

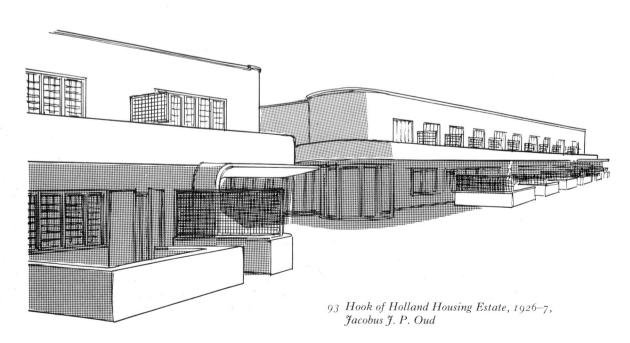

93 Hook of Holland Housing Estate, 1926–7, Jacobus J. P. Oud

into laying out low-cost housing estates and city planning. He was followed by the architect *J. M. van der Meij* (1878–1949), whose work was national and as near to Art Nouveau as was ever approached in Holland. A typical example of his contribution at this time is the *Scheepvaarthuis* (the Dock Offices or Terminal) on the *Prins Hendrik quay* in *Amsterdam* (1913). This is a most unusual building, angular, powerful, dramatic and intimately personal. It is built of dark brick with decoration in iron scrolls and twirls. The roof is covered by lighter-coloured ceramic tiling.

From just before the First World War till about 1925, the leading architects were *Michael de Klerk* (1884–1923) and his colleague *Pieter Lodewijk Kramer* (1881–1961) (**97**). Their work was of the expressionist school like that of their contemporary German counterparts. They laid out a number of large housing estates from 1913, especially in *Amsterdam*, including the *Eigen Haard Estate* (**Plate 31**). The buildings are all in brick with unusual, simple, three and four-storey façades

employing the material skilfully in curves and rounded corners. The work is national, romantic and, even now, does not appear old-fashioned. Certainly, such buildings, low-cost as they were, have stood up to the extensive wear and tear that they received much better than their post-war equivalents – a tribute to the building standards of the time. A little later, in 1918–23, came the *De Dageraard Estate* in Amsterdam, of similar treatment (**95**, **Plate 32**).

Willem Dudok (1884–1974) was an architect with a modern but personal, particularly Dutch style. He was city architect at *Hilversum* for a number of years and his *town hall* here (**94**), one of his best works, was much imitated all over Holland. The building, in brick, is plain, almost stark, but beautifully proportioned and designed. His other contributions to the city include the *Bavinck School* and the *public baths*.

The work of two other Dutch architects, *Jacobus Johannes Pieter Oud* (1890–1963) and *Gerrit Thomas Rietveld* (1888–1964), was contemporary with

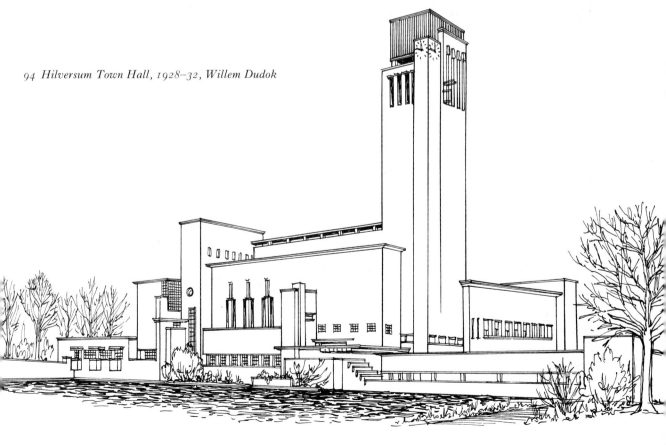

94 Hilversum Town Hall, 1928–32, Willem Dudok

that of Dudok but was more strongly influenced by the purist modern approach. Both men were members of the Dutch group of artists known as *De Stijl*, which sought to establish a form of non-representational art unrelated to past styles. The movement was founded in 1917 by the painters Piet Mondrian and Theo van Doesburg, who also designed several buildings. In both art and architecture, this movement profoundly influenced the modern work, as at the Bauhaus, from the 1920s onwards. Whereas the buildings of Kramer, de Klerk and even Dudok were modern in appearance, as were those of their Scandinavian contemporaries Östberg and Eriksson (p. 134), they were fundamentally simplified forms of past styles. The contribution of Oud and Rietveld, like that of Le Corbusier (pp. 122–3), Gropius (p. 85) and Loos (p. 96) was introducing the uncompromising shape of the future.

Oud became city architect at *Rotterdam* in 1918, and was particularly involved in the design of several housing estates there, notably the *Spangen Housing Estate* (1918) and the *Tuschendijken Estate* (1920). The buildings here were in brick, uncompromisingly plain and stark, all past decorative forms totally abandoned. In the Oud *Mathenesse Estate* (1922) Oud's style had matured and become

less negative and empty in its plainness. It showed greater care in detail and subtle form. This maturity was continued and developed in his best work, which was the layout of white rendered housing terraces and shops at the *Hook of Holland* (1926–7) (**93**). Typical of his later, still further mellowed work is his *Shell Building* in *The Hague* (1938).

Rietveld is known chiefly for his private houses, such as the *Schröder House* in *Utrecht* (1924), which showed an affinity with Le Corbusier's designs of the same time – flat roofs, uncompromising cubic shapes, balconies and white rendered finish: a style ideally suited to Mediterranean sunshine but not to northern Europe (**96**). Just before he died Rietveld designed the *National Van Gogh Museum* in Amsterdam, which was completed in 1973.

In the post-war period, architecture began to get under way again after 1950. The first major task that the Dutch had to face was the rebuilding of the devastated city of *Rotterdam*, where so much fine architecture by men such as Oud and Dudok had perished. In the centre of the city it was a case of starting from scratch. Unfortunately, as in the case of Germany and Italy, the need was so great that architectural and planning opportunities were

95 *De Dageraard Housing Estate, Amsterdam, 1918–23, Kramer and de Klerk*

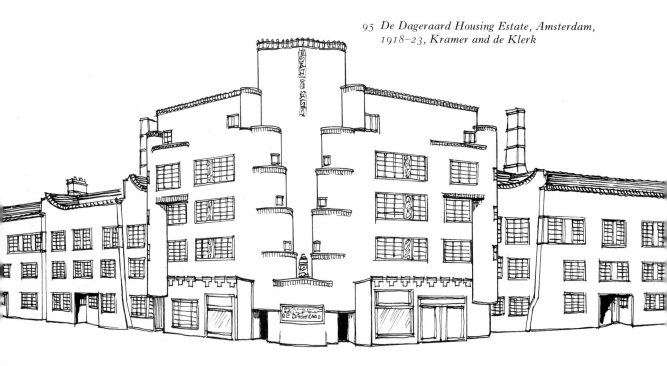

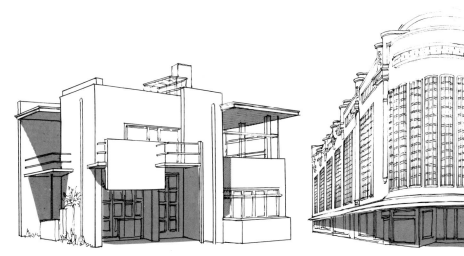

96 *Schröder House, Utrecht, 1924, Gerrit Rietveld*

97 *Bjenkorf Department Store, The Hague, 1924–6,*
    P. L. Kramer

missed in an endeavour to house the population and build offices and civic structures quickly. This work, and that of later decades, though reasonably good, is not of the original character that had been shown in the inter-war years in Holland.

One new factor was developed here in the early 1950s, the *pedestrian precinct*, of which the *Lijnbaan* is the prototype (**98**). Such precincts have now become commonplace in the cities of western Europe, but in 1953 this was an unusual and

progressive development. Much of the work of reconstruction here was under the leadership of *J. H. Van der Broek* (1898–1978) and *J. B. Bakema* (b. 1914). Also of interest, in the centre of Rotterdam, is *S. Paul's Church*, the *Central Station*, the *Exchange* and the new *Bijenkorf Store*, which was one of the later works of *Gropius* in 1955–7. It is very plain on the exterior except for a metal, sculptured decoration in contemporary style on the Coolsingel façade. This contains

98 *Lijnbaan, Rotterdam, 1953, Van der Broek*
    and others

motifs appropriate to Rotterdam such as fisher-
man's netting, anchors and lines of rigging, all in
iron and copper. Inside, all the floors are the same
as one another, with woodframed ceilings containing light panels. Columns support this ceiling and
the walls are plain. The restaurant, on the top
floor, is simple and attractively coloured and
decorated.

Belgium

It was in Belgium that the Art Nouveau mode was
introduced into architecture by *Baron Victor
Horta* (1861–1947) in his *Tassel House* in *Brussels*,
completed in 1893. In the United States, Louis
Sullivan had been incorporating an Art Nouveau
style of ornament into his buildings and Louis
Comfort Tiffany was producing decorative work
in this style. Also, Gaudì was developing in Spain
his own personal version in the ironwork on his
Barcelona palaces of the late 1880s (pp. 46–7), but
the Brussels house was a complete Art Nouveau
entity, mature and fully developed. On the street
façade this was evidenced in the plastic curving of
the window area and especially in the balcony
ironwork, but it was in the interior that the Tassel
House was so remarkable. This was especially so in

99 *Staircase hall, Tassel House, Brussels, 1893,
Baron Victor Horta*

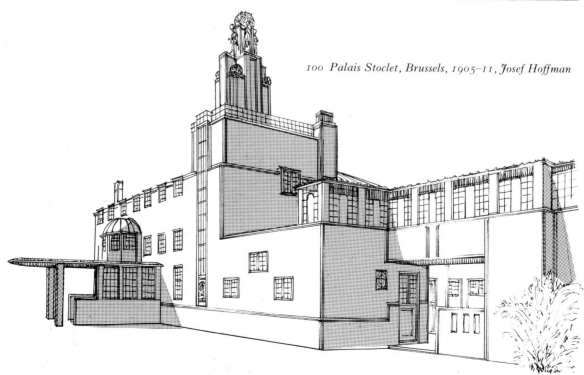

100 *Palais Stoclet, Brussels, 1905–11, Josef Hoffman*

the staircase hall where the ironwork of the supporting column and the balustrade create a free-flowing design, its tendrils twining plant-like up to the ceiling and the staircase. Originally, the wall decoration echoed this naturalistic format in colour (**99**).

Horta went on to build several more town houses in Brussels: the *Frison House* (1893–4) and, in 1895, the largest and finest of his domestic work, the *Hôtel Solvay*. The façade here is more characteristic Art Nouveau than in the earlier houses and, despite differences in their personal style, has much in common with Gaudì's Barcelona houses (p. 47). In the same year was built the *Baron van Eetvelde* house. Others followed but later examples, the *Wiener House* of 1919 for instance, moved away from Art Nouveau, for which the fashion had then passed.

Horta's most notable structure was the *Maison du Peuple* in *Brussels* (1896–9). This building occupies an unusually formed site within an irregularly-shaped open square. The façades are curved and generally concave. Art Nouveau is used here both architecturally and in the decorative handling of the work in metal, stone and brick. Horta's most famous building was the *Innovation Department Store* (1901), destroyed only a few years ago by fire. The front was entirely of glass and iron, set in a granite frame.

The long career of *Henri van der Velde* (1863–1957) was different. In the 1890s he worked as a decorator in Art Nouveau style, chiefly for exhibitions, then in 1899 moved to Germany, where he designed several shop and department-store interiors, such as the *Hohenzollern Kunstgewerbehaus* in *Berlin*. In 1902 he left Berlin to take up the invitation to be in charge of the School of Applied Arts in Weimar, a school that Gropius finally took over to create the Bauhaus. Van der Velde went to Switzerland in 1917 and returned to Belgium in 1925. His influence after this was chiefly in the academic field.

Post-war architecture in Belgium is not noteworthy. Among the more interesting examples is the *Church* of the *Pères du S. Sacrament* at *Sleihage*, built in the early 1960s. It is a 12-sided church and has triangular windows all round. The ceiling is entirely in dull black and the rest of the church interior is in black marble, stainless steel and glasswork. There is no colour. The exterior has steel roofing and a flèche.

Britain

Like Holland, architects in Britain showed little inclination to dabble with Art Nouveau, though in interior decoration, fabric design, stained glass, painting and craftwork it was a temporary phase. The nearest approach to Art Nouveau in architecture was the work of such architects as *C. Harrison Townsend* as in his *Whitechapel Art Gallery* (1900) (**101**) and *Bishopsgate Institute* (1893–4), both in London, and *Charles Rennie Mackintosh* (1868–1928), the Scottish architect, whose outstanding contribution was the highly original *Glasgow School of Art* (p. 14).

But it was as a decorator that Mackintosh created the remarkable interiors in his houses such as *Hill House, Helensburgh* (1902–3) and, most notably, in the various *tea-rooms* in *Glasgow* that he designed for Miss Cranston between 1897 and 1904. In these he remodelled the interiors, designing coloured window glass, lighting effects and furniture very much on the Belgian and French Art Nouveau pattern. Most characteristic of these were the *Willow Tea Rooms* in *Sauchiehall Street* of 1904.

101 Whitechapel Art Gallery, London, 1900, Charles Harrison Townsend

102 The City Centre, Cardiff, comprising city hall, art gallery and law courts, 1897–1920, Lanchester, Stewart and Rickards

103 Brick and half-timber building, including bank and library, Port Sunlight Estate, Cheshire

Most architecture in England until after the Second World War was eclectic. Some fine traditional buildings, erected in brick and stone, and predominantly in a simplified form of classicism, were however created. Up till 1914 the best work was in neo-Baroque style, similar to the Paris Grand and Petit Palais. The extensive layout of the *Cardiff City Centre* (**102**), the *Central Hall, Westminster* and the *Town Hall* at *Deptford* are all by the firm of *Lanchester, Stewart and Richards*. They are good designs with excellent detail, and the city centre in Cardiff, in particular, has stood the test of time well.

In the years 1918–39, within the eclectic framework, fine buildings were produced by architects like *Sir Reginald Blomfield, Sir Ernest Newton* and *Sir Guy Dawber*.

The outstanding figure of the time, however, was *Sir Edwin Lutyens* (1869–1944). His work was traditional, generally on a classical basis, streamlined and simplified and, as with work of all great architects, definably personal. He worked in all fields; civic, housing, ecclesiastical. Like Sir Christopher Wren, he adapted the simplified classicism of his day to essentially English patterns. He showed this at first entirely in house building. These were the last of the great country houses, following on the tradition of Norman Shaw and C. F. A. Voysey (pp. 13–14). His best houses, mostly built before 1914, were *Heathcote, Ilkley*, 1906, of local stone, the *Deanery, Sonning*, 1899–1901, of brick, and *Tigbourne Court, Hambledon, Surrey*, 1899, also in brick (**104**). He built few town houses, but of contrasting styles in his housing estates were the traditional brickwork of *Hampstead Garden Suburb*, begun 1908, and his low-cost council scheme in *Page Street, Westminster*, begun 1928 (**106**). The Hampstead work was the central area of the suburb, comprising the two *churches* and the *Institute Buildings*. It is well designed and attractively blended into the surroundings. The Page Street scheme, on the other hand, is much more original. Lutyens used light grey bricks, Portland stone and white cement to produce a chequer board pattern in successive rectangular blocks on courtyard layout. The effect is austere, modern and entirely non-eclectic, apart from its white-painted sash windows. It is one of his most original works.

In the early 1920s Lutyens turned to large civic schemes and developed his classical theme. One of his best works is *Britannic House* in *Finsbury Circus*, London (1920-6). Typical of his simpler, more streamlined approach, in the next decade is

104 Tigbourne Court, Hambledon, Surrey, 1899,
Sir Edwin Lutyens

105 *Peter Jones' Department Store, London, 1936–9,*
William Crabtree

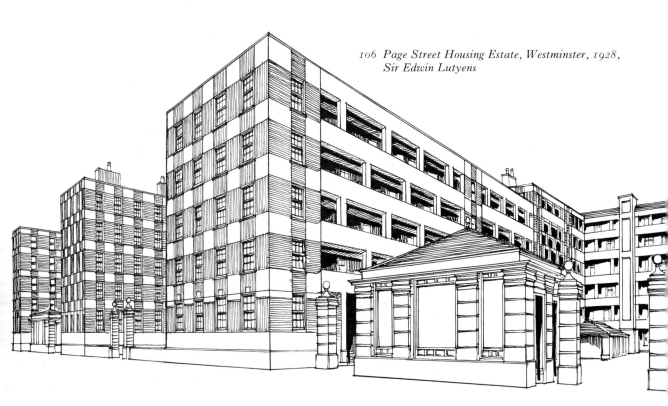

106 *Page Street Housing Estate, Westminster, 1928,*
Sir Edwin Lutyens

the *Reuter Building* in *Fleet Street*, also London. He built a number of these large, plain yet elegant classical structures, particularly as architect to the Midland Bank.

Outstanding examples of Lutyens' industry vary from the extensive scheme at *New Delhi* in *India* to the *Cenotaph* in *Whitehall*. One of his last works was the *Metropolitan Cathedral of Christ the King* in *Liverpool*: an immense classical/Byzantine structure of which only the crypt was built, surviving under the modern cathedral podium (pp. 119–20).

Another traditionalist was *Sir Giles Gilbert Scott* (1880-1960), grandson of the nineteenth-century Sir George. In a large number of churches, together with work on abbey, cathedral and university-chapel restoration and rebuilding, Scott evolved a simplified Gothic style as Lutyens had done with classical form.

His outstanding contributions were in widely different fields: the *Anglican Cathedral of Liverpool* and power station design. Scott won the competition for Liverpool Cathedral in 1901 at the age of 21. It is a fine design, Gothic in modern dress but much more alive and rich than Maufe's emasculated version at *Guildford Cathedral*. It is a red sandstone building with a high vault and impressive tower. The high cost and difficulty of finding sufficient funds and the skilled labour delayed its completion, the nave largely completed only in 1978. It is undoubtedly the last of the great cathedrals in Gothic style and, though perhaps an anachronism, is a worthy swan song.

In 1929, Scott set the pattern for *power station* design in Britain with his brick building at *Battersea*, fronting the River Thames in London. He continued with this type of work till late in life; at the age of 79 he was consulting architect for the *nuclear power station* at *Berkeley*. In the years 1939–45 he was architect for the new *Waterloo Bridge* in *London*, built of reinforced concrete faced with Portland stone slabs: a design of sophisticated simplicity making full use of modern materials and means of construction. He was later consultant for the *Forth Road Bridge* near Edinburgh.

The work of *Sir John Burnet* was more modern. *Adelaide House* at *London Bridge* (1924) and the *Kodak Building* in *Kingsway* (1911) both in London are early examples of steel framing with the structure visible in the façade design. In the period 1920–39 came the plain block architecture evidenced by *Senate House, London University* (1933-7). The best example of this type is the *Headquarters* of *Transport Executive*.

Genuine modern architecture was unusual in England before 1945. The few examples built were chiefly by foreigners who were political refugees and came to seek asylum in Britain. Although they would have liked to stay in the country, they mainly emigrated further, mostly to the United States, because the architectural opportunities for modern architecture in England were so limited. They included Walter Gropius, who came in 1934, and designed buildings at *Impington Village College*, Cambridgeshire with *Maxwell Fry* and departed for the United States in 1937. Erich Mendelsohn came in 1933, built the *De la Warr Pavilion, Bexhill-on-Sea* (**107**) in 1936 with *Serge Ivan Chermayeff* (b. 1900) (from the Caucasus), then departed for Palestine and later to the United States. Another emigré was *Berthold Lubetkin* (b.1901) from the Caucasus who founded the firm of *Tecton* which built the well-known *Highpoint*

107 De la Warr Pavilion, Bexhill-on-Sea, 1935–6, Mendelsohn and Chermayeff

Flats at *Highgate* in North London (1938) and created the sculptural Penguin Pool in moulded concrete at the Zoological Gardens, Regents Park. Other flats of a modern type include the *Isokon Flats* at *Hampstead* (1933–4) by *Wells Coates* (1895–1958) and *Kensal House* (1936), *Ladbroke Grove*, a low-cost scheme by *Maxwell Fry* (1899–1987). Steel-framed buildings with glass curtain-walling were not common in England before the Second World War. An exception was the pharmaceutical factory erected at *Beeston* for the *Boots Pure Drug Company* by *Sir Owen Williams*. On a new site (1930–2) he designed the two sections of the factory, the 'wets' for liquids, creams and pastes and the 'drys' for powders, tablets and lozenges. Williams used the 'mushroom' form of construction, where the reinforced concrete supporting piers spread outwards at the top to carry the slab floors above. Façades of these were glass curtain-walled (**108**). Another, very successful design of this type was *Peter Jones' department store* at *Sloane Square* in London (1936–9, *William Crabtree*) (1905–91) (**105**).

Modern architecture in the post-war years in England compares favourably with that of other countries in quality of building, planning and layout in general housing schemes, civic structures and schools, and especially in the New Towns. These are, in general, better built and more imaginatively planned and designed than the Swedish prototypes, for instance (p. 136). There is, however, a general monotony in the great quantity of building and an over emphasis on the

108 A corner of the 'Drys' factory for manufacture of pills, powders, tablets etc., Boots Pure Drug Company, Beeston, 1938, Sir Owen Williams

rectangular block, due to the dependence on the steel construction method. As in Germany, most of the outstanding examples have come since 1960.

Among the skyscraper blocks, the *Millbank Tower* on the Thames Embankment in *London* (1963) by *Ronald Ward and Partners* and *Centrepoint*, also in London, at *St Giles' Circus* (1962–6) by *R. Seifert and Partners* are the most unusual and interesting. The Millbank Tower is of steel and glass, Centrepoint of reinforced concrete. This

109 The National Theatre, London, 1967–76, Denys Lasdun

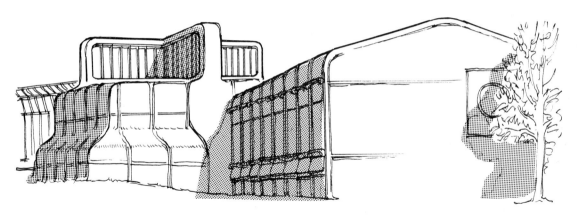

110 Olivetti Training Centre, Haslemere, 1969–72,
    James Stirling

latter, honeycomb-patterned, 370 ft (115 m) tower is a London landmark. The same architects have designed a lower, but not dissimilar, structure for *Grand Metropolitan Hotels* in *Knightsbridge*.

The most original building in Britain in the 1960s was the new *Roman Catholic Cathedral* of *Liverpool*, built 1962–7 by *Sir Frederik Gibberd* (1908–84) to replace Lutyens' abandoned design. It is constructed on circular plan – the centrally-planned church of Renaissance ideals – but this is no eclectic building. It is like an immense marquee, with a glass lantern and metal crown above (**111**). The cathedral is built on the podium of the intended classical cathedral and has sacrament chapel and altar outside where open-air services can be held on the great podium space in front. Inside, the cathedral emanates, by the handling of its spatial features and both natural and artificial

111 Metropolitan Cathedral of Christ the King,
    Liverpool, 1962–7, Sir Frederick Gibberd

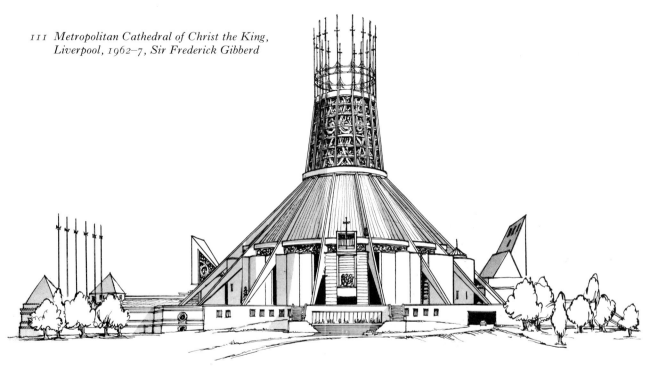

Plate 33 Lloyds of London, 1980–6, Richard Rogers,
Photograph Janet Gill

Plate 34 The Thames Barrier, London

lighting, the spiritual quality to be felt in the great
Medieval cathedrals. There is no white light. The
natural lighting comes entirely from the lantern,
whose glass ranges through all the spectrum
colours, and the narrow strips of coloured glass in
the nave walls. Chapels are inserted into these
walls all round, squeezed in between the great
sloping buttresses that offset the thrust of the
2,000-ton (2,030-tonne) lantern. This lighting is
rich and glowing even on a dull, wet Liverpool day.
In sunshine, it becomes magical. The altar is set in
the centre of the circular, grey, patterned floor.
Round it are concentric rings of pews and, above, is
suspended the delicate metal *baldacchino*.

From the mass of dull building created to house
the new universities, extensions and technical
colleges of Britain, more interesting well-designed
examples include the *Arts Faculty Buildings* in
Sidgwick Avenue, *Cambridge* (1961) by *Sir Hugh
Casson* (b. 1910) and *Neville Conder* and the new
University of York begun in the 1960s by *Robert
Matthew* (1907–75). This lay-out was well planned
and landscaped on a new site and has some

pleasant, attractive buildings. More original is the
work at *Durham University*, where some of the new
buildings front the A1 trunk road. These façades
have been kept blind to cut out noise and dirt, and
advantage is taken of the natural lighting on the
opposite elevation.

The most publicized of the new Universities,
that of *Sussex*, is built on a fine site of rolling
country between the Downs and the sea at Falmer,
near Brighton. The chief architect, *Sir Basil
Spence* (1907–76), has used a brick-and-concrete
format, combining the two media skilfully in an
arcaded style. This can be seen in the first building
here, *Falmer House* (1962–3), which has a central
court on traditional English University pattern.
The flattish arches are repeated, though the
balance and proportions differ, on each of the three
floors. The architect's *Meeting House* is also
interesting, especially inside. There are two floors,
the lower one for relaxation and reading and the
upper a circular chapel, illuminated through the
coloured glass extending round the walls. As at
Liverpool Cathedral, the colours run through the

whole spectrum. There is an oculus above in the sloping ceiling.

Sir Basil Spence repeated his brick and concrete arched theme in the *Household Cavalry Regiment Buildings* in *Knightsbridge* in London. This façade is successful: a sophisticated improvement on the buildings at Sussex University, though the controversial tower is more mundane.

The Durham University buildings and these two Spence examples are sometimes designated as 'brutalist', but none of them obtrudes offensively and they possess a refinement that seems to be absent in more classic 'brutalist' buildings such as the *Park Hill Development, Sheffield* (1961), the *Tricorn Centre* at *Portsmouth* (1967) (*Owen Luder*) and the *Queen Elizabeth concert hall* on London's riverside. All of these are of raw, unrelieved concrete in massive thrusting blocks.

In the 1970s and 1980s Britain has produced architecture in all the current modes. There is a strong reaction against modernism which shows itself in a return to classicism, generally of an innocuous nature. The work of *Quinlan Terry* is characteristic of this approach. Of much greater variety and originality is the contribution of *James Stirling* (b. 1926), who, in the 1960s, especially in university building, used mainly glass and steel in a severely modern manner. In the *Olivetti Training School* at *Haslemere* (1969–72) he turned to plastic 'wet-look' (**110**) but in his most notable and immensely popular design, that for the *Staatsgalerie* complex in *Stuttgart,* the architect has returned to a human scale, to colour and traditional forms in an ingenious handling of space and light (**Plate 30**). Two younger architects, *Norman Foster* (b. 1935) and *Richard Rogers* (b. 1933) are better known for their work in the high-tech field, Foster especially for the black glass-enveloped *Willis, Faber and Dumas* office headquarters in *Ipswich* (1975) and the *Hong Kong and Shanghai Bank* metal and glass skyscraper (completed 1986) towering over Hong Kong's waterfront, and Rogers for his *Centre National d'Art et de la Culture Georges Pompidou* in *Paris* (completed 1976) and the later, refined version of this type of structure, *Lloyds of London Headquarters*, 1978-86 (**Plate 33**), designed to permit continuous expansion of accommodation as required. Built of gleaming silver stainless steel, polished aluminium and grey concrete, this unusual building wears its domestic functions on the exterior in a profusion of heating and ventilating pipes, as well as its glass-walled observation lifts. Its lacework atrium resembles a latter-day Crystal Palace.

France

French architects tended to use Art Nouveau purely as a decorative medium on apartment blocks, shops and department stores and the interiors of restaurants. Little survives of this work. An exception was *Henri Guimard* (1867–1942) who, apart from his apartment blocks such as the *Castel Béranger* (1896–7) in *Rue La Fontaine* in Paris, is noted especially for his *Paris Métro* station entrances (1899–1904) in which he used metal decoratively in sinuous Art Nouveau manner. In 1902 *Auguste Perret* (1874–1954) designed an impressive masonry apartment block at *119 Avenue Wagram* in *Paris* on the façade of which Art Nouveau ornament was carved round the window openings of the upper storeys. The *Church of S. Jean de Montmartre* in *Paris* (begun 1897), by *Anatole de Baudot*, was the first major reinforced concrete building. It also embodies a Gothic version of Art Nouveau decoration. Some of the Paris department stores built in the early years of the twentieth century were designed with glass-and-metal façades, using Art Nouveau forms of decoration, somewhat in the manner of Horta's *L'Innovation Store* in Brussels (p. 113). The best of these is the *Samaritaine Department Store* in the Rue de la Monnaie of 1905 by *Frantz Jourdain*.

Two of the earliest exponents of *modern architecture* were practising in France: *Auguste Perret* (1874–1954) and *Tony Garnier* (1867–1948). Perret's was the greater contribution in actual building and he is especially noted for his development of the technique of building in reinforced concrete (pp. 75–6). While iron and steel were the chief structural developments of the nineteenth century, reinforced concrete belongs to the twentieth. Perret was interested in experimentation with this material and concentrated from early in his career in its use and the types of design that would be most suitable for its employment. A very early example was his *apartment block* at *25 bis Rue Franklin* in Paris (1902–3). Constructionally the building was a breakthrough, being made up in a reinforced concrete skeleton of horizontal and vertical members, the concrete façade faced with faïence mosaic.

113 Swiss Pavilion, Cité Universitaire, Paris, 1931–2, Le Corbusier

112 Church of Notre Dame, Royan, 1954–9, Guillaume Gillet

Perret's most original concrete structure is the *Church of Notre Dame* at *Le Raincy* on the outskirts of Paris (**114**, **118**). On the exterior there is an interesting very tall slender tower of diminishing stages, but it is the interior that is magnificent. It is a wide, light church, the shallow-vaulted roof supported on slender columns. The whole structure is in concrete apart from the glass window panels, which extend the full height of the walls all round the church. They provide a symphony of colour, culminating in deep blue behind the altar. Because of the slenderness of the columns and the richness of the glass, this church possesses a spiritual atmosphere and unimpeded sight and sound of and from the altar for everyone. It became the prototype for churches all over Europe for decades, from Moser in pre-war Switzerland (**78**) to Spence's post-war Coventry Cathedral and recent churches in France such as the *Church of S. Rémy* at *Baccarat*.

Tony Garnier is known chiefly for his project for an industrial town designed in the early years of the century. He called it the *Cité Industrielle*, and it represented his ideas for an ideal city in the age of technology. It was, like Sant' Elia's *Città Nuova*, years ahead of its time. Garnier illustrated glass curtain-walling, building on *pilotis* and with flat roofs. The shapes are simple blocks and the material chiefly concrete. Garnier envisaged pedestrian precincts, community centres and schools, with traffic and industry separated from leisure and living areas. He was city architect in Lyons for many years and tried to use some of his themes during his working life in practical structures. He was full of new ideas and had a fertile imagination.

Since 1920 French architecture has been dominated by the world-famous Swiss architect *Charles Edouard Jeanneret* (1888-1965), usually known as *Le Corbusier* a name he adopted in 1920. He was one of the great world leaders of modern architecture, along with Gropius, Mies van der Rohe and Frank Lloyd Wright.

Le Corbusier became established as an architect with advanced, original ideas immediately after the First World War. He specialized in house design and in low-cost housing and planning for flats and estates. He developed a practical, ideal form of house design and construction using modern materials, adaptable to the individual commission from a limited selection of parts. The houses were generally two-storeyed, the upper floor supported on *pilotis* (usually circular concrete columns), a concept that has dogged modern architecture ever since. The form of the building was uncompromisingly constructed of horizontals and verticals, it had wide, long glazed areas, open plan areas within, often the full height of the building. Roofs were flat, sometimes with roof gardens, walls whitewashed. Le Corbusier coined the phrase 'a house as a machine for living in'. By this he did not mean that it was an impersonal machine but that it should function as efficiently and be of as well-designed form as a pupose-built machine would be. He was absorbed in the social problems of housing people in cities and developed his ideas in his book *Urbanisme*, published in 1925.

In the 1930s the economic depression hit France badly, and building was severely curtailed. In these years Le Corbusier worked out many projects, but most of his actual building was outside France. He worked in South America, North Africa, India and on such designs as the *Ministry of Education Building* in *Rio de Janeiro* (1936–45) and the *Centrosoyuz* in *Moscow* (1930, p. 146, **Plate 43**).

Immediately after the Second World War Le Corbusier won even greater international fame for the development of his *Unité d'Habitation* theme. The first of these was built in the *Boulevard Michelet* on the outskirts of *Marseilles* in 1947–52

114 Church of Notre Dame, Le Raincy, near Paris, 1922–3, Auguste Perret

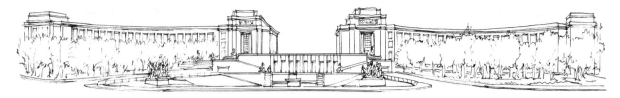

115 Palais de Chaillot, Paris, 1937, Carlu, Boileau, Azema

(**117**). It was his answer to the problem of successfully accommodating large numbers of people in a small space at a low cost. The scheme comprises one immense rectangular block, carried on a double row of massive, central supports rather than slender *pilotis*. It contains 350 flats in eight double storeys, with a storey for shops half way up and communal facilities on the roof. This is certainly a 'machine for living in'. Claimed as an architectural masterpiece, it nevertheless strikes a chill to the heart to imagine living in such a 'machine'. Whether the building is aesthetically satisfactory is very much a matter for personal taste. Though posterity will no doubt accord to both Le Corbusier and the *Unité* an important place in the history of modern architecture, it may well re-write the excessive eulogies with which the first *Unité* was greeted by the architectural world.

A second was built in *Nantes* (1952–7), a third in *West Berlin* (1957) and the fourth at *Briey-la-Forêt* (1960).

In 1950 Le Corbusier turned to ecclesiastical architecture. First he built his world famous, highly-personal and original *pilgrimage Church of Notre Dame du Haut at Ronchamp* (**116**). Finding much more universal favour than the *Unités*, the church is massive, rough-cast, essentially plastic. An interesting silhouette is seen from all angles, and each form and mass is balanced exactly to give a satisfying design. The interior is also unusual. The surfaces are all of rough-cast concrete, and the lighting is carefully arranged to shine through the tiny windows set in the thick walling. These windows are of irregular shapes and sizes and are filled with coloured glass. The whole interior is curved or sloped at differently-designed angles, all

116 Church of Notre Dame du Haut, Ronchamp, 1950–5, Le Corbusier

dominated by the massiveness of the curved, tent-like roof. The studied sophistication of the work soon becomes apparent after the first fleeting impression of rural simplicity.

Le Corbusier's second ecclesiastical commission is quite different and has more in common with the stark, raw concrete of his *Unités*. This is the *Dominican Convent* of *La Tourette* at *Eveux-sur-l'Arbresle*, near Lyons, begun 1956. The entire complex of conventual buildings and church is of plain concrete, inside and out. The exterior is particularly 'brutalist'; stark and uncompromising. The interior of the church is a large rectangle, tall and rather narrow, the choir at a higher level than the nave. The crypt is painted in rich, strong colours and is lit by oculi in the ceiling. The colours from this chamber, which can be seen from the plain grey main church, contrast vividly with it. The whole church has atmosphere, much of which is due to the carefully-planned indirect natural lighting. The artificial lighting is equally necessary and carefully thought out. Much of it comes from the floor, angled in many directions to illuminate varied vistas and planes. Nearly all the surfaces of walls, window openings and floor are subtly sloped, the angles being meticulously worked out to give the optimum visual effect (**Plate 35**).

The work of men like Perret and Le Corbusier was, however, untypical of architecture in France until after 1950. The resistance mounted by the architectural establishment was formidable. Led by academic centres such as the École des Beaux Arts in Paris, the commissions were successfully kept out of the hands of younger architects trying to establish modern architecture. Building in France in the first half of the twentieth century was more traditional than anywhere except England, and the quality of this traditional work was inferior, especially compared to work by such

117 Unité d'Habitation, Marseilles, 1946–52, Le Corbusier

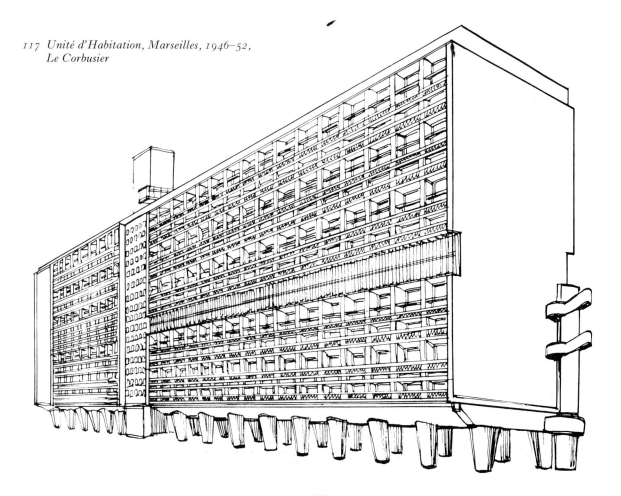

*Plate 35 Interior of the Monastery Church of La
Tourette at Eveux sur l'Abresle, France,
1955–9, Le Corbusier*

with traditional tall blocks. The appallingly low
standard of workmanship and materials more than
cancels out, from the point of view of living
conditions, any architectural merit that the scheme
may have had. Carefully taken photographs, with
calculated lighting effects, of the models and the
buildings when brand new give a false impression
of the arid reality.

Another such instance is the new town of *Marly-
le-Roi*, just west of Paris. It is small with an
unimaginitive centre, monotonously laid out with
low-level, poorly-constructed shops round an apo-
logy for a piece of sculpture. As a new design for
living, it compares unfavourably with most European examples, especially such English ones as
Crawley or Stevenage New Towns. Also the
subject of praise from architectural critics, but a
no-less-unimpressive new town, is that at *Bagnols-
sur-Cèze*, twinned with the pleasant old Provençal
small town. A privileged layout, built for the
workers from Marcoule nuclear power station and
awarded the 1960 *Prix d'Urbanisme*, the story is
one of similar mediocrity and lack of quality. A
much better new housing development in France
is the new town built to house the workers from the
site of the natural gas discovery at *Lacq* in the
Pyrenees. This is a much better scheme, using high
quality materials and workmanship, especially in
the church, the town hall and individual houses on
the upper slopes.

Apart from Le Corbusier's work and the layout
by the aged Perret in the rebuilding of Le Havre,
the most interesting examples of modern architecture in France are in some new churches and the
UNESCO building in Paris. Interesting new
churches include that of *S. Agnes* in *Fontaine-les-
Grès* by *Michel Marot*, the *Church* of *Sacré Coeur* at
Audincourt by *Maurice Novarina* and, by far the
most interesting, the *Church of Notre Dame en son
Immaculée Conception* at *Royan*. Designed by
Guillaume Gillet, built in 1954–9 entirely in reinforced concrete, this is the modern successor to
Perret's work at Le Raincy and has much in
common with the present-day Finnish churches,
like that at Tampere (p. 144, **112**). It is a dramatic
and successful design outside and in. It is large and
on an oval plan. It possesses two features from
medieval, southern French/Spanish origins; on
the exterior the base splays outwards like the castle
at Coca in Spain and, inside, the two levels of
galleries are set into the thickness of the piers and

architects as Lutyens. Typical of the 1930s is the
vapid emptiness of such structures as the *Palais de
Chaillot* (**115**) and the *Museum of Modern Art*,
both built in 1937 in *Paris* (**Plate 37**).

After the Second World War the State provided
financial support for housing schemes and modern
architecture became the accepted style. Little
advantage was gained from this. A number of
planned estates were built on the periphery of
cities and a few new centres established. Architecturally the designs are often original and interesting, but the quality of workmanship, building and
landscaping and the shoddiness of the materials
employed is poorer in France than in any country
in Europe, including Greece, Yugoslavia and
Rumania, which are genuinely poor countries.

Typical of these housing estates is the *Cité des
Courtillières* at *Pantin*, a suburb of *Paris*. Built
about 1970, it soon became shabby. The design is
ingenious and unusual, with six-storey long blocks
winding sinuously around the site, interspersed

Plate 36 The entrance pyramid to the Louvre under construction, Paris, 1988 Photograph J. M. Webber

buttresses like the chapels in Albi Cathedral in southern France (Vol. 2). The interior décor is most effective. All is in grey concrete except for the focal point of rich light shining through the coloured glass behind the altar.

The UNESCO *Headquarters Building* in *Paris* (1953–8) is notable. Designed and built by an international group of architects, *Marcel Breuer*, born in Hungary but a citizen of the United States, *Bernard Zehrfuss*, a Frenchman, and *Pier Luigi Nervi*, an Italian, it is a Y-shaped building, eight storeys high. It is an interesting conception, containing some fine halls and rooms, finely built and finished with quality materials.

As long as he was President of France Charles de Gaulle succeeded in keeping high-rise structures out of the centre of Paris, but under his successor, Georges Pompidou, this policy changed, and the rebuilding of more central and inner suburban areas introduced such designs as in, for example, the *Place de la Bastille* and the extensive development of the *Quartier de la Défense*. The scheme at Défense continued over a long period of time; centrally, it comprises office buildings, apartment blocks and shops rising high above a great concrete platform which is pedestrianized. Beneath this flows the segregated motor traffic. An early, notable structure here is the *Centre National des Industries et Techniques* – the CNIT building – an innovative design providing almost 1 million square ft of space.

In the Hi-tec field of architectural design *Piano and Rogers* won the competition for the cultural centre designed also to cover a million square ft of space, this time on a car-park site in the area of Les Halles. Called the *Centre National d'Art et de Culture Georges Pompidou* (but more colloquially known as the Beaubourg), this predecessor of the Lloyds building (pp. 120–1) was completed in 1977. Still a very popular place to visit, it is more colourful than Lloyds but now appears shabby and, as it seems not possible to clean the exterior glass of the high travelator walkways, the magnificent view from within is foggily obscured.

The most successful, despite controversy, of such glass and metal structures is the Louvre pyramid. The decision to create a *Grand Louvre* was taken in 1981 by the then recently elected President, François Mitterand, the aim being to provide much more exhibition space in a coherent redesigning of the museum interior and cater for the needs of the ever-expanding tourist industry. This was to be achieved by utilizing the space beneath the Cour Carrée and that bordered by the buildings erected in the time of Napoleon III (p. 19).

The architect chosen in 1983 was the Chinese-American *Ieoh Ming Pei* who decided to build a 71-ft (21.6-m) high transparent pyramid set in the middle of the courtyard which would constitute the main entrance to the revised museum (**Plate 36**). There is no doubt that the pyramid is incongruous in this setting of florid, nineteenth century stonework but it is not obtrusive for the

Plate 37 Sculptural decoration on the exterior of the Museum of Modern Art, Paris, 1937

courtyard is large and the pyramid only half the height of the surrounding ranges. There is also no doubt of its success as such an entrance and in the resulting creation of the reorganized galleries below ground.

The Iberian Peninsula: Spain

Art Nouveau in Spain is embodied in the work of Antonio Gaudì but in a manner personal to the architect and which went much further towards individual and original design than the Art Nouveau movement ever achieved.

Gaudì's work of the late nineteenth century, including his masterpiece, the Sagrada Familia, has been described earlier (pp. 47–9). In the twentieth century his style developed, becoming more plastic and flowing, as is evidenced in his later portal on the Sagrada Familia (**Plate 13**).

Gaudì's two chief buildings showing these characteristics are the apartment blocks in *Barcelona*; the *Casa Battló*, and the *Casa Milá* at numbers *43 and 92 Paseo de Gracia* respectively (**119**). Both were built 1905–7. The former is a tall and narrow block of six storeys. The latter is much larger, occupying a corner site and containing two

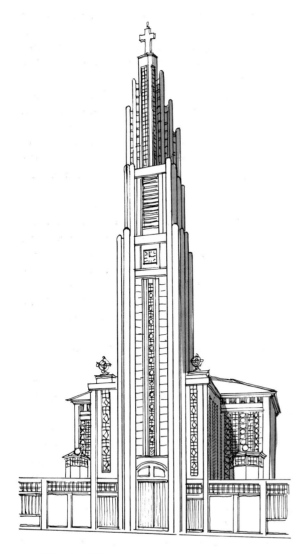

118 Church of Notre Dame, Le Raincy, near Paris, 1922–3, Auguste Perret

courts. The façades are undulating like waves. There are no horizontal or vertical lines or planes; all is movement. The chief motif is the sea, not only in waves but also in fronds of plant life, seaweed and rocks. This maritime element is seen mainly in the iron balconies on each floor. The building is not to everyone's taste but it is one of the few genuinely original and different works of the time and completely non-eclectic.

Although Gaudì was famed and respected in his own time, he had no real followers. His was an individual contribution, not the basis of a large movement, as was, for example, the Bauhaus. Most of the other architectural work in Spain before the Second World War was traditional. Typical is the vast Baroque pile of the *General Post Office* in *Madrid* (1913, *Palacios*), the classical monument to *King Alfonso* in the *Retiro Park* in the city (1922) and the neo-Gothic *Cathedral* at *Vitoria*, begun 1906 and continued after a long period of inactivity, after 1946. This is a large cathedral, well-designed and built on traditional cruciform lines with apsidal choir ending. It is, despite the high-quality workmanship, an unenterprising and uninteresting building.

Since 1950 most of Spanish architecture has been in the modern idiom, though the totalitarian regime, which, until 1975, still controlled the country, showed a tendency towards traditional building. One example of this is the *National Monument* of *Santa Cruz* of the *Valley of the Fallen*, built near the Escorial in the Guadarrama Mountains. Initiated by General Franco, it was consecrated in 1960. Covering $3\frac{1}{3}$ acres (1.3 ha.) and situated at nearly 6,000 ft (1800 m) above sea level, the monument comprises a great sculptured cross above a curving, arcaded entrance that leads into a basilica hewn out of the mountain side. The whole scheme is on the gigantic scale and simplified classical style so beloved of dictators, whether fascist or communist. The interior of the basilica is a rectangular chamber, barrel vaulted and with an immense cupola at the far end, decorated all over by mosaic pictures in the Byzantine tradition of style and subject. The work is treated in a fairly modern manner, but is based entirely on traditional precepts. The quality of the materials is good and the craftsmanship technically adequate.

In the genuinely modern style Spanish work is of fair quality only, and there are few outstanding examples. Typical are the tall blocks in the *Plaza*

España in *Madrid*, modern hotels such as the *Grand Hotel Zurbaran* in *Badajoz*, banks such as the *Banca Catalana* (1965–8) in *Barcelona*, blocks of flats like that in the *Calle Muntaner* in *Barcelona* (1965–7) and new university building such as that at *San Sebastian*, begun in 1964 by *Miguel de Oriol*. Prolific development schemes abound along the miles of coastline of the Mediterranean from Barcelona in the north-east to Cádiz in the south-west. *Gandía*, near Valencia, and *Benidorm*, near Alicante, are typical. These architectural mushroom growths are appearing all round the warm sandy beaches of Europe, especially those undeveloped before 1945. Such work is monotonously similar from Spain to Bulgaria.

Modern buildings in Spain that have received some particular architectural acclaim include the *Torres Blancas* apartment blocks on the *Avenida de América* at the entrance to Madrid, built 1965–8 by *Saénz-Oiza*, and one or two churches. The Torres Blancas have balconies made in flat, cylindrical shapes, which, when piled one above the other, give a superficial resemblance to the famous Chicago cylindrical towers. The Spanish examples are, unfortunately, much more impressive on the photographic page than in reality, as they are poorly proportioned, dull and dark.

There are two churches of some interest in *Vitoria*. The finer of these is the *Church of the Coronation of Our Lady* by *Miguel Fisac*. The interior is very plain, of natural wood and stone. The surfaces are curved in Baroque fashion to give movement, but the effect is different due to the excessive simplicity of the décor. The lighting from the slit windows on one side is effective. The *Church of Our Lady of the Angels* by *Ferrer* and others has an unusual form. The exterior is a pyramid covered with blue-grey tiling with a separate, concrete campanile that is an integral part of the neighbouring apartment block. One wonders how the occupants of the latter appreciate the ringing of the bells. The interior of the church is vast and barn-like and is much less interesting.

The post-modern movement in Spain is particularly active in Catalonia, often referred to as the '*Barcelona school*'. Notably original in his ideas, an interesting blend of nostalgia and modern, is *Levi Ricardo Bofill* (b. 1939), who founded the *Taller de Arquitectura* in *Barcelona* in 1960, a studio or workshop for a team of architects. Characteristic of Bofill's bold and dramatic concepts is his *Palais*

*119 Casa Milà, Barcelona, Spain, 1905,
Antonio Gaudì*

d'*Abraxas*, an unusual housing scheme near *Paris*
(1978–83), at Marne la Vallée designed on circular
plan, and his *Le Viaduc* housing scheme at *St
Quentin-en-Yvelines* (1974), built out like a bridge
over water, reminiscent of the sixteenth-century
Château of Chenonceaux. In 1984 Bofill designed a
projected Olympic Ring Stadium and Sports
Palace Complex for the 1992 *Olympic Games* in
Barcelona. Also in the city, *Bertran Pep Bonet* (b.
1941) formed an architectural partnership in 1965
called *Studio PER* comprising four architects
working in the same accommodation but in related
schemes, the others being *Cristian Cirici, Luis
Clotet* and *Oscar Tusquets*. Like Krier in Austria,
Bonet's work lies chiefly in the housing field.

Portugal

As in Spain, the totalitarian régime in Portugal
showed its preference and power in such buildings
as the immense, austere *Pantheon* in *Lisbon*,
inaugurated by Dr Salazar as a temple to honour
great Portuguese citizens, for example Vasco da
Gama. This is a perfect, centrally-planned church
on classical principles with drum and dome rising
on pendentives supported on Composite Order
piers. It is correct but cold and uninspired.

In post-war modern architecture there are
examples such as can be seen in any city of Europe,
for example, the housing development on the
Avendia Infante Santo in *Lisbon* by *Pessoa*. More

original and of general interest is the *Discovery Monument* at *Belém*, overlooking the Tagus, on the fringe of the city of Lisbon. Completed in 1960, it commemorates the great Portuguese explorers of the fifteenth and sixteenth centuries. The architect was *Cottinelli Telmo* and the sculptor *Leopoldo de Almeida*.

Scandinavia: Denmark

Before the First World War, Danish architects tended to turn away from eclecticism towards *Nyrop's* (p. 67) style of romantic nationalism, or to a mixture of this and Art Nouveau. One of Nyrop's later works is his chunky, personal version of Romanesque decorated with Art Nouveau, the *Elijah Church* in *Copenhagen* (1906–8).

Another Scandinavian architect whose work is individually personal and national is *P. V. Jensen Klint* (1853–1930). Sometimes he benefited from Gothic inspiration, sometimes Art Nouveau. His style is plastic and monumental. His best-known work is the *Grundtvig Church* in *Copenhagen*, built as a memorial to N. F. S. Grundtvig, the hymn writer, educationalist and priest. The church is entirely of brick (between five and six million of them), including the altar, pulpits and decoration. The tall façade is Expressionist in design (**121**) but the interior, in a simplified Gothic form and in similar vein to Sir Edward Maufe's later Guildford Cathedral in England, has a magnificent simplicity, its tall piers rising in unbroken line to the lofty quadripartite vault; it is a moving interior of great dramatic intensity.

From about 1915–16 the Danes, like the other Scandinavian countries, returned to Neo-classicism. Leading architects in the years up to 1930 included *Carl Petersen* (1874–1923) and *Hack Kampmann* (1856–1920). Petersen designed the *Faaborg Museum* in simple classical style. Kampmann is best known for his *Police Headquarters Building* in *Copenhagen* (1918–24). A stark, grey structure on the exterior, built on a triangular site,

120 Concert Hall, Tivoli, Copenhagen, 1956, Hans Hansen and Fritz Schegel

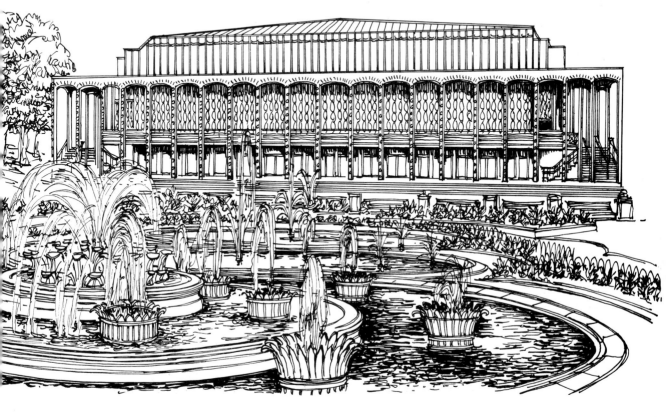

*Plate 38 Fountain in shopping precinct, Rødovre, near
Copenhagen, post-1956*

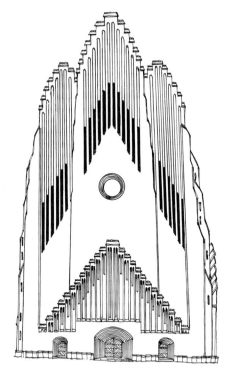

*121 Façade, Gruntvig Church, Copenhagen, designed
1913, built 1920–40, Jensen Klint*

122 Town Hall, Aarhus, 1937, Arne Jacobsen

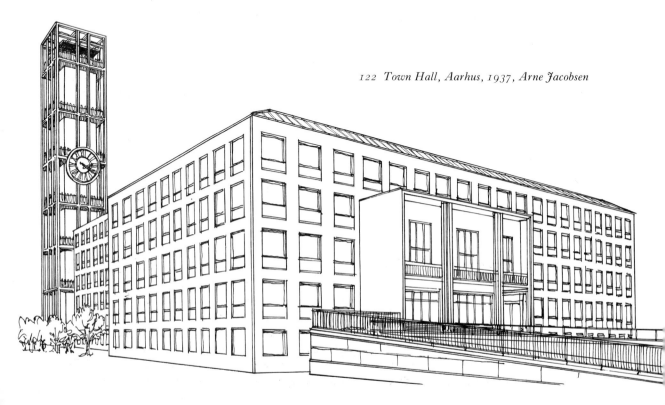

it contains two beautiful courts, especially the circular one. This is handled in plain but correct classicism, with coupled Doric Order columns on the ground arcade and plain classical windows on two storeys above. It is reminiscent of the courtyard of Charles V's Renaissance palace at the Alhambra (Vol. 3).

In the 1930s Denmark, like Sweden, turned towards Bauhaus designs and functionalism. Architects explored the possibilities of reinforced concrete and adapted their national material – brick – to similar designs. Typical examples built in this decade were *Broadcasting House* in *Copenhagen* (1937–45, by *Vilhelm Lauritzen*), the *Copenhagen Stadium* (1934, by *Hansen* and *Jørgensen*) and housing estates and blocks of flats like those on *Tuborvej*, a suburb of Copenhagen (1940–2, by *Baumann* and *Hansen*).

A good example of quality brickwork in this plain style is *Aarhus University*. A competition was held for this in 1931 and *Kay Fisker, C. F. Møller* and *Poul Stegmann* were appointed to design a number of buildings. The university, which is still being added to, is pleasantly situated on a rolling site about 1½ miles (2 km) from the centre of the city and is laid out with a lake, trees and flowers. Although building has continued intermittently between 1932 and 1958, designs are remarkably homogeneous. Only the very latest buildings are noticeably different; the remainder are all in yellow brick, very plain block designs with tiled roofs and rectangular simple fenestration. Much of the original work of the 1930s has had to be rebuilt. The Royal Air Force bombed the buildings during the Second World War because they were occupied by the Gestapo.

The best-known Danish architect of the period 1935–70 is *Arne Jacobsen* (1902–71). He was strongly influenced by the work of Le Corbusier and Mies van der Rohe. He adopted functionalism early and produced a series of buildings during these years. His designs became even plainer as time passed, as is evidenced by the starkly plain, repeated glass walling of the façade of his *Town Hall* in *Rødovre* (new suburb of Copenhagen), built in 1956. Jacobsen's work, like that of all Danish architects of quality, was very national. Within the confines of plain modern architecture, his buildings are notable for their excellence of materials, finish and superb quality of proportion. He worked in concrete – plain or marble-faced –

brick and glass-and-steel curtain walling. His designs are recognizable for their individuality, their sparing use of decoration and careful calculation of scale. His best-known inter-war building is *Aarhus Town Hall* (**122**). It is interesting to compare this with the one at *Søllerød* (1942) and the final example at *Rødovre*. He also designed the 21-storey steel-and-glass skyscraper in *Copenhagen* for *Scandinavian Airlines*, combining their needs with the *Royal Hotel* (1960), as well as an even plainer glass office block in *Nyropsgade* (1955).

Other modern work of interest, all in or near Copenhagen, is the *Restaurant* and *Club Pavilion* along the waters' edge at *Langelinie* (1958, *Eva* and *Nils Koppel*), the *Concert Hall* in the *Tivoli*, a replacement for one lost during the war (**120**), the interior of the *Church of S. Knud Lavard* in the suburb of *Lyngby* (1956–7, by *Carl Frederiksen*) and the *town centre* of the new scheme at *Rødovre*, which has a particularly attractive under-cover shopping precinct laid out with cafés around fountains, trees and seats (**Plate 38**).

Sweden

The early years of the twentieth century were a time of romantic nationalism in Sweden, as in Finland. Sweden became known for her simple, brick, clean-lined structures, built mainly between 1910 and 1930. At the same time, in the first decade of the century, Swedish architects were still building (like their colleagues elsewhere in Europe) in styles more closely derived from the past. *Ferdinand Boberg* (1860–1946) evolved a Swedish form of Art Nouveau, an example of which can be seen in his *General Post Office* in *Stockholm* (1903). Its newly-cleaned pale pink façade gleams in the evening sunshine, clearly delineating the Art Nouveau decoration on the principal entrance and the wall panelled ornament. The *Royal Dramatic Theatre* in *Stockholm* (1907) by *Frederik Lilleqvist* (1863–1932) is a rich, ornate example of a simplified classicism. In its articulation and column supports the exterior shows the influence of Wagner's work in Vienna (pp. 94–5).

In the years 1910–30 Swedish architects tried to break away from eclecticism into a more modern approach. They developed a romantic nationalist style which, while still eclectic, was couched in such simple, elegant terms that it was not so obviously derivative. As in Denmark and Finland, there was an emphasis on a return to national materials, clearly displayed. In Sweden, this was generally brick, designed on clean lines with carefully rationed use of ornament. In the 1930s and 1940s such architecture was classified as modern. It is now seen to be fully traditional and has much in common with the works of traditional architects in other countries, Sir Edwin Lutyens in England, for instance. In both cases, the designs are essentially national.

The best known work in this style is the *Stockholm City Hall*, begun in 1911 and opened in 1923 (**125**). It was built to the designs of *Ragnar Östberg* (1866–1945) and is a brick structure with a tall, elegant tower. The buildings are grouped round two courtyards. The interiors are interesting, especially the Golden Hall, 144 ft (44 m) long and decorated with mosaic. The City Hall is Stockholm's most famous landmark. It has a magnificent setting; the waters of Lake Mälaren enclose it on two sides. Less imaginative and elegant but similarly in simplified eclectic vein is the work of *Carl Westmann* (1866–1936), which can be seen in his *Law Courts in Stockholm* (1912–15). This also shows Medieval origins; its interiors are vaulted and darkly mysterious.

In the 1920s a number of architects returned to Neo-classicism in a modern simplified form. *Ivar Tengbom* (1878–1968) was a leader in this respect. Tengbom had earlier designed in romantic nationalist mood as in his brick Högalid Church in Stockholm which is a landmark with its tall Baroque towers, but his *Concert Hall in Stockholm* (1926) is a prototype of Neo-classicism. This has a lofty, simple portico of Corinthian columns with multi-sided shafts. In front is the *Orpheus Fountain* by Carl Milles (1936) (**Plate 39**).

Two ecclesiastical buildings that belong to the period of romantic nationalism but which, though partly eclectic, are essentially original works are the *Engelbrekt Church* in *Stockholm* and the *Masthugg Church* in *Göteborg*. Both have some affinity with the Grundtvig Church in Copenhagen (p. 131). The Engelbrekt Church (**123**) is very tall and powerful. In its setting on the top of a rocky hill, it reminds one of Lars Sonck's Finnish churches (p. 139), though the exterior is less plastic. The Stockholm church by *Lars Israel Wahlman* (1870–1952) is of brick. Built in 1910–14, it has one tall, simple tower. The interior is reminiscent of Sonck,

with the great parabolic arches spanning each arm of the cross. The decoration is restrained, chunky and imaginative. The altar wall is painted and gilded, the originally designed wooden pulpit set in stone. Granite is used for the arches and pillars, wood for the barrel vaulting. There is considerable contrast between the massive, arched interior and the soigné verticality of the outside.

The *Masthugg Church* in *Göteborg* (Gothenburg) (**126**) was designed by *Sigfrid Eriksson* (1879–1958) and built in 1914. It is unusual, massive and severe, its monumental tower rising on the skyline of the hills bordering the river. The exterior is of red brick on a base of granite blocks on an L-shaped plan. Inside, the brick is whitewashed. Piers support semicircular, plain arches and the roof is of open timber construction in whole logs, not rafters. It is an interesting church, original and monumentally simple.

*123 Engelbrekt Church, Stockholm, 1906–14,
Lars Israel Wahlman*

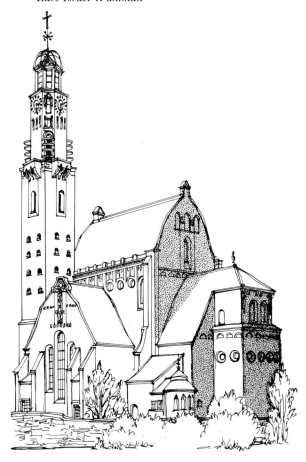

124 Stockholm City Library, 1924–8, Gunnar Asplund

125 Stockholm City Hall, 1909–23, Ragnar Östberg

126 Masthugg Church, Göteborg, 1916,
Sigfrid Eriksson

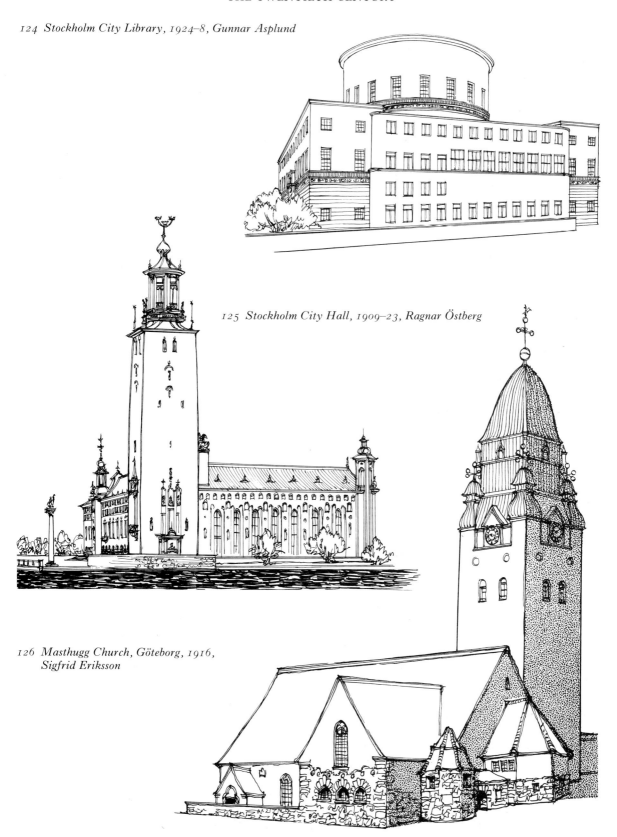

Plate 39 Orpheus fountain, outside Concert Hall in Stockholm, 1936, Carl Milles

From 1930 onwards some Swedish architects were beginning to design in functionalist style, trying out such newer materials as glass and concrete, and modelling their works on those of Le Corbusier and Gropius. A leading architect of the period 1920–40 was *Erik Gunnar Asplund* (1885–1940). He had studied extensively in Italy and Greece and his earlier work was a severe interpretation of Neo-classicism. His best-known design in this form is the *Stockholm City Library* (1924–8) (**124**). The lending library in the rotunda has a fine interior. He then advanced to glass and steel construction and developed a modern style. His extension to the *Göteborg* (Gothenburg) *Town Hall* dates from 1937.

Also in Göteborg is the civic layout in the *Götaplatsen* where architectural development over

the years 1923–36 can be seen in one scheme. A number of architects were employed here, with the *Art Museum* in the centre (1923), flanked by the neo-classical *City Theatre* (east), built by *Carl Bergsten* in 1934 and, west, the *City Concert Hall* (1935–6) by *Einar Eriksson*. The sculpture of the central fountain and the theatre caryatids is typical of the date.

Osvald Almqvist (1884–1950) was one of Sweden's early functionalist architects. The Power Station at Hammerfors (1929) and the industrial School for Boys at Domnarvet (1930) are characteristic of his work. *Sven Gottfrid Markelius* (1889–1972) was even better known in this field, and his Concert Hall in Hälsingborg (1932) was a pace-setter.

Post-war architecture in Sweden received considerable acclaim in the 1960s. Swedish architects were praised for their high standards in building, planning and research, their use of prefabricated unit construction and, especially, for their new towns such as those on the periphery of Stockholm at Vällingby and Farsta. But, as with the romantic nationalism of the 1920s, it was realized later that this work was less original in planning and conception than had been thought. It appeared so outstanding simply because Sweden, a neutral country in the Second World War, had been able to develop her building of this type much earlier than the countries that had suffered the devastation of their cities.

In fact, Swedish post-war architecture has produced some remarkably banal results from such high-powered planning and automation. The advanced methods of construction seem to have created only dull, circumscribed buildings, markedly so in contrast to the lively, original and beautifully-finished work of the Finns. *Vällingby New Town*, for instance, today gives an impression of a small, unnotable town centre, with functional and well-constructed buildings, but drab in both style and hue. The whole town displays a marked lack of imagination, in appearance and design. Everything is in grey and dun. Concrete and dull-brown brick prevail. The churches are as unecclesiastical as garages and as unwelcoming. They look as though they were produced as cheaply and quickly as possible. *Farsta New Town* is similar but poorer, both architecturally and in quality of building and workmanship. Though later, already it is shabbier than Vällingby. In both towns the main housing near the centre is in stark, high-rise concrete blocks, built, like so many others in different countries, before the planners of Europe 'discovered' that most people prefer, and need, to live in low-rise blocks or even small houses.

Norway

During the first 30 years of the twentieth century, traditional forms of architecture held the field. There were two bases: first, the traditional form, mainly wood, of Norwegian building through the centuries; second, the international revival of Gothic or classical form. In the first of these, the *'dragon style'* continued from the *fin de siècle* movement (p. 69). Private houses, large and small, were built in this manner, especially in the mountains.

In an international traditional manner *Bredo Greve* designed the *Technical University* at *Trondheim* in 1910. A Gothic Revival building, this is very northern European in its dour, monumental

127, Plate 40 View and detail of Oslo City Hall, 1933–50, Arneberg and Poulsson

façade, solidly built in rough-hewn granite blocks. Chief architect of this school of work was *Olaf Nordhagen*, who carried out the extensive restoration and reconstruction work necessary at this time on *Trondheim Cathedral*, the great Gothic monument of Norway (Vol. 2). Nordhagen built the *Library* at *Bergen*, which is also of rough-hewn blocks and in a simplified Romanesque style. His most interesting achievement is in the immense hydro-electric *power station* at *Rjukan*, deep in the mountains of central/southern Norway. This is in a modern Baroque, a monumental design in large stone blocks, set into the hillside. It has columns with modern capitals and sparing classical decoration. The village *church* of 1914–15 is in similar vein to traditional Norwegian style, blending suitably into the wild landscape.

A simplified form of classicism, akin to the contemporary English kind, was used for public buildings. *Haugesund Town Hall* (1931, *Munthe-Kaas*) is one example, *Magnus Poulsson's Shipping Offices* in the railway station square in *Oslo* (1917) another.

In the late 1920s and early 1930s the ideas of the Bauhaus and functionalism percolated through to the north. An early skyscraper building based on these ideas is the *Horn Building* in *Egertorvet*, Oslo (1929). Other structures were built by *Lars Backer*, *Gudolf Blackstad* and *Munthe-Kaas*. The outstanding example, which illustrates the Norwegian national approach, is the famous *City Hall* of *Oslo* (**127**, **Plate 40**). This immense building in red brick stands near the waterfront, where the whole area is laid out with lower buildings, fountains and gardens.

It was begun in 1933, but the interior was not completed till 1950. The walls of the large hall and galleries are covered with paintings and tapestries depicting Norwegian life and art. They are of varying standard, some naïve and garish, others more successful. The latter are refreshingly charming and show nothing of the decadence to be seen in more recent mural work in the civic buildings of capitals further south, for example the UNESCO Building in Paris.

Post-war Norwegian architecture is entirely modern and takes several of the accepted forms. A good and well-designed example of the very simple approach is the large *government building complex* in *Oslo* in Henrik Ibsen's Gate by *Erling Viksjø*, from 1958. There is a tall 14-storey block, with decoration incised on the plain end wall, adjoining low curved blocks, which include the new post office. The treatment is of good quality, light-coloured pebble rough concrete. The first new buildings for the *University of Oslo*, at *Blindern* outside the city had been built in the late 1930s, in red brick, by *Bryn* and *Ellefsen*. These are in plain, functionalist style. The whole complex has been greatly enlarged since the war in the usual pattern of tall and low rectangular blocks in glass, steel and brick. The layout is successful, the quality of building good – very similar to new universities in other northern countries.

In more nationally traditional style is a late work by *Magnus Poulsson*. His modern *church* at *Gravberget*, in the woods near the Swedish border (1955), is Norwegian timber church-building at its best, using traditional methods but on modern lines. Another, more recent, church is the one at *Eystein* on the *E.6 Arctic Highway* near Hjerkinn. This is of white rubble-covered concrete with purplish grey roofing and a wooden sculptured figure under the rose window (**128**). It is a charming, well-built church, entirely suited to its lonely surroundings on the high mountain plateau.

Norway has built several satellite towns since the war; *Lambertseter* near Oslo, for example, and new towns to replace those destroyed by the Germans in the invasion of 1940 at places like

128 Eystein Church, Norway, c. 1970

Kristiansund and *Molde* in the lonely island area west of Trondheim. While the designs are good but not outstanding, the workmanship, quality of materials and landscaping is excellent.

Finland

Russia finally conquered Finland and removed the country from the sphere of Swedish influence in 1809, at the same time granting autonomy to the Finns. In architecture a renascent nationalism was reflected in a return to building in local materials and traditional structural methods. Three architects, in particular, showed great talent and originality in this work: *Sonck, Saarinen* and *Lindgren*. Their buildings are strongly plastic, with dramatic massing. The material, whether stone or timber, is ruggedly handled and left in great blocks or beams. There are picturesque towers and roofs based on Finnish Medieval churches and castles. *Lars Sonck* (1870–1956) is the most personal of the group. His buildings are always clearly stamped with his characteristic style and handling. His *Cathedral* at *Tampere* is his best work, built 1902–7 in rough-hewn granite blocks. It is a large building, finely built and proportioned, sited on a hill. The grey of the granite contrasts pleasingly with the red tiled roofs and spires (**131**, **Plate 42**). The interior is quite different. It is a Romanesque structure but decorated in a mixture of Byzantine and Art Nouveau motifs. The quality of workmanship, the lighting, colour and spatial handling are magnificent.

Sonck's other great church is the *Kalliö Church* in *Helsinki* (1909–12). It also is very large, crowning a steep hill, and it has an immensely tall central tower and eastern apse, which dominate the Helsinki skyline. This church too is built of rugged, grey blocks. The exterior is dramatic and sombre; the interior, in contrast, is wide and brightly lit. Its interior is plainer than that of Tampere Cathedral but it has a characteristic gallery and capitals. It shows Sonck moving away from national romanticism towards a more modern approach. Highly personalized is his *Telephone Exchange* in *Helsinki* (1905), a building constructed of vast, rugged granite blocks and with his individual style of decoration in window shafts, especially in the oriel window in the tower. This massive style of building in granite blocks is reminiscent of Henry Hobson Richardson's struc-

tures of the 1880s in the United States, for example his Allegheny County Jail in Pittsburgh and his Marshall Field Wholesale Store in Chicago (**Plate 41**).

Eliel Saarinen (1873–1950) joined Lindgren in partnership. Until his emigration to the United States in the early 1920s, Saarinen was the most outstanding architect in Finland in this period of fine building. His most famous structure is the *Railway Station* at *Helsinki* (**130**), from which he gained an international reputation. This too is in granite blocks, rugged, dramatic and stark. Inside, the decoration is somewhat Art Nouveau, superimposed on great Romanesque arcuated construction. Saarinen's *National Museum* in *Helsinki* (1905) is typical of the Finnish national style of the time, but his *Town Hall* at *Lahti* (1912) shows his progression towards the internationality of modern architecture.

Finland gained complete independence in 1917. The urge of her artists to express their national feelings in their several media quickly evaporated. In the 1920s, as in the other Scandinavian countries, Neo-classicism returned to Finland, this time in a plainer version comparable to Lutyens in England and the earlier work of Asplund in Sweden. *Kalliö's Municipal Theatre* in *Tampere* (1912) is a traditional example, but *J. S. Sirén's Parliament Building* in *Helsinki* (1927–31) is typical of the formal, simplified classicism. The monumental block is approached by an immense flight of steps on which is an impressive, lofty colonnade.

By 1930, the Neo-classical phase was passing and Finland adopted modern architecture. In the years before the Second World War, the country was beginning to establish its position as a leading nation in this field; after 1945 its European preeminence was confirmed.

Finland's greatest modern architect, *Alvar Aalto* (1898–1976) studied at the Helsinki Polytechnic and graduated in 1921. After a few early designs in simple classical form, he soon moved towards functionalism, setting aside all purely decorative features and concentrating on fundamental structure. Two of his works of the interwar years became classics in modern architecture and made him internationally famous. Highly original was his *City Library* at *Viipuri* (1927–35), where he first used his acoustic system of insulating wood strips in ceiling design. Viipuri was Finland's second city but was lost to the country when it was ceded to the Soviet Union in the Second World War. The library was seriously damaged but has now been rebuilt. Aalto's other outstanding building of the time is the *Tuberculosis Sanatorium* at *Paimio* (1929-33) – a most original, plastic design.

Another important contributor to Finland's modern building before 1939 was *Erik Bryggman* (1891–1955). He graduated from the Helsinki Polytechnic in 1916 and spent much of his working life in *Turku*. In the years 1930–40 he designed his best works, which include the *Library* for the *Abô Akademie* in 1935–6 and many houses. His most original and successful work is the *Cemetery Resurrection Chapel* at Turku (1939). Built in the cemetery on the outskirts of the city, it is a simple,

white, rectangular structure with a colonnade and tower. The interior is most effective. Covered by a flattish barrel-vaulted ceiling, there is a colonnade and windows along one whole side, while beside the altar at the far end is a tall, large, plain window, which not only floods the whole interior with light but also makes one feel as though the pine woods outside are really part of the interior. This ability to blend and affiliate architecture with natural surroundings is an especial and beautiful quality of Finnish architecture and one not confined to modern work alone.

A number of other architects were designing good-quality modern structures in the 1930s. *Pauli Blomstedt* (1900–35) was responsible for the *Finnish Savings Bank* in *Helsinki* and the pleasant,

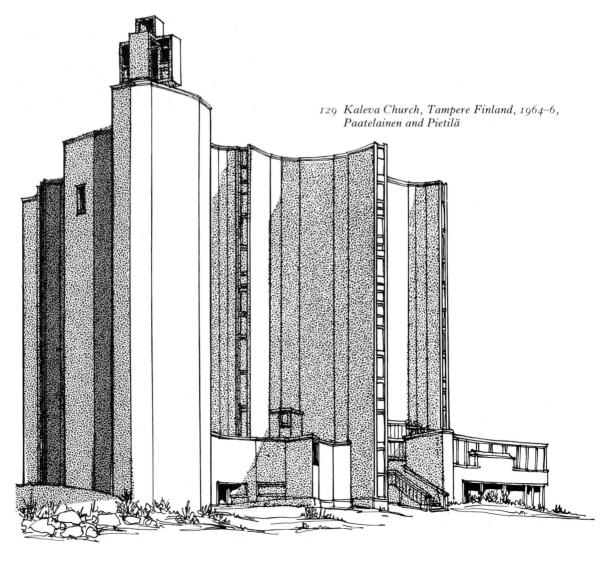

129 Kaleva Church, Tampere Finland, 1964–6, Paatelainen and Pietilä

Plate 41 (left) Telephone Exchange detail, Helsinki, 1905, Lars Sonck

Plate 42 (right) West Doorway, Tampere Cathedral, 1902–7, Lars Sonck

130 Railway Station, Helsinki, 1904–14, Eliel Saarinen

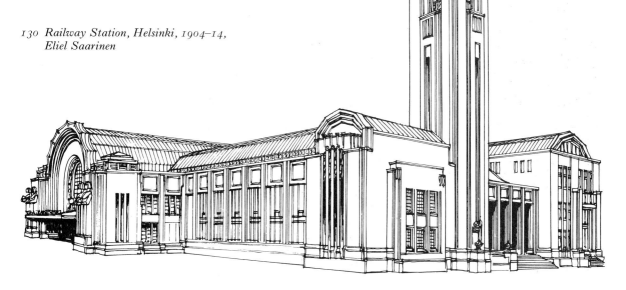

distinguished, luxury hotel at *Hämeenlinna*, the *Aulanko Hotel*, which is built beside the lake in most beautiful surroundings. This, like most of Finland's buildings of the period, is plain, white and well proportioned. A good example of the years just before the war is the *Stadium at Helsinki*, built for the Olympic Games of 1940 (though the games had to be cancelled). This and the Olympic Village were the most modern structures of their kind at this time.

After 1945, Finnish architecture began to realize the promise of originality that had shown itself in the 1930s. The modern style has continued a steady progress since. Led by Alvar Aalto and supported by his talented colleagues, a Finnish school of architecture has evolved. It is characteristic and national, expressing in which, to the Finns, is the most important of the arts a contemporary fulfilment of both functional and aesthetic perfection. In Finland, as in other countries, there is a quantity of average, typical modern architecture in simple but monotonous block formation, but the proportion of interesting, vital ideas, schemes and projects is greater than elsewhere. The Finns have adapted their modern architecture to suit their difficult climate and not to obtrude on their landscape. The architecture is, as it should be in any age, an integral part of the environment, providing what is needed for the comfort, inspiration and efficiency of mankind but never offending or causing distress to the beholder and user. Finnish modern architecture, apart from its fine designs, interesting form and detail, has an unusually high standard of quality in building and finish. It maintains a uniform standard not reached by any other European country. That this is possible in a country where most of it is in extreme cold and darkness for much of the year, where the population is less than five million and not wealthy, should shame those richer lands of the west whose performance has been markedly so much lower.

After a war in which Finland lost a large section of her territory to the Soviet Union, the country faced the problem of housing and employing, within its reduced borders, over 400,000 people who had been displaced by the Russians. This represented, at that time, one-eighth of the population. In addition, Finland, like other countries participating in the war, had lost many buildings and had several years of leeway to make up. The task of so much building by so small a nation was

formidable, and work of the 1950s is accordingly noted more for quantity than quality, though the standards here never fell as low as in a number of similarly-placed European countries at this time. As the urgency slowly abated, the work of the 1960s showed much more originality and enterprise. Finnish architects are skilled in the handling of wood – their national material – as well as brick and reinforced concrete. Shortage of steel means a greater use of these materials and less rectangular block skyscraper building.

Of the new towns and housing centres, *Tapiola* is justly famous. About 5 miles (8 km) from Helsinki, it covers a large area of land and is spread out to make attractive use of existing trees and the countryside. The houses and other buildings are sited naturally and pleasantly, not laid out in formal rectangles. The satellite town was begun in 1952, its chief architect *Aarne Ervi* (1910–77), who designed the central area. The lay-out comprises a large lake with swimming pools and fountains and behind it a pedestrian precinct shopping area and a 13-storey tower block, which has a restaurant and terrace on the top floor. The housing is of mixed development, pleasingly planned and built. The only poor building is the church, its exterior mercifully hidden by trees. The interior is a bright cube, devoid of any atmosphere, built in grey breeze-blocks and boarded concrete.

Among the many other fine new town centres and housing developments are the *Central Square* at *Vaasa* (1963) by *Viljo Rewell* (1910–64), the island site at *Säynätsalo* (1950-2) by Alvar Aalto, the predominantly civic *development* at *Kotka* and nearby *Sunila* and the *town centre* at *Seinäjoki* (**132**). This is an extensive complex, begun in 1951 and still continuing. A number of buildings of the civic centre are designed by Aalto, of which the *Church* and the *Theatre* have been built. The church is of brick, painted white and has a tall, slender, separate campanile. The theatre is faced with purple ceramic tiling. It is an unusual shape and a most effective design supported on its simple colonnade. There are also two *libraries* and *halls*.

Alvar Aalto has contributed extensively to the high quality of the architecture of post-war Finland. Among his other works are the *Church* at *Vuoksenniska*, near Imatra (1959), the *Enso-Gutzeit* office block (1962) and his *House of Culture* (1958) both in Helsinki. At the end of the war, he was responsible for re-planning the town of *Rova-*

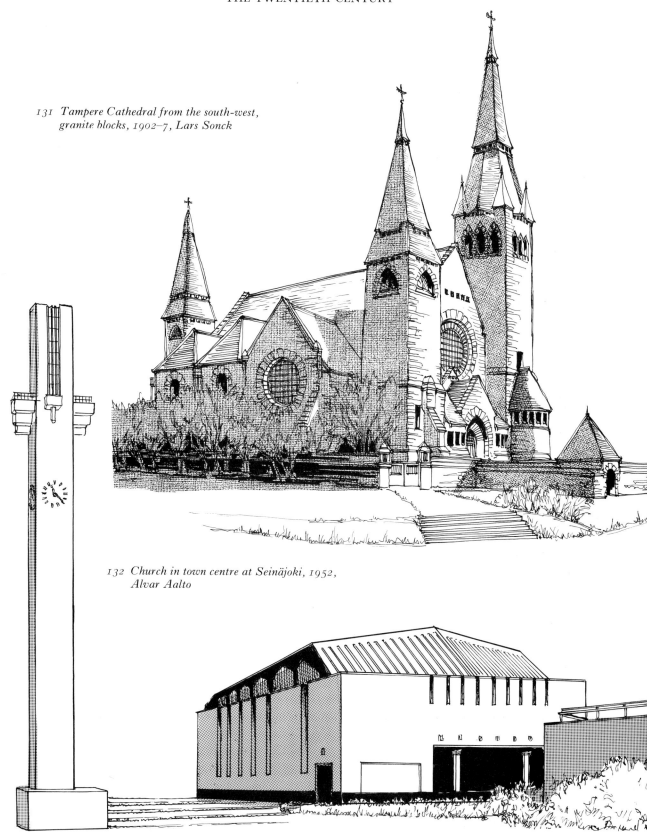

131 *Tampere Cathedral from the south-west,*
granite blocks, 1902–7, Lars Sonck

132 *Church in town centre at Seinäjoki, 1952,*
Alvar Aalto

niemi, adminstrative capital of Finnish Lapland. This town, close to the Arctic Circle, was almost totally destroyed by German forces in 1944. It was rebuilt according to Aalto's plans, and three of the more important civic buildings were designed by him: the *library, conference centre* and *town offices* (1965 onwards). Rovaniemi is an important centre for long-distance travel communication, and in the rebuilt town all the skills and knowledge of a technological age have been tapped to make living and working there pleasant during the long winter ice and darkness: triple glazing for windows and excellent artificial lighting, for instance. Aalto's versatility and national qualities are shown particularly at the new *Technical University* at *Otaniemi*, between Helsinki and Tapiola. There are many buildings of red brick and grey granite laid out on a large, rolling and wooded site. There are close affinities here with Sussex University in England (p. 120). Quite different, however, are Aalto's *university centre* and *auditorium group*, which dominate the scene.

Of the many great post-war Finnish architects must be mentioned *Aarne Ervi, Aarno Ruusuvuori, Reima Pietilä* and *Raili Paatelainen*. Ervi's work at Tapiola has been referred to (p. 142). He was also responsible for some new *University* buildings at *Turku* where he built the *Library* in 1954. Among other works, two of the other architects have been responsible for designing two of the most original and satisfactory churches in modern materials and idiom erected anywhere in post-war Europe. Acoustically, liturgically and aesthetically they are exciting and functional. Ruusuvuori created the *Church* at *Hyvinkää* (just north of Helsinki) in unusual triangular tent-like form, in shining white concrete and glass, set in the woodlands on the edge of the town. The interior is striking, with its windows, galleries and roofing echoing endlessly, but not repetitively, the triangular motif. In sunlight especially, the interior lighting effects through the beautiful glass panels are dramatic.

The *Kaleva Church* at *Tampere*, built on a grassy mound in the suburb of that name, stands on a triangular site in a new housing estate. It was the work of Paatelainen. The walls of multi-planes and curves are of uniform height and are faced with cream coloured, composition tiling, which gives a glowing, oatmeal consistency all over and delineates clearly the undulating character of the exterior (**129**).

The interior is rather like the church at Royan in France (p. 146), but here there is no gallery. The immense height lends an overwhelming impression of light and space. This is Baroque architecture in a modern idiom. The simple materials of concrete and plain pale-coloured wood are handled imaginatively and in a fine tradition of craftsmanship. The undulating ceiling is in a darkish concrete and ribbed. The walls are plain white concrete, and the window glass is also plain. The pews, choir stalls, organ casing and altar sculpture are of beautifully-finished wood.

East Europe:
The Soviet Union

Before the First World War Russian architecture was still based on the classical tradition, generally in a heavy, over-ornamented Baroque style tinged with oriental and Byzantine forms.

Typical is the *Kiev Opera House* of 1901 by *Shretera*. It is set in a square laid out with four-storey apartment blocks in the same decorative style. Art Nouveau was seen chiefly in paintings, interior decoration and, above all, choreography. In architecture its effect was limited, its chief exponent being *Schekhtel*. The finest structure of the period is the *Kazansky Railway Station* in *Moscow* by *Alexei Shchusev* (**134**). It is derivative, but its origins are manifold, eastern and western, ancient and medieval. It is a richly-decorated, colourful and successful design.

The Revolution of 1917 provided not only the chance for society to be transformed but also tremendous opportunities artistically to break from the eclecticism of the past and provide new designs that would both reflect and encourage the new society. The younger architects, in particular, saw this as a great chance to create an art form in building worthy of the ideas of a Workers' State. From 1920 it became clear to all such architects that modern architecture was the building style for socialism. The State now took responsibility and handled the financial support for all building: civic, town planning, industrial, technical, housing and education.

There was, for some years, more discussion than action. Partly this was due to administrative disorganisation and the Soviet Union's economic position after the war and the Revolution. Money was not available in sufficient quantity. *Constructi-*

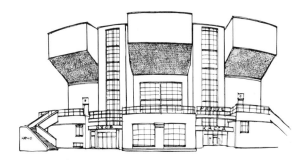

133 Workers' Club, Ivan Rusakov House of Culture, Moscow, USSR, 1927–9, Konstantin Melnikov

vism was one of the themes of the new architecture, led by such men as Eliezer M. *(El) Lissitzsky* (1890–1941), who had studied at Darmstadt before the war. The theory was that this new architectural form would express the collective aims and desires of the masses in art and building. Materials must be produced by Soviet industry. New materials – glass, steel, concrete – were correct and nothing must be on or in a building that was not strictly functional or useful. The exponents of this theme were convinced that such buildings would have beauty and satisfaction that would inspire and educate all the people. The structures would be a blend of the greatest achievements of man in science, technology and art. Unfortunately, little was ever built, and experience showed, as decades passed, that 'the masses' resolutely preferred their buildings in familiar traditional style, of traditional

materials not glass and concrete and with plenty of decoration on them: a revelation manifested to well-intentioned modern architects not only in the Soviet Union.

The years 1925–32 were a time of trial and experiment in modern architecture in the Soviet Union. There was not a great deal of contact with the West and therefore little to guide architects in their new theories. Of the older men, established in their profession before 1917, some began to adapt themselves to the new régime and continued to build in a semi-traditional vein. These included *Shchusev, Shchuko* and *Zholtovsky*. Many others emigrated to the west.

Of the younger men who established themselves and designed in modern manner were the *Vesnin brothers* (Alexander, Leonid and Victor), who evolved a number of projects of which little was actually built. The most successful of these younger men was *Konstantin Melnikov*. With the radical changes in social structure and methods of government, the types of buildings erected had changed too. Private houses, churches and cathedrals were no longer needed. Instead were built

134 Kazansky Railway Station, Moscow, USSR, 1913–26, Alexei Shchusev

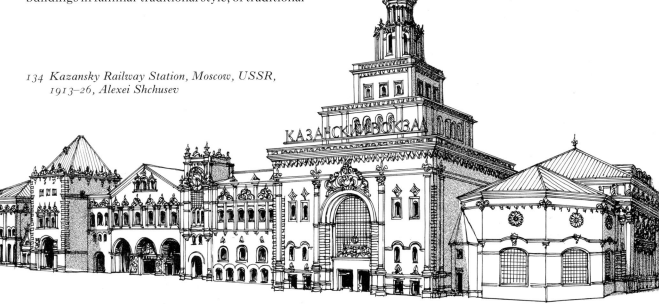

Plate 43 Centrosoyuz adminstrative building (now Central Statistical Office of the USSR), Moscow, 1929–36, Le Corbusier together with Pierre Jeanneret and the Soviet architect Nikolai Kolli

Plate 44 CMEA Complex (buildings of the Council for Mutual Economic Assistance), 1964–8, Mikhail Posokhin, Ashot Mindoyantz and Vladimir Suirsky

palaces for the Soviets (probably the nearest equivalent to town hall and council offices), communal housing and, a specifically communist type of building, the *workers' club*. This was a multi-purpose building. It included theatre, cinema, library, facilities for study, reading, discussion and light entertainment. This was the class of building for which Melnikov became well-known; he built seven between 1925 and 1929, of which several survive, including the *Club Rusakov* in *Moscow* (**133**) 1925–6. Melnikov's designs for these and other structures were, considering he and his colleagues had so little contact with the West, surprisingly similar to the functionalist ideas of the Bauhaus. The Moscow club is very plain, angular and built of modern materials.

Later modern architects in the Soviet Union had some Western examples to study, as, for example, the *Centrosoyuz*, now the Ministry of Light Industries, built in *Moscow* 1929–36 by *Le Corbusier*. This large building of glass and steel curtain-walled façades and terminal blocks of concrete on *pilotis* still survives. It is now a familiar design but was a prototype in 1929 (**Plate 43**).

Several new projects were designed in the 1920s by younger architects, but by the early 1930s support for modern architecture began to weaken. The Soviet Union lost its first idealistic fervour for communist principles and under Josef Stalin became a dictatorship. As in the parallel contemporary régimes in Germany and Italy, attenuated classical architecture became the accepted style.

To the frustration of the modern architects, the 'masses' much preferred this. In the nineteenth century classicism had been the prerogative of the privileged classes, now it was ubiquitous, backed by government decree and popular support. Now, in simplified form, it was available, with thanks, for all. Chief examples in the 1930s were the *Moskva Hotel* (1936, *Shchusev*), the *Supreme Soviet of the Ukraine* at *Kiev* (1938, *Fomin*) (**Plate 46**), the extensive layout of shops and apartments in *Gorki Street*, the *main street* of *Moscow* (1938, *Mordinov*), and the *Lenin Library* in *Moscow* (1938, *Shchuko* and *Gelfreikh* (**135**). These are all well-designed and built classical structures comparable with Western examples of the time.

The most impressive construction in this style was to be the *Palace of the Soviets* in *Moscow*. A competition was held in 1934; 200 architects entered, many from western Europe; including Gropius, Mendelsohn and Le Corbusier. The Soviet hierarchy decided on a traditional building and appointed *B. Iofan, V. Shchouko* and colleagues to carry out their Russian design. The model showed a fantastic, vast-scale, classical structure in diminishing stages, overlooking the Kremlin and dwarfing it. The total height of the building was to be 1,365 ft (417 m), the tallest in the world. This included a totally out-of-scale immense statue of Lenin 325 ft (100 m) in height. The Palace was to contain museums, an amphitheatre, halls, an auditorium, library and government rooms. The work had not progressed far when Hitler's armies invaded the Soviet Union. After 1945 the climate of opinion had changed, the building was never erected and Moscow gained a large open-air swimming pool on the site.

However, the Stalinist form of classical architecture – a mixture of Baroque, nineteenth-century heavy grandeur and the large-scale approach traditional to the Russians – continued to develop after 1945 and lasted until the early 1960s. Typical are the immense skyscrapers, owing something to the early twentieth century American pattern, which were erected as universities, government offices and hotels, not only in the Soviet Union but in all the eastern European satellites as well. In *Moscow* is the greatest of them all, the *Lomonosov State University*, built on the Lenin Hills on the fringe of the city (**136**). There is also the very similar *Hotel Ukraina* in *Moscow*, the apartment block in *Vassaniya Square* and the *Traffic Ministry* at the Red Gate, all of the 1950s. In *Kiev*, the main street, the *Kreshchatik*, was rebuilt in this style in the 1950s, after almost total destruction during the War, with many civic buildings, as was also *Stalinallee* in *East Berlin*. This was the first main street to be rebuilt after the War; it is now called *Karl Marx Allee*. All this work is classical in basis, especially fenestration and decoration, but there is an oriental and Byzantine quality also, blended with the American skyscraper central tower and steeple designs of the period just before the First World War in New York, such as the Woolworth Building (1913).

An admirable achievement in the Soviet Union has been the building of the *Moscow Underground Railway* system or *Metro*. It was begun before the war and has been continued since. Apart from being technically and administratively an efficient system (a rarity in the Soviet Union), it is aesthetically the most original in the world. Each station is different in design and décor. The most interesting pre-war station is *Dynamo*, built 1938 by *Tschetschulin*, which has a fine sculptured

135 The Lenin Library, Moscow, 1929–41, Shchuko and Gelfreikh

136 The Lomonosov State University, Hill of Lenin, Moscow, 1949–53, Rudniev, Chernisev, Abrosimov, Chrjakov and Nasomov

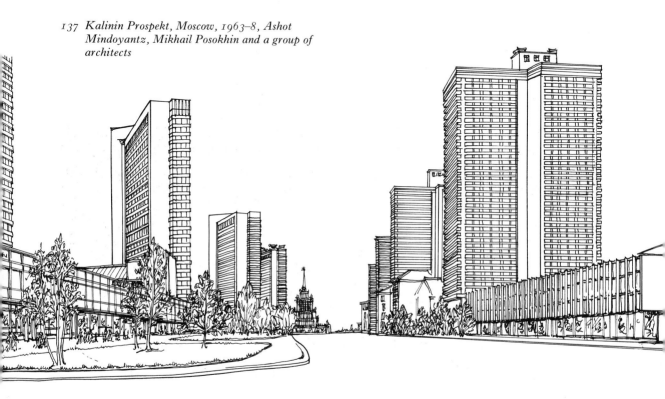

137 Kalinin Prospekt, Moscow, 1963–8, Ashot Mindoyantz, Mikhail Posokhin and a group of architects

Plate 45 (above) Dynamo Station, Moscow Underground, 1938, Tschetschulin

Plate 46 (below) Supreme Soviet of the Ukraine Building, Kiev, 1938, Ivan Fomin

Plate 47 Hotel Kosmos, Moscow, 1980, Victor Andreyev, Trifon Zaikin and Vladimir Steiskal

exterior building on classical pattern (**Plate 45**). Of the post-war stations, Komsomol and the Botanic Gardens are among the best. *Komsomol* was built in 1952 by *Shchusev* and *Warwarin*. It is of fine quality in materials and craftsmanship, but more Edwardian than of the 1952 vintage. The ceilings are rococo and Baroque decorated plaster; the semi-apsidal entrance for the trains is ornamented by ceramic tile murals representing Soviet work and achievement on one side and, on the other, the story of the building of the Metro showing both men and women labouring at laying track. The *Botanic Gardens Station* (1952, *Gelfreikh* and *Minkus*), now re-named *Prospekt Mira*, is in Baroque/Byzantine classical form, with a lattice-patterned barrel-vaulted ceiling in stucco supported on immense, squat columns with vast Corinthian-type figured capitals. The scheme is in white marble and glazed white ceramic tiling with gilt decoration. The upstairs booking hall is like an ornate Edwardian version of a Nile temple with Egyptian lotus columns and capitals. All the

stations are derivative but the variety, quality and robust vitality compel admiration.

Since 1960 the Soviets have turned to the international mode of modern architecture. They have taken to glass, steel and concrete boxes that differ little from those elsewhere in Europe except that what is being built in Moscow in the 1980s is similar to what was erected in western Europe in the 1970s and earlier. The *Kalinin Prospekt* in *Moscow* (**137**) is the show boulevard of shops, offices and apartments. It looks much like a street in any capital of western Europe, but the road is far wider and longer and the individual flats are much smaller and less well equipped, especially in the bathrooms, heating, hot water systems and kitchens. But they represent progress to Soviet citizens. There is also, in the centre of the city an elegant 31-storey tower set in an extensive building complex. Erected 1964-8 by *Posokhin, Mindoyantz* and others, it contains offices, a conference hall and hotel with curving façades to offset the monotony of the usual glass box. It is an elegant, well-designed structure of glass and steel (**Plate 44**). A link between these latest achievements and the Stalinist building era is provided by the *Palace of Congresses* in the *Kremlin*, built 1960–1 by *M. V. Posokhin*. This is a plain, functionalist type modern building, with much in common with Arne Jacobsen's town halls (p. 133). It is a beautifully finished structure in fine materials. Representative of the 1980s in the city is the semi-cylindrical tower of the Hotel Kosmos (**Plate 47**). On truly Russian scale, the hotel can accommodate 3,500 people

Romania and Bulgaria

The development of architecture during the twentieth century in Romania and Bulgaria shows the strength of influence from both the Soviet Union and the West. In Romania, the stronger influence has probably been from the West, in Bulgaria,

from the East. Classical-style architecture from the inter-war years still survives in Bucharest, though widescale demolition of buildings of all periods has been taking place in recent years in this city. This is of the same type of plain classicism, stripped of decoration and using only the orders and fenestration that was usual in the Soviet Union in the 1930s.

In post-war years Romania took up modern architecture earlier than the Soviet Union. Certainly Stalinist skyscrapers were built under Soviet influence; the immense *Casa Scinteia* in *Bucharest* (**139**) is the chief example. This occupies a fine site but the proportions are less satisfactory than the Moscow examples; it is too stumpy and squat. Apart from these buildings, which are not numerous, much of Romanian modern architecture is of good quality. In *Bucharest* there is a simple, elegant *Exhibition Pavilion* at the entrance to the *Village Museum*. The *State Circus* has a waved

138 Alexander Nevsky Cathedral, Sofia, Bulgaria, 1904–13, A. N. Pomerantsev

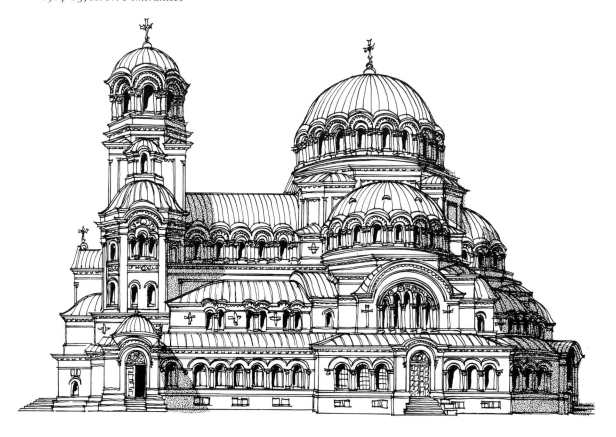

139 Casa Scinteia, Bucharest. Centre for printing and publishing in Romania

concrete roof after the style of Nervi in Rome (p. 105). In the centre of the city, in the *Piata Palatulei* (Palace Square), is an entirely modern layout comprising a domed *Congress Hall* and apartment blocks of different proportions and sizes. The ensemble is an attractive one with plenty of space and excellent landscaping of trees, lawns and flowers. This is in marked contrast to French equivalents. The Congress Hall is faced with cream-coloured stone set in stainless steel framing. Below the shallow dome are blue-grey mosaic panels.

There are many new *hotels* in the country built to attract the fast-growing tourist trade. The *Carpaţi* in *Braşov* is a good example. On the beaches round the Black Sea coast entire new resorts have been created on mere sand spits. The building of the large hotels and blocks of flats, together with the landscaping and successful growing of trees and flowers, especially roses, has been a remarkable technical and scientific feat. Like the Israelis, the Romanians have made the sand blossom. *Mamaia* is the best known of these resorts, 5 miles (8 km) north of Constanţa. Its sea front extends over a great distance along the sand spit, while the great lake of Siutghiol lies inland behind. In building more than 30 hotels here, as well as apartments, the Romanians had to begin from nothing and provide drinking water, electricity and drainage. The sea front is laid out in gardens with shops, post office, hairdressing salons and supermarkets; only cafés and restaurants are rare. The quality of building is good, if a little monotonous.

Bulgaria, a near neighbour of Romania, has for centuries been more strongly influenced by Russian art and architecture. The great *Cathedral of Sofia, Alexander Nevsky* (**138**) was built by a Soviet architect in honour of the Soviet liberators of the day. It is a large, flamboyant, impressive cathedral, its newly-gilded domes gleaming in the sunshine. The exterior is well proportioned and architecturally simple in structure though richly decorated in Byzantine tradition. The interior is even more Byzantine. Ionic marble columns divide the narthex from the five-aisled nave with its vast square piers. The windows are small but numerous. The entire interior is painted with scenes from the Bible; the style of these paintings varies from Byzantine formality to modern realism. From the interior of the great crossing cupola the bearded Pantocrator gazes down sternly like a Russian Tsar admonishing his people. The marble archbishop's throne has an impressive canopy over it, supported on columns with Byzantine drilled-hole capitals (Vol. 1), which, in turn, stand upon the backs of lions.

In *Sofia* also is the *Russian Orthodox Church* of *St Nikolai* (1913, by the Russian architect *Preobrajensky*). Much smaller than the cathedral, this is an interesting architectural pile, tall, dramatic and very Byzantine. With its small gilded onion domes surrounding the tall steeple topped by another such cupola, it is reminiscent of the cathedrals in the Moscow Kremlin (Vol. 1). There is a fine tall entrance porch decorated with paintings and mosaic.

As in the Soviet Union, classical architecture in different guises has been built for much of the twentieth century. The style before the First World War was, as in Russia, heavily-ornamented

Baroque, for example the *National Theatre* of *Sofia* of 1907. An inter-war example is the *University*, built in 1931 by the French architect *Breançon* on Petit Palais lines. The building has much more the appearance of belonging to the 1900–10 era in Paris than 1931. After 1945, the massive sky-scraper classicism of Stalinism came to Sofia in the buildings in *Lenin Square*, while the *Stadium* shows the very plain version of the Palace of Congresses type in Moscow.

Since 1955–60 modern architecture has been built in quantity in Bulgaria and, in particular, along the Black Sea coast in resorts like *Varna*, which are much like their Romanian equivalents.

Greece and Yugoslavia

Greek architecture has developed along Western lines. A poor country, the quantity of building was not extensive until after 1945 when the tourist trade began to increase quickly. A number of the better-known examples of modern architecture in Greece, especially in *Athens*, are by foreign architects; the *United States Embassy*, for example, by *Walter Gropius* and his Collaborative, and also the *Hilton Hotel*. Many of the numerous hotels built all over the country are well designed, comfortable and fine. They are by Greek architects, who have created varied designs on original lines and all carefully suited to their location. The interior décor is particularly attractive and unusual. The *Xenia* chain of hotels is a good example as at, for instance, the island of *Mykonos* (**140**) and at *Nauplia* in the *Peloponnese*. A hotel on more brutalist lines in its exterior structure and appear-ance is the *Amalia Hotel* at *Delphi*, built in 1966 by *Valsamakis*. This is particularly well designed for its magnificent site and for the interior, which is ideally suited to the climate.

Yugoslavia has followed a similar pattern. Again, the poverty of the country has been restrictive and, poised politically between East and West, the Western influence has been slower to develop than in Greece. Modern architecture of the 1950s in Yugoslavia was drab and dull, lacking good materials and original ideas. The work of the 1960s is much better, though the quality of finish and plumbing is still not always good. There has been much new building along the resorts of the whole *Adriatic Coast*, with problems of terrain even more difficult than those of the Romanians at Mamaìa. Here the mountains make communica-tions, transport and siting a problem, but the Yugoslavs are overcoming the difficulties and making some fine resorts.

Hungary

Hungarian architecture before the First World War was still strongly influenced by Austria. There was some sign of Art Nouveau and still much eclecticism. A typical building surviving in war-damaged *Budapest* is that of *Ibusz*, the State Tourist Organization, built in 1909.

140 Xenia-Lite Hotel, Mykonos, Greece, 1960s, Aris Konstantinidis

In the years since 1945 Hungary has, like the other countries of the communist bloc, been influenced by the Soviet Union. A severe, but late, use of classicism is the *Railway Station* façade at *Györ* (1959), which has completely plain columns like Piacentini's Via Roma in Turin of 1938 (p. 105). Above the columns is a sculptured panel notable for its Soviet influence. The *National Theatre* in *Budapest* is a structure of the 1960s. This indicates the now completely modern approach with its semi-abstract, all-over decoration to the rectangular block façade.

From the later 1960s onwards, as Hungary began to follow more Western political policies, architecture reflected these moves. The tourist trade increased markedly, and a rash of new hotels were built to serve this influx, notably in *Budapest* and in holiday areas such as the *Lake Balaton* region. Typical were the *Hotel Duna-Intercontinental* in Budapest, architect *József Finta* (1967–9), a 360-room plain, modern design in concrete, steel and glass built on the river bank, and the *Hotel Budapest*, situated on the *Buda* site of the Danube, by *György Szragh* (1967), which is a circular design predating the similar Grand Metropolitan Hotel in Knightsbridge in London (Seifert, 1974). Hungary also produced some 'brutalist' boarded concrete structures (p. 76), for example, the *Hospital and Clinic* at *Kazincbarcika* by György Janossy (1967) and some fine modern churches not dissimilar to those which Finland made famous (p. 144). Typical was the *Roman Catholic Church* at *Hollóhaza* by *László Csaba* (1967). This is very geometrical and stark on the exterior. Built of reinforced concrete, the body of the church is pyramidal in form and, adjacent, is a tall triangular tower.

Czechoslovakia

The pattern of architectural design followed here had much in common with that in Austria. The Art Nouveau manner was led by *Jan Kotěra*, a pupil of Wagner (pp. 94–5). He and his colleagues designed a number of houses and stores.

Soon after the First World War, the ideas of modern architecture percolated to Czechoslovakia and, from 1921 onwards, a number of 'functionalist' architects were practising. These included *Josef Fuchs*, *Jaromír Krejcar* and *F. M. Černy*. The *Prague Sample Fairs Palace*, built 1924–8 by Tyl and Fuchs, was an early example of glass curtain-walling.

By 1925–7 modern architecture was establishing itself in Czechoslovakia and designs were in advance of most countries of western Europe, with the exception of Germany, Switzerland and Italy. Buildings such as department stores, hotels, churches and civic structures were being erected under such architects as *Polaček*, *Gočár*, and *Bohuslav Fuchs*, whose Avion Hotel at Brno (1927) was typical.

In the 1930s, as in many western European countries, large *housing estates* were planned and built. A modern example of the time was the *Baba* residential district of Prague, laid out 1928–32 by *Pavel Janák*. This still exists, though it appears old-fashioned today in its severe 'functionalist' blocks, almost totally devoid of decorative or architectural relief. A new town was planned at *Zlín* – now *Gottwaldov* – where both industrial development and appropriate housing with educational and shopping needs were provided. It was designed by *František Gahura* who was also responsible for the glass and steel department store *Centrum* in Brno, built in 1946–52 and *Vladimir Karfík* and largely built 1928–39; an innovation at this time.

The Second World War did not cause great devastation to most Czech towns and cities and, as architects had not been forced to emigrate for political reasons to the same extent as in Germany, the modern architectural tradition survived in Czechoslovakia. In 1945, however, the power of the new régime from the East established the usual stranglehold on artistic endeavour and enterprise. A period of architectural stagnation followed from which there was only just emerging a new energy and initiative when the Soviet occupation of the country in 1968 put an end to hopes of its success.

In the 1960s a new generation of younger architects were beginning to design in the current modern mode. Before this the Stalinist Moscow style of skyscraper blocks had been *de rigueur* for large commissions in Czechoslovakia as elsewhere in eastern Europe (**136** and **139**). The *International Hotel* in Prague is a typical example, being a facsimile, on smaller scale (as befits a satellite country), of the Hotel Ukraina in Moscow. Among the talented new group of architects was *Karel Prager*, who designed the glass curtain-walled *Institute of Macromolecular Chemistry* of the Czechoslovak Academy of Sciences in the Petřiny district of Prague in 1964. This is an area of the city that has been developed as a new dormitory suburb since 1955. Another building, this time of low-level design, planned in a curving elevation, is the *Soviet Chamber of Commerce* in *Prague*, designed in 1964, by *Holuša, Kulišták* and *Leniček*.

The most interesting of Prager's designs is the new *Parliament House* in *Prague*, next to the National Museum at the head of Wenceslaus Square. The new building is square in form and carried out in glass, metal and stone. Tragically, the architect, still in his thirties, was deprived of his commission and disbarred from his profession because of his sympathetic support for the previous, Dubcek, régime.

Poland

Because of the extensive devastation of nearly all Polish cities in the Second World War, it is difficult to find good examples of early twentieth-century architecture. Naturally, the Poles, when rebuilding their cities, have attempted to restore and re-create the great periods of their architectural heritage – the Middle Ages, Renaissance and Baroque eras – and twentieth-century work has been replaced by building styles current after 1960.

Modern architecture did not develop early in Poland and most of the buildings in the modern style erected in the inter-war years were by foreigners. These included *Hans Poelzig's* water tower in *Poznan*, 1910, *Hans Sharoun's* hostel at *Wroclaw* (1929) and *Erich Mendelsohn's* store in the same city. The last of these, built by Mendelsohn as the *Peterdorff Store* in 1927 (p. 87), miraculously survives and illustrates how far ahead of its time this design was, with its glass, metal and concrete construction, horizontal emphasis and curving corner turning.

Little new building of note appeared in the years after 1945; too great an effort was needed to provide shelter and work for the homeless population. This was especially true of the capital, Warsaw, 80 per cent of whose buildings were destroyed or gutted. In the late 1950s and early 1960s Polish architecture, as elsewhere in Eastern Europe, was dominated by Moscow. The *Palace of Culture* in Warsaw, designed 1952–6 by *Rudniev*, one of the architects of the Lomonosov State University in Moscow (**136**), shows the usual approach of this type of building. In the later 1960s, modern building, also very much on Soviet pattern, has been erected. *Workers' flats* in housing estates are, like those in Leningrad and Moscow, dull and blockish, while the *boulevards* of *Warsaw*, like *Marszalkowska*, show offices, flats, cinemas, and so on laid out just like Moscow's Kalinin Prospekt (**137**) and East Berlin's Karl Marx Allee (p. 94).

There are now signs that more interesting architecture is being designed and studied. The interior of the main hall at *Warsaw airport*, for example, shows a livelier approach, as do one or two of the new *churches*. In certain cities the slowly developing tourist trade with the West is encouraging more interesting designs in hotels along Western lines, for example, the *Cracovia Hotel* in *Cracow* and the *Orbis-Monopol Hotel* in *Wroclaw*.

Glossary

The bold reference figures in brackets refer to illustrations in the book

Abacus The top member of a capital, usually a square or curved-sided slab of stone or marble (**17**)

Abutment The solid mass of masonry or brickwork from which an arch springs or against which it abuts (**Plate 7**)

Acanthus A leaf form used in classical ornament

Ambulatory A passage or aisle giving access in a church between the choir, with high altar, and the eastern apse

Anthemion A type of classical ornament based upon the honeysuckle flower

Apse Semicircular or polygonal termination to a church most commonly to be found on the eastern and transeptal terminations (**25**)

Arcade A series of arches, open or closed with masonry, supported on columns or piers (**37**)

Architrave The lowest member of the classical entablature

Arcuated construction Wherein the structure is supported on arches

Articulation The designing, defining and dividing up of a façade into vertical and horizontal architectural members (**3**)

Ashlar Hewn and squared stones prepared for building

Astylar A classical façade without columns or pilasters

Attic In Renaissance and later classical architecture an upper storey above the cornice (**45**)

Baldacchino A canopy supported on decorative pillars, suspended from the roof or projecting from a wall and carried on brackets, set over an altar or throne

Barrel vault A continuous vault in round section like a tunnel (**54**)

Cantilever A specially shaped beam or other member – for example, a staircase tread – which is supported securely at one end and carries a load at the other, free, end or with the load distributed evenly along the beam. A cantilever bracket is used to support a cornice or balcony of considerable projection. The cantilever principle is widely used in bridge design

Capital The crowning feature of a column or pilaster

Caryatid Sculptured female figure in the form of a support or column (**1**)

Centering A structure, usually made of wood, set up to support a dome, vault or arch, until construction is complete

Chevet Term given to a circular or polygonal apse when surrounded by an ambulatory from which radiate chapels

Chevron ornament Romanesque decoration in zig zag form

Cimborio Spanish term for lantern or fenestrated cupola

Clerestorey, Clearstorey The upper storey in a church generally pierced by a row of windows

Conch The domed ceiling of a semicircular apse (**13, 54**)

Console A decorative scrolled bracket used in classical architecture to support a cornice

Cornice The crowning member of a classical entablature

Coupled columns In classical architecture where the wall articulation is designed with the columns in pairs (**27**)

Crocket A projecting block of stone carved in Gothic foliage on the inclined sides of pinnacles and canopies

Crossing The central area in a cruciform church where the transepts cross the nave and choir arm; Above this space is generally set a tower or cupola

Cruciform A plan based on the form of a cross

Curtain wall In modern architecture this is in general used to describe an external non-loadbearing wall composed of repeated modular elements generally of glass in metal framing (**105**)

Cusp Point forming the foliations in Gothic tracery

Drum The circular or poly-sided walling, usually pierced with windows, supporting a dome (**51**)

Engaged column One that is attached to the wall behind it

Entablature The continuous horizontal lintel made up of mouldings and supported by columns characteristic of classical architecture (**21**)

Entasis Taken from the Greek word for distension, this is a carefully and mathematically calculated convex curving along the outline of a column shaft. It is designed to counteract the optical illusion that a shaft bounded by straight lines appears to be concavely curved. In Greek and high-quality Renaissance work the column sides appear to be straight, so slight is the entasis. In later, especially nineteenth-century mass-produced, buildings the curvature is often exaggerated, appearing crudely convex and bulbous

Ferrovitreous construction Buildings constructed with glass and iron (**11, 42**)

Fillet A narrow flat band that separates mouldings and column flutes

Finial Ornament finishing the apex of a roof, gable, pinnacle, newel, canopy, etc.

Flèche French term for a slender spire commonly found over the crossing on a church

Flute Vertical channelling in the shaft of a column (**21**)

Frieze The central member, plain or carved, of the classical entablature

Giant Order Used in Mannerist, Baroque and later classical architecture where the order spans two storeys of the elevation (**58**)

Greek cross plan A cruciform ground plan in which all four arms of the cross are of equal length

Intersecting vault Where two vaults, either of semicircular or pointed section, meet and intersect at right angles; the most usual instance is in the crossing of a church

Intercolumniation The space between columns (**19**)

Kokoshniki Term used in Russia for the series of arches set in rows, generally in Byzantine construction; derived from *kokoshnik*, the name for a traditional headdress worn by Russian women and which the series of arches are thought to resemble (**138**)

Lancet window A tall, one-light, narrow window with a sharply-pointed arch head characteristic of thirteenth-century Gothic style; lancets may be designed singly or in groups, usually three, five or seven (**Plate 7**)

Lantern Structure for ventilation and light, often surmounting a dome or tower (**31**)

Latin cross plan A cruciform church plan where the nave is longer than the other three arms

Lierne From the French *lier* – to tie; a short intermediate rib in Gothic vaulting which is neither a ridge rib nor rises from the impost

Lintel The horizontal stone slab or timber beam spanning an opening and supported on columns or walls

Loggia Open-sided gallery or arcade

Lunette A semicircular-headed opening, window or panel, often to be found above a door (**1**)

Mansard roof One with two angles of slope, one steeper than the other, named after the seventeenth-century French architect François Mansart (**14**)

Modillion A scrolled bracket used as a console but set horizontally not vertically

Module A unit of measurement by means of which the proportions and detailed parts of a building may be regulated. In classical architecture the column shaft diameter (or half diameter) was so used; in the twentieth century Le Corbusier proposed a system of measurement based upon the proportions of the human male figure, which he called the system *Le Modulor*. The module is essential to modern mass-produced building parts

Monolithic column One where the shaft is of one piece of stone, marble or wood in contrast to one made up from drums

Narthex In an Early Christian or Byzantine church, or a more modern version of such a design, a vestibule extended transversely across the western end of the building. The narthex was originally separated from the nave by a screen or wall and set apart as an area for women and penitents

Parabolic arch or vault A structure formed in the shape of a parabola, that is, a plane curve formed by the intersection of a cone with the plane parallel to its side. This form was developed mainly in the twentieth century most commonly in reinforced concrete material, though brick has also been used for such forms (**68**)

Pediment In classical architecture the triangular low-pitched gable above the entablature that completes the end of the gabled roof; pediments are also used as decorative features above doors, niches and windows (**26**)

Pendentive Spherical triangles formed by the intersecting of a dome by two pairs of opposite arches, themselves carried on piers or columns (**13**)

Peristyle A row of columns surrounding a court or cloister, also the space so enclosed

Pilaster A column of rectangular section usually engaged in the wall

Pilotis A term in modern architecture derived from the French word for pile or stake; popularized by Le Corbusier in his designs for apartment blocks and houses supported on such piles (**113, 117**)

Podium A continuous projecting base or pedestal

Polychromy The use of different colours in a variety of materials to give a decorative effect, both externally and internally, to buildings (**Plate 3**)

Propylaeum An important entrance gateway in Greek architecture as, for example, the entrance to the Athenian acropolis (**17**)

Quadriga A sculptured group surmounting a building or monument that is in the form of a chariot drawn by four horses abreast (**17**)

Rotunda Building of circular ground plan often surmounted by a dome; a circular hall or room (**87, 111**)

Rustication A treatment of masonry with sunk joints and roughened surfaces (**18**)

Saucer dome A dome of segmental form and without a supporting drum (**13**)

Segmental arch or vault Where the curve is formed as a segment of a circle, with its centre below the springing line (**78**)

Shaft The column of an order, between capital and base

Spandrel Triangular space formed between an arch and the rectangle of outer mouldings as in a doorway, generally decorated by carving or mosaic (**52**)

Stylobate The platform upon which the columns of a Greek temple stand (**20**)

Stucco An Italian word for decorative plasterwork. *Stucco duro* was the hard plaster used by Renaissance craftsmen in Italy, which, in addition to lime and gypsum, contained powdered marble

Tierceron An intermediate rib in Gothic ribbed vaulting that extends from the vault springing to the ridge rib (**55**)

Tracery The ornamental stonework in the head of a Gothic window (**Plate 3**)

Transept The arms of a cruciform church set at right angles to the nave and choir and generally aligned north and south

Triforium The first-floor intermediate stage of a Gothic church between the nave arcade and clerestorey. The triforium is usually arcaded and may have a passage behind this to facilitate access all round the building at this level

Tympanum The face of a classical pediment between its sloping and horizontal cornice mouldings. Also used to describe the area between the lintel of a doorway and the arch above it. Tympana are generally carved and/or sculptured or are decorated with mosaic (**21, 26**)

Vault Arched covering (**54**)

Vaulting bay The rectangular or square area bounded by columns or piers and covered by a stone vault

Vaulting boss A carved decorative feature set over the intersections of a ribbed vault to hide the junctions

Vault springing The point at which the vault ribs spring upwards from the capital, corbel or impost

Volute A spiral or scroll to be seen in Ionic, Corinthian and Composite capitals

Voussoir The wedge-shaped stones that compose an arch

Bibliography

General

ALLSOPP, B., BOOTON, H.W. and CLARK, U., *The Great Tradition of Western Architecture*, A. and C. Black, 1966

BALCOMBE, G., *History of Building Styles, Methods and Materials*, Batsford, 1985

BENEVOLO, L., *The History of the City*, The MIT Press, 1986

BERTON, K., *Moscow*, Studio Vista, 1977

BRAUN, H., *Elements of English Architecture*, David and Charles, 1973
English Abbeys, Faber, 1971

BRUNSKILL, R., *Traditional Buildings of Britain*, Gollancz, 1982

BRUNSKILL, R., and CLIFTON-TAYLOR, A., *English Brickwork*, Ward Lock, 1977

CAMESASCA, E., *History of the House*, Collins, 1971

CICHY, B., *Great Ages of Architecture*, Oldbourne, 1964

CIOCULESCU, S., *et al, Romania*, Meridiane Publishing House, Bucharest, 1967

CLIFTON-TAYLOR, A., *The Pattern of English Building*, Faber, 1972
English Parish Churches as Works of Art, Batsford, 1974

CLIFTON-TAYLOR, A., and IRESON, A. S., *English Stone Building*, Gollancz, 1983

COBB, G., *English Cathedrals, the Forgotten Centuries*, Thames and Hudson, 1980

COLVIN, H. M., *A Biographical Dictionary of British Architects, 1600–1840*, John Murray, 1978

COOK, G. H., *English Monasteries in the Middle Ages*, Phoenix House, 1961

COOK, O., *The English House Through Seven Centuries*, Whittet Books, 1983

COPPLESTONE, T., Ed., *World Architecture*, Hamlyn, 1963

CURL, J. S., *English Architecture: An Illustrated Glossary*, David and Charles, 1977

DE BREFFN, B., *Churches and Abbeys of Ireland,* Thames and Hudson, 1976

DOBRZYCKI, J., *Cracow: Landscape and Architecture*, Arkady, Warsaw, 1967

DUNBAR, J. G., *The Architecture of Scotland*, Batsford, 1978

DUNLOP, I., *The Royal Palaces of France*, Hamish Hamilton, 1985

DYNES, W., *Palaces of Europe*, Hamlyn, 1968

FABER, T., *A History of Danish Architecture*, Det Danske Selskab, 1964

FENWICK, H., *Scotland's Abbeys and Cathedrals*, Hale, 1978

FLEMING, J., and HONOUR, H., *The Penguin Dictionary of Decorative Arts*, Penguin, 1977
A World History of Art, Macmillan, 1982

FLEMING, J., HONOUR, H., and PEVSNER, N., *The Penguin Dictionary of Architecture*, Penguin, 1980

FLETCHER, B., *A History of Architecture*, Butterworth, 1987

FOSTER, M., Ed., *The Principles of Architecture*, Phaidon, 1983

GARDINER, S., *An Introduction to Architecture*, Leisure Books, 1983

GIROUARD, M., *Life in the English Country House*, Yale University Press, 1978
Cities and People, Yale University Press, 1985

GOMBRICH, E., *The Story of Art*, Phaidon, 1972

HAMILTON, G. H., *The Art and Architecture of Russia*, Pelican History of Art Series, Penguin, 1954

HARRIS, J., and LEVER, J., *Illustrated Glossary of Architecture*, Faber, 1966

HARVEY, J., *Cathedrals of England and Wales*, Batsford, 1978

HILLING, J. B., *The Historic Architecture of Wales*, University of Wales Press, 1976

HINDLEY, G., *Castles of Europe*, Hamlyn, 1968

HOGG, G., *Priories and Abbeys of England*, David and Charles, 1972

JACOBS, J., Ed., *Horizon Book of the Great Cathedrals*, Hamilton, 1969

JANKOWSKI, S., and ROFALSKI, P., *Warsaw: A Portrait of the City*, Arkady, Warsaw, 1979

JONES E., and WOODWARD, C., *The Architecture of London*, Weidenfeld and Nicholson, 1983

JONES, E., and ZANDT, E. VAN, *The City: Yesterday, Today and Tomorrow*, Aldus Books, 1974

JORDAN, R. F., *Western Architecture*, Thames and Hudson, 1985

KAVLI, G., *Norwegian Architecture*, Batsford, 1958

KNOX, B., *The Architecture of Poland*, Barrie and Jenkins, 1971

KOSTOV, S., *A History of Architecture: Settings and Rituals*, Oxford University Press, 1985

KOSTROWICKI, I. and J., *Poland*, Arkady, Warsaw, 1980

KRINSKY, C. H., *Synagogues of Europe*, The MIT Press, 1986

LLOYD, D., *The Making of English Towns*, Gollancz, 1984

LLOYD, N., *History of the English House*, The Architectural Press, 1975
  History of English Brickwork, Antique Collectors' Club, 1983

MAGUIRE, R., and MURRAY, K., *Modern Churches of the World*, Studio Vista, 1965

MITCHELL, A., *Cathedrals of Europe*, Hamlyn, 1968

MUSCHENHEIM, W., *Elements of the Art of Architecture*, Thames and Hudson, 1965

NORBERG-SCHULZ, C., *Meaning in Western Architecture*, Studio Vista, 1986

NORWICH, J. J., Ed., *Great Architecture of the World*, Mitchell Beazley, 1975

NUTTGENS, P., *The Story of Architecture*, Phaidon, 1983
  The World's Great Architecture, Hamlyn, 1980

OLSEN, D. J., *The City as a Work of Art: London, Paris, Vienna*, Yale University Press, 1986

PETZCH, H., *Architecture in Scotland*, Longman Group, 1971

PEVSNER, N., *An Outline of European Architecture*, Penguin, 1961;
  Founding Ed., *The Buildings of England, Ireland, Scotland and Wales* (many vols.), Penguin
  A History of Building Types, Thames and Hudson, 1986

PEVSNER, N., and METCALF, P., *The Cathedrals of England*, Penguin

PLACZEK, A. K., Ed., *Macmillan Encyclopedia of Architects* (4 Vols.), Collier Macmillan, 1982

RAEBURN, M., Ed., *Architecture of the Western World*, Orbis Publishing, 1980

RAHIVES, F., *Cathedrals and Monasteries of Spain*, Kaye, 1966

RICHARDS, I., *Abbeys of Europe*, Hamlyn, 1968

RICHARDS, J. M., *Who's Who in Architecture from 1400 to the Present Day*, Weidenfeld and Nicholson, 1977
  800 Years of Finnish Architecture, David and Charles, 1978

ROSENAU, H., *Social Purpose in Architecture*, Studio Vista, 1970

SAUNDERS, A., *The Art and Architecture of London*, Phaidon, 1984

SITWELL, S., *Great Houses of Europe*, Weidenfeld and Nicholson, 1961

Great Palaces of Europe, Weidenfeld and Nicholson, 1964

STAMOV, S., Ed., *The Architectural Heritage of Bulgaria*, State Publishing House Tehnika, Sofia, 1972

STANKIEWICZ, J., *Gdansk*, Arkady, 1971

STANLEY, C. C., *Highlights in the History of Concrete*, Cement and Concrete Association, 1979

STIERLIN, H., *Encyclopaedia of World Architecture*, Macmillan, 1983

TRACHTENBERG, M., and HYMAN, I., *Architecture from Pre-History to Post-Modernism*, Academy Editions, 1986

WATKIN, D., *A History of Western Architecture*, Barrie and Jenkins, 1986

WATKIN, D., and MELLINGHOF, T., *German Architecture and the Classical Ideal 1740–1840*, Thames and Hudson, 1987

WEST, T. W., *A History of Architecture in France*, Unversity of London Press, 1969
  A History of Architecture in Italy, University of London Press, 1968

YARWOOD, D., *The Architecture of Italy*, Chatto and Windus, 1970
  The English Home, Batsford, 1979
  The Architecture of Britain, Batsford, 1980
  English Interiors, Lutterworth Press, 1984
  Encyclopaedia of Architecture, Batsford, 1985
  Chronology of Western Architecture, Batsford, 1987
  The Architecture of Europe, Spring Books, 1987

ZACHWATOWICZ, J., *Polish Architecture*, Arkady, 1967

The Nineteenth Century

BEAVER, P., *The Crystal Palace*, Hugh Evelyn, 1977

BRADLEY, I., *William Morris and His World*, Thames and Hudson, 1978

BRIGGS, A., *Victorian Cities*, Odhams Press, 1963

BULLOCK, N., and READ. J., *The Movement for Housing Reform in Germany and France 1840–1914*, Cambridge University Press

CROOK, J. M., *Victorian Architecture*, Johnson Reprint, 1971
  The Greek Revival, John Murray, 1972
  William Burges and the High Victorian Dream, John Murray, 1981

CURL, J. S., *The Egyptian Revival*, George Allen and Unwin, 1982

EGBERT, D. D., *The Beaux-Arts Tradition in French Architecture*, Princeton University Press, 1980

HITCHCOCK, H. RUSSELL, *Early Victorian Architecture in Britain* (2 Vols.), The Architectural Press, 1954

Architecture, Nineteenth and Twentieth Centuries, Pelican History of Art Series, Penguin, 1982

HOBHOUSE, H., *Thomas Cubitt, the Master Builder,* Macmillan, 1971

KELLY, A., *Mrs Coade's Stone,* Images, 1990

LOYRETTE, H., *Gustave Eiffel,* Rizzoli, New York, 1985

MIGNOT, C., *Architecture of the Nineteenth Century in Europe,* Rizzoli, New York, 1984

PUGIN, A. W. N., *Contrasts,* Republished Leicester University Press, 1969

PORTOGHESI, P., *L'eclettismo a Roma 1870–1922,* De Luca, Rome, n.d.

RICHARDS, J. M., and MARÉ, E., *The Functional Tradition in Early Industrial Buildings,* The Architectural Press, 1958

RICHARDSON, M., *Architects of the Arts and Crafts Movement,* Trefoil Books, 1983

ROBINSON, C., and HERSCHMAN, J., *Architecture Transformed, 1839 to the Present,* The MIT Press, 1987

SCHINKEL, K. F., *Collected Architectural Designs,* Academy Editions, 1982

STANTON, P., *Pugin,* Thames and Hudson, 1971

STROUD, D., *The Architecture of Sir John Soane,* Studio, 1961

The Twentieth Century

ACHLEITNER, F., *et al, Neue Architektur in Österreich, 1945–1970,* Bohmann, Vienna, 1969

ALTHERR, A., *New Swiss Architecture,* Gerd Hatje, Stuttgart, 1965

ARTS COUNCIL OF GREAT BRITAIN, *Lutyens,* 1988

ARUP, O., and PARTNERS, *40th Anniversary of the Founding of the Firm,* Academy Editions, 1986

BACHMANN, J., and MOOS, S. VON, *New Directions in Swiss Architecture,* Studio Vista, 1969

BACULO, A. G., *Otto Wagner,* Edizioni Scientifiche Italiane, Naples, 1971

BANHAM, R., *The New Brutalism,* The Architectural Press, 1966

BENEVOLO, L., *History of Modern Architecture,* Routledge and Kegan Paul, 1971

BÉRET, C., *Architectures en France, Modernité, Post-Modernité,* Centre de Création Industrielle, 1981

BESSET, M., *New French Architecture,* The Architectural Press, 1967
    Who was Le Corbusier?, Albert Skira, Geneva, 1968

BLIJSTRA, R., *Dutch Architecture after 1900,* P. N. van Campen and Zoon, Amsterdam, 1966

BÖDE, P. M. and PEICHL, G., *Architektur aus Österreich seit 1960,* Residenz Verlag, Salzburg and Vienna, 1980

BOESIGER, W., *Le Corbusier* (8 Vols.), Thames and Hudson, 1970

BOFILL, R., *Taller de Arquitectura,* Rizzoli, New York, 1985

BOOTH, P., and TAYLOR, N., *Cambridge New Architecture,* Leonard Hill, 1970

BORSI, F., and GODOK, E., *Vienna 1900: Architecture and Design,* Lund Humphries, 1986

BROOKS, H. A. Ed., *Le Corbusier,* Princeton University Press, 1987

BURCHARD, J., *Post-War Architecture in Germany,* The MIT Press, 1966

CAFFÉ, M., and SEBESTYÉN, G., *Development of Constructions in Romania,* Meridiane Publishing House, Bucharest, 1964

CALDENBY, C., and HUTTIN, O., *Asplund,* Rizzoli, New York, 1986

COLLYMORE, P., *The Architecture of Ralph Erskine,* Granada, 1982

COOPER, J., Ed., *Mackintosh Architect,* Academy Editions, 1984

CURTIS, W. J. R., *Modern Architecture since 1900,* Phaidon, 1987

DOSTAL, O., PECHAK, J., and PROCHAZKA, V., *Modern Architecture in Czechoslovakia,* Nakladatelstiví Českolovenských Výtvarných Umělců, Prague, 1967

EMERY, M., and GOULET, P., *Guide Architecture en France,* Groupe Expansion, 1983

FABER, T., *New Danish Architecture,* The Architectural Press, 1968

FANELLI, G., *Architettura Moderna in Olanda 1900–1940,* Marchi Bertolli, 1968

FEO, V. DA, *URSS Architettura 1917–1936,* Riuniti, 1963

FEUERSTEIN, G., *New Directions in German Architecture,* Allen and Unwin, 1956

FLEIG, K., *Alvar Aalto,* Les Editions d'Architecture, Artemis, Zürich, 1970

FRAMPTON, K., *Modern Architecture,* Thames and Hudson, 1987

GALARDI, A., *New Italian Architecture,* The Architectural Press, 1967

GANS, D., *The Le Corbusier Guide,* Princeton Architectural Press, 1987

GIRBAU, L. D., *Arquitectura Española Contemporanea,* Editorial Blume, Madrid, 1968

GREGOTTI, V., *New Directions in Italian Architecture,* Studio Vista, 1968

GROPIUS, W., *Scope of Total Architecture*, Allen and Unwin, 1956

HITCHCOCK, H. RUSSELL, *Architecture, Nineteenth and Twentieth Centuries*, Pelican History of Art Series, Penguin, 1982

HOLLEIN, H., *et al, Hollein*, Architecture and Urbanism Publishing Company, 1985

HOLMDAHL, G., *et al, Gunnar Asplund Architect 1885–1945*, Svenska Arkitekters Riksförbund, Stockholm, 1950

IKONNIKOV, A., *Russian Architecture of the Soviet Period*, Raduga Publishers, Moscow, 1988

JENCKS, C., *Late-Modern Architecture*, Academy Editions, 1980
    Post-Modern Architecture, Academy Editions, 1984
    Modern Movements in Architecture, Penguin, 1985

JENŠTERLE, J., *Recent Architecture in Slovenia*, Modern Galerija Ljubljana, 1968

JOEDICKE, J., *Pier Luigi Nervi*, Edizione di Comunità, Milan, 1957
    Architektur in Deutschland '85, Karl Krämer Verlag, Stuttgart, 1986

JONES, C., *Marcel Breuer*, Thames and Hudson, 1962

KOPE, A., *Town and Revolution, Soviet Architecture and City Planning 1917–35*, Thames and Hudson, 1970

KULTERMANN, U., *New Architecture of the World*, Thames and Hudson, 1966
    Zeitgenössische Architektur in Osteuropa, DuMont-Buchverlag, Cologne, 1985

LAMPUGNANI, V. M., Ed., *Encyclopaedia of 20th Century Architecture*, Thames and Hudson, 1986

LE CORBUSIER, *Towards a New Architecture*, The Architectural Press, 1970
    The City of Tomorrow, The Architectural Press, 1971
    The Modulor, Faber, 1977
    Le Corbusier: Early Works by Charles Edouard Jeanneret-Gris, Academy Editions, 1987
    Le Corbusier: Architect of the Century, Arts Council of Great Britain, 1987

LEVY, J. M., *Contemporary Urban Planning*, Prentice-Hall, New Jersey, 1988

LISSITSKY, EL, *Russia: An Architecture for World Revolution*, Lund Humphries, 1970

LUTYENS, M., *Edwin Lutyens*, John Murray, 1980

MACFADYAN, D., *Sir Ebenezer Howard and the Town Planning Movement*, Manchester University Press, 1970

MÜNZ, L., and KÜNSTER, G., *Der Architekt Adolf Loos*, Anton Schroll, Vienna and Munich, 1964

MURRAY, P., and TROMBLEY, S., Ed., *Modern British Architecture since 1945*, RIBA Magazines Ltd, 1984

NERVI, P. L., *New Structures*, The Architectural Press, 1963

NUTTGENS, P., Ed., *Mackintosh and his Contemporaries*, John Murray, 1988

PAWLOWSKI, C., *Tony Garnier*, Centre de Recherche d'Urbanisme, Paris, 1967

PEDERSEN, J., *Architekten Arne Jacobsen*, Architiktens Vorlag, Copenhagen, 1957

PEHNT, W., *German Architecture*, The Architectural Press, 1970

PEICHL, G., *Editorial Gustavo Gill*, Barcelona, 1987

PETER, H., *Modernes Deutschland*, Mosaik Verlag, Hamburg, 1968

PEVSNER, N., *The Sources of Modern Architecture and Design*, Thames and Hudson, 1981
    The Pioneers of Modern Design, Penguin, 1982

PROBST, H., and SCHÄDLICH, C., *Walter Gropius*, Ernst und Sohn, Berlin, 1988

RAÈV, S., Ed., *Gottfried Böhm*, Karl Krämer, Stuttgart, 1987

RAY, S., *Il Contributo Svedese all' Architettura Contemporanea e l'Opere di Sven Markelius*, Oficina Edizioni, Rome, 1969

RICHARDS, J. M., *An Introduction to Modern Architecture*, Penguin, 1956

ROSSI, A., *Buildings and Projects*, Rizzoli, New York, 1985

RUSSELL, F., Ed., *Art Nouveau Architecture*, Academy Editions, 1983

SAARINEN, E., Architecture and Urbanism Publishing Company, 1984

SAFDIE, M., *Building in Context*, Process Architecture, 1985

SUDJIC, D., *New Architecture: Foster, Rogers, Stirling*, Thames and Hudson, 1986

TAFURI, M., and DAL CO, F., *Modern Architecture*, Faber, 1986

WAGNER, O., *Sketches, Projects and Executed Buildings*, The Architectural Press, 1987

WEAVER, L., *Houses and Gardens by E. L. Lutyens*, Antique Collectors' Club, 1981

WEBB, M., *Architecture in Britain Today*, Country Life Books, 1969

WHITTICK, A., *Eric Mendelsohn*, Leonard Hill, 1964
    European Architecture in the 20th Century, Leonard Hill, 1974

WINGLER, H. M., *Bauhaus*, The MIT Press, 1980

WINTER, J., *Modern Buildings*, Hamlyn, 1969

Index

Buildings are listed under the names of towns or villages. Persons are generally listed under the surname. References to line and plate illustrations are printed in **bold** type.

71010